BACKPACKER.
THE COMPLETE GUIDE T

BACKPACKING

Field-Tested Gear, Advice, and Know-How for the Trail

FALCON®

Guilford, Connecticut

An imprint of Globe Pequot

BACKPACKER is a registered trademark of Active Interest Media.
Falcon and FalconGuides are registered trademarks and Make Adventure Your Story is a trademark of Rowman & Littlefield.

Distributed by NATIONAL BOOK NETWORK

Copyright © 2017 by Rowman & Littlefield

British Library Cataloguing-in-Publication Information available

Library of Congress Cataloging in Publication Data available

ISBN 978-1-4930-2597-8 (paperback)
ISBN 978-1-4930-2598-5 (ebook)

♾™ The paper used in this publication meets the minimum requirements of American National Standard for Information Sciences—Permanence of Paper for Printed Library Materials, ANSI/NISO Z39.48-1992.

CONTENTS

PREFACE

A heated house that provides T-shirt weather in winter. A fridge filled with fresh food. A car that can zip you across town to visit a friend. The comforts of modern living are undeniably appealing, and I enjoy them just as much as you. But I learned long ago that there's such a thing as being *too* comfortable.

It takes a certain kind of person to reject the luxury of modern plumbing, if only for a weekend, and turn back the clock on "progress." But that's exactly what we're doing when we head into the wilderness with all of our essentials on our backs. Backpackers experience the world the way our ancestors did, with nothing between us and the wild. That means a lot of pretty views, of course, but that's not all. You can see a pretty view by driving to the edge of the Grand Canyon. It's a powerfully different thing to shoulder a pack and hike over the edge.

Traveling into the backcountry sparks something in our DNA that's as old as humankind. And modern science is finding that it's good for us to reconnect with it. Researchers have found that backpacking makes you smarter (really), and that time spent in nature has measurable benefits for happiness and health. If backpacking could be packaged and sold in a pill, there would be lines at every pharmacy.

But drug makers won't figure this one out. Instead, the prescription is a pair of boots. Fortunately, there's no better time for this miracle cure. Backpacking gear is better than ever, making the wilderness more accessible than ever.

Does that mean every trip will be easy? No. I won't kid you: Even if you follow every bit of advice in the pages that follow, there will be times when you feel the cold, feel the hard ground, feel real hunger. Even the best stuff can't entirely take the rough out of roughing it. And there's real comfort in that.

Dennis Lewon
BACKPACKER editor-in-chief

White Chuck Mountain, North Cascade Range, Baker
Snoqualmie National Forest. THINKSTOCK.COM

INTRODUCTION

Welcome to the golden age of backpacking.

Back in the early 1970s, it was perfectly normal to carry a 60-plus-pound external-frame pack the size of a small refrigerator for a few nights out. If it rained, you pulled on a poncho or, if you were serious, a waterproof cagoule that hung below the knees. In cool weather, backpackers wore scratchy wool everything and protected themselves from wind and snow with a heavy cotton nylon–blend jacket. Feet were shod with heavy leather boots that took months to break in, though it was mostly the feet that ultimately succumbed. It took dozens of stakes to pitch the A-frame tents, and they still elicited little sleep in a storm. Since there weren't many options on the market, much of the gear was made at home on a sewing machine.

Nowadays, with a little prudent shopping, it is quite reasonable to carry a svelte 30-pound pack for a multiday hike. The clothing, for good weather and bad, is actually comfortable and performs well when used

Backpacking can take you to some of the world's most beautiful places.
STEPHEN GORMAN

ix

properly. Even "heavy" boots are half the weight of yesterday's models and break in faster, while many people don't even need that much protection. Tents set up easily and provide superior protection, even in howling gales.

Backpacking today is easier and more comfortable than ever. Of course the trails are just as steep and the miles just as long, but the new gear truly makes them melt under your feet. If you are of the persuasion that life is too short not to be enjoyed, it is now painless to pack in a gourmet meal, even a fine wine, to remote locations with incredible views. Or you can trim your pack down to the bare necessities for fast and light trips into distant ranges that would require many extra days with old-school technology.

While proper gear selection and usage are vital to a happy backpacking experience, there are also many tricks of the trail that will make your hikes safer and more comfortable. These are most important when venturing outside your home region, where you may be less familiar with environmental hazards.

In this book we will give you an overview of your equipment options in different categories, looking first at basic backpacking gear such as packs, tents, sleeping bags, and accessories. Then we will discuss clothing options for a variety of environmental conditions, followed by chapters on trip planning, hiking techniques, and navigation. Leave No Trace principles, water purification, fires, and camping in bear country are covered in chapter 6. Food packing, meal basics, recipes, stoves, and cook gear are covered in the chapter on camp cooking, followed by chapters on backcountry hazards and weather, backcountry first aid, and outdoor survival—topics of paramount importance to backpackers.

People go backpacking for many reasons. Some like to get away from the city, others wish to explore or take photographs, and many enjoy it for mental and physical fitness. But the common theme for everyone is having fun. The more pleasurable the experience, the more you will do it. Hopefully you will also share the rewards of wilderness with future generations and embrace the protection of the environment we share.

Shenandoah National Park. THINKSTOCK.COM

Rough Ridge Overlook, North Carolina.
THINKSTOCK.COM

CHAPTER 1
EQUIPMENT

Perhaps you've heard the expression "lighter is better." That's true to a point, but a more accurate version of the expression would advise "lighter is better, but silly light is dumber." Gear enters the domain of "silly light" when it falls apart, fails to keep you warm and dry, or when a couple of ounces can make a dramatic increase in comfort.

Home sweet home—with a view.

When it comes to pack weight, the Big Three are your shelter, your sleeping system, and your pack. If you want to significantly reduce the load you carry, these are where the easiest savings can be achieved.

After these major items, it helps to have a decent scale, since the savings will be in ounces instead of pounds. But the ounces do add up, and you won't have to go to such extremes as cutting a toothbrush handle in half or trimming the edges off topo maps. Long experience has taught us to never trust manufacturers' weights when it comes to what you actually carry. If you keep track of your base pack weight (everything minus the clothes on your back and food, water, and fuel) on different trips, you will learn where cuts can safely be made.

Consider backpacking equipment an investment in yourself. In the long run, it is usually less expensive to purchase higher quality gear that will handle your needs for years to come. Buying cheaper products that perform poorly and soon require upgrades can be a costly mistake.

TENTS

The first decision in picking an appropriate tent is deciding how many people you need to accommodate. Typically, a two-person tent offers the greatest versatility, since it is light enough for solo trips and roomy enough for car camping too. Larger three- to four-person tents can offer a good weight-to-volume ratio for families; however, the largest models require a lot of flat, open space, which can sometimes be difficult to find.

If you will be backpacking in regions with considerable rain, then be sure to look for a roomy vestibule that can shelter your gear and allow cooking. A big vestibule is also important if you hike with dogs—a wet, muddy pooch does not make a pleasant tent mate.

In general, backpacking tents fall into one of three categories: double-wall domes, double-wall tunnels, and ultralight single walls. Double-wall tents have an outer fly of waterproof fabric that covers an inner tent made of bug-proof mesh and ripstop fabrics. These offer the greatest versatility and comfort, since you can leave the fly off on starry nights, and the design reduces condensation to a bare minimum. Single-wall tents can be significantly lighter, but they rely on airflow to prevent condensation.

Dome tents feature two, three, or four intersecting poles (the more poles, the stronger the tent but also the heavier) and resemble an igloo. It is actually a misnomer to call dome tents "freestanding," because in reality they require at least three or four stakes for proper performance. Dome tents do provide the greatest livability, particularly when you're cooped up inside during a storm, and you can easily pick them up to relocate. Due to their shape, domes also perform the best when winds come from multiple directions. For these reasons, a double-wall dome tent is likely your best buy when starting out.

A convertible double-wall dome tent offers greater flexibility but is heavier than a single-wall dome.
CLYDE SOLES

Tunnel tents have two or three non-intersecting hoops, like a Conestoga wagon, and rely entirely on front and rear stakes for support. These provide maximal space with minimal weight because they contour to the body (low and narrow at the feet, wide and tall at the hips, lower and narrower at the head). When well staked, tunnel tents can be quite storm worthy; however, side winds and heavy snow can be problematic.

Single-wall tents come in all sorts of shapes, but the most common for backpacking are A-frame styles that rely on trekking poles for support. While remarkably lightweight, these tents often require many stakes and careful pitching. Without adequate ventilation, there will be considerable condensation by morning that can soak sleeping bags. Because of these issues, and the fragile fabrics used, a single-wall tent is probably not a good choice for your first tent.

Whether double or single wall, one of the major innovations in tent construction in recent years is the advent

This tunnel tent with a large vestibule provides a lot of living space for minimal weight. CLYDE SOLES

of silicone-treated nylon fabrics (called silnylon). Compared to traditional urethane-coated fabrics, silnylons can be far lighter yet stronger, reducing tent weights considerably. The main trade-off is higher cost. Since silnylon is very slippery, some people apply seam sealer to the floor for traction to keep sleeping pads in place.

No matter the style, there is no such thing as a "four-season" tent unless you always camp in the tropics. A tent that is warm enough and sturdy enough for winter camping is far too hot and heavy for backpacking in summer. Even the "convertible" tents that strip down for warm weather tend to be several pounds heavier than a true summer tent yet only marginally adequate for winter; they are best in spring and fall.

When comparing weights of tents in catalogs, ignore the "minimal weight" because it is so stripped down that the tent is useless (read the fine print). The most accurate number is actually the "packaged weight," since that is closer to what you will end up carrying on the trail. As a rule of thumb, a two-person backpacking tent should have a packaged weight of no more than 6 pounds; less than 5 pounds is preferable, and less than 3 is possible.

Many tents now have a fast-packing option if you purchase the matching ground cloth (sometimes called a footprint). This allows the fly to be set up while leaving the tent body at home, saving several pounds. It sounds nice, but you may find you want the bug and storm protection of a tent. Or, if the weather is nice, perhaps you would rather have a view of the stars than the inside of a tent fly.

Rather than purchase a custom footprint to protect your tent floor from abrasion, you can save money and around 0.5 pound by using a thin sheet of plastic or Tyvek. Simply buy a rectangle at a hardware store that is large enough to fit under your tent and vestibule, and then trim it slightly smaller so that rain will not pool under your tent.

The accessories that come with most tents are frequently inadequate for the backcountry. For example, most stuff sacks will be far too small once the tent is wet from rain or condensation. The skewers provided are often a cheap grade of aluminum that bends at the mere sight of a rock. Guy lines made of black cord are ideal for tripping you at night; white is better, but reflective cord rules.

Tent Alternatives

Two alternatives to a traditional tent are tarps and camping hammocks. When bugs are not an issue, a silnylon tarp can offer a very lightweight rain shelter that is easy to pitch among trees; just string a taut ridgeline and stake out the corners. However, the weight savings are negated if you must carry mosquito netting, and they are impractical above tree line. Other tarps might be set up using trekking poles; the advantage here is that any time you can use one item for two purposes, you are saving weight.

A camping hammock gives one person protection from bugs and rain and can be set up in locations too rugged or sloped for tents.
CLYDE SOLES

Hammocks designed for camping simply require two stout trees, so there is virtually no impact on the terrain, and even rocky slopes are not a problem. These are strictly one-person affairs, and emptying your bladder during the night is problematic. Not for everyone, hammocks can be a good choice for "stealth camping," since you don't need a normal tent site.

SLEEPING BAGS AND PADS

The first step in picking a sleeping bag is deciding upon a temperature rating. Just as there is no such thing as a four-season tent, there are no year-round sleeping bags. In general, for backpacking in spring, summer, and fall, you will be best served by a bag rated to 20°F and weighing less than 2.5 pounds. This is warm enough for chilly nights yet not sweltering when opened up like a blanket. If the temps really drop, you can augment the rating by wearing additional clothing.

Temperature ratings are highly subjective, since many factors affect them, including your metabolism, level of fatigue, and thermal efficiency of your sleeping pad. Mainstream sleeping bag manufacturers now use a rating system adopted in Europe with three ratings on the tag: a Comfort Limit at which most women are comfortable, a Lower Limit at which most men are comfortable, and an Extreme Rating, which is the lowest a woman might survive the night. Check carefully so you understand the rating of any bag you're considering; beware of ultralight bags with extravagant claims.

As for insulation material, high-grade goose down is still the first choice. A sleeping bag with 800-plus fill power down is significantly lighter and more compressible than any alternatives. If price is a prime consideration, then opting for 650-plus fill down won't mean a huge weight increase in a three-season bag but becomes very noticeable in winter bags. With a quality tent and a good stuff sack (see pages 4, 8), keeping down bags dry is not that difficult in all but the most extreme conditions. Plus, most down today has a water-resistant treatment that helps it retain loft in wet conditions.

Still, if you will be backpacking in notoriously wet regions, particularly when using single-wall tents or tarps, then synthetic insulation can be a better option. The best of the modern synthetics rival 650-plus fill down for weight, bulk, and cost, but not longevity or comfort on warmer nights. The inexpensive synthetic bags offer mediocre performance and value, though they beat the pants off anything available three decades ago. By the way, people who claim "warm when wet" have obviously never slept in one; "tolerably uncomfortable" is a more accurate description, so it behooves you to keep any sleeping bag dry.

Shell fabrics compose a major portion of total bag weight and compressibility. Since durability is pretty much a nonissue, go with the

Left to right: 1. This ultralight mummy filled with high-quality down gives the best weight-to-warmth ratio. 2. For maximum weight savings, this semi-rectangular bag has no bottom fill; it attaches to a pad for insulation from the ground. 3. A wearable sleeping bag has armholes and a leg opening with a draw cord so you can perform camp chores. 4. For wet weather camping, it is wise to use a synthetic-filled sleeping bag—the best ones are now starting to rival down for minimal weight and bulk. CLYDE SOLES

lightest fabrics you can afford. Generally, microfiber nylons deliver the best performance. However, if you will spend a lot of time camping at or near below-freezing temperatures, a waterproof/breathable outer shell can help minimize condensation problems.

Mummy-style sleeping bags that have a hood and a tapered shape offer the best thermal efficiency. However, bags that are too tight or with partial-length zippers can prevent a good night's sleep; a few extra ounces will make life better. When camping mostly in above-freezing conditions, semi-rectangular bags without a hood offer great comfort.

Many hikers underestimate the importance of their pad to a good night's sleep. When they shiver through a cold night, the sleeping bag is often blamed when the real culprit is the inadequate pad. Like the walls of your home, pads are rated with an R-value. Anything less than an R-value of 2 is completely inadequate for cold ground and ensures a night of suffering even with a winter bag. Lesser ratings can be fine for hot weather, but you need at least an R-5 pad for sleeping on snow.

Closed-cell foam pads are, frankly, best suited to those with masochist tendencies (like alpinists). Similarly, three-quarter-length pads sound

Left to right: 1. A good self-inflating pad offers comfort, warmth, and convenience. 2. Although a down-filled air mattress takes longer to inflate, it is incredibly comfortable and compact when rolled. 3. This high-end air mattress requires a lot of puffing but is lighter and more compact than other pads. 4. A hybrid between a closed-cell and self inflating pad provides reasonable comfort and good durability. 5. This folding closed-cell pad has dimples to provide a bit more cushioning from hard ground; it's lightweight and inexpensive. Simply lay it out and go to bed.
CLYDE SOLES

good for reducing weight in theory but often equate to more tossing and turning during the night. Sleeping pads are an area where you can go silly light and hurt yourself or carry a few extra ounces and get a great sleep. Be willing to carry a tad more weight for a minimum of 1.5 inches padding underneath the full length of your body. You won't regret it.

Your sleeping bag should come with a storage sack (use it) and a stuff sack (upgrade it). Do yourself a favor and purchase a silnylon waterproof stuff sack that has sealed seams and a roll-top closure; this is lighter and gives better protection. If you have a bulky sleeping bag, compression stuff sacks can help reduce volume; however, they are heavy, complicated, and don't make that much of a difference.

For hot weather you might consider using a sleeping bag liner made of cotton or silk. These keep your bag clean and can be used alone when it's sweltering. You can also augment the warmth of your sleeping bag with thermal liners that can boost the rating by 10°F to 20°F.

BACKPACKS

Of the Big Three, we cover packs last because your prior decisions affect this one. With a lighter and more compact tent and sleeping bag, you can get away with a smaller and less-supportive pack—at least for some trips. If you will be carrying climbing gear into the Cirque of the Towers or a large-format camera into the Teton wilderness, then a more substantial pack is needed.

The starting point for pack selection is volume, because too small is frustrating and too large means you often bring the kitchen sink. Most people will find that a 4,000-cubic-inch pack has sufficient volume for extended weekend backpacking trips (two to three nights out). Those going spartan might get by with 3,000 cubic inches, while those with bulkier gear may need as much as 6,000 cubic inches.

Volume dictates the amount of support required, though it is better to err on the side of more. Packs with a minimal frame may only weigh 2

For fast and light trips, a good no-frills pack carries all your gear with minimal weight and still has features you need. On longer trips, or when extra gear is required, a large internal-frame pack carries heavier loads comfortably; this one (right) has an outer pocket that detaches to become a daypack. CLYDE SOLES

OUTDOOR GEAR REPAIR KIT

BACKPACKER
THE OUTDOORS AT YOUR DOORSTEP

Step by Step Techniques to Maximize Performance and Save Money

COMPLETE GUIDE TO OUTDOOR GEAR MAINTENANCE AND REPAIR

KRISTIN HOSTETTER

You spend a lot of money on your gear, and you want it to last. The best investment you can make is to pick up a copy of *Backpacker Magazine's Complete Guide to Outdoor Gear Maintenance and Repair* by longtime gear editor Kristin Hostetter. It includes step-by-step techniques to maximize the performance of your gear and save you money. For in-the-field repair situations, the following items are what Kristen carries in her backcountry repair kit:

O-rings: If you're using a liquid-fuel stove on any given trip, always pack a few spare O-rings just in case.

Zip-lock bag: No need to get fancy. A freezer-weight zip-lock bag is the lightest receptacle for your repair kit, plus it's waterproof and see-through, so you can get at the goods quickly.

Seam Grip: There are 1,001 uses for this awesome adhesive, so never leave home without a small tube.

Buckles: Pack a replacement for your pack's hip belt, a Slik Clip (designed to join any two pieces of webbing), and a ladder lock with a slit (making it easy to install without sewing).

Alcohol prep pads: Use these to clean any fabric surface before making a repair.

Tent pole repair sleeve: Tough to improvise and a godsend if you break a pole, this aluminum sleeve is key. Wrap a bit of duct tape around the sleeve and use the tape to affix the sleeve in place. And always keep a few more feet of the silver stuff wrapped around your water bottle or trekking pole for other repair emergencies.

Tear-Aid patches: This is excellent repair tape. Be sure to get "Type A," which works on pretty much all fabrics. ("Type B" adheres only to vinyl.)

Multitool: The Leatherman Juice S2 is fully featured (with scissors, pliers, and sundry screwdrivers and blades), but at 4.4 ounces, it's light enough that you don't mind carrying it.

Even a frameless pack needs contoured shoulder straps and good ventilation for comfort (note the hip belt pocket on the red pack, a tremendously useful feature). The best internal-frame packs are fully customizable, so you can dial in the fit for maximum comfort. CLYDE SOLES

pounds but can lead to sore shoulders and hips for all but the most hard-core ultralight backpackers. On the other hand, many over-built packs weigh 6 to 8 pounds and ensure a tortoise-like pace. Somewhere in the region of 3 to 4 pounds is likely a good choice for many backpackers.

External-frame packs have gone the way of dinosaurs, though they are still the best choice for carrying 80-plus-pound loads. At the opposite extreme, frameless packs that rely on the sleeping pad for "support" are all the rage in the ultralight community. However, frameless packs require truly minimalist packing and they're typically made with ultralight materials that need TLC to avoid damage.

Internal-frame packs run the gamut from clean and elegant to complex monstrosities designed by the marketing department instead of users. If possible, try a pack on in the shop with the appropriate weight inside and wear it around for at least a half hour to notice the subtle pressure points. Be sure to have the salesperson show you how to make all the fit adjustments so you can make tweaks on the trail.

When looking at backpacks, pay attention to the little things that get used a lot. Hip belt pockets are super handy to carry items you may want during the day; if you use a hydration bladder, you'll want a pack that includes that feature. Everybody's preferences will vary. If you like to bushwhack, avoid mesh side pockets that snag on every branch. Packs with dark interiors become black holes that make finding gear needlessly difficult; light-colored fabric really helps.

Keeping your gear dry while hiking in the rain is a bit of an art. For the most part, pack covers are rather heavy, flap in the wind, snag on bushes, and still don't work well due to condensation and perspiration from your back. A more reliable system is to use a pack liner—either a purpose-built liner with sealed seams or a white compactor trash bag—and double-bag critical items like your sleeping bag and warm clothes. This also protects from accidental submersion during a stream crossing, as well as leaky fuel bottles or hydration bladders.

STOVES AND COOK GEAR

The Romans knew that an army marches on its stomach. Backpackers too know that food fuels their hikes. But more than that, food sets the mood and tenor of your trips. Some decide to go hard-core and eat flavorless yet easy-to-prepare meals. Others prefer to enjoy delectable treats during the day and a four-course gourmet repast accompanied by adult beverages at dinner. But whatever you choose for your backcountry fare, you will need a good backpacking stove as well as some cook gear to make your meals. What follows is a concise discussion of stoves and cook gear. Dig into chapter 7 for further coverage of campsite cooking techniques.

Stoves

Gather a dozen backpackers together and it's almost certain the topic of conversation will turn to stoves. For whatever reason, many backpackers have a stove fetish and end up with a collection. The primary fuel options are butane, white gas, and alcohol, with some stoves capable of burning multiple fuels.

With proper understanding of use and limitations, the majority of backpackers will be well served by stoves that use screw-on butane (actually either isobutane or a butane-propane blend) cartridges. These are generally easy to operate and reliable; however, the basic models do struggle in cold weather. More-sophisticated stoves use inverted canisters and preheating to improve performance in the cold.

White gas stoves have long been the preferred option for many backpackers due to their efficiency as well as the availability and affordability of fuel. Although it's hard to beat the convenience and safety of butane stoves, once you learn a particular stove's quirks and how to maintain it, white gas stoves do crank out a lot of heat no matter the temperature. If you will be cooking for more than two or three people, white gas stoves are likely your best option.

In cold weather, a white gas stove with a pump inside the fuel bottle (rear) is the most reliable option; efficiency can be increased further with high-performance aluminum pots. In warmer weather, butane stoves (center) offer the greatest convenience and are compact enough to fit inside the cookset. Some stoves are designed to use either white gas or butane (front); with an integrated windscreen and pots designed to capture heat, this is a good system for any weather. CLYDE SOLES

Eating out of the pot isn't always an option, so a collapsible bowl can simplify mealtime. An aluminum knife, fork, and spoon can be lighter and more durable than plastic versions. Leave the antique Sierra cup at home and carry a modern insulated mug that won't spill and will keep your drink warm. CLYDE SOLES

Alcohol stoves are popular among ultralight backpackers because the stoves are simple and light; long-distance hikers appreciate the ready availability of ethanol and methanol. However, these stoves are slow to boil water, perform poorly in wind or cold temperatures, seldom have heat control, and the fuel burns with an invisible flame when accidentally spilled.

Stoves that integrate with pots have increased in popularity, though they are not necessarily superior to well-chosen separate components. When picking a butane or white gas stove, be sure that the pot supports are sheet metal with teeth instead of round rods, since pots are less likely to slide off accidentally.

No matter the stove and cookset, a vital component is an effective windscreen. It is best to purchase one designed for the stove, since it can also increase efficiency. Improvised windscreens can work, but care must be taken to prevent overheating the fuel tank on some stoves to prevent an explosion.

Cook Gear

Pots and a windscreen should be considered an integral part of your cooking system. Proper selection can significantly increase fuel efficiency, especially when cooking in the wind. Backpacking pots are made from aluminum, stainless steel, or titanium.

The best pots are aluminum with a hard anodized coating for durability and ease of cleanup. Look for a textured base to help prevent dinner sliding onto the ground. Stainless-steel pots can take more abuse than other materials, but that factor isn't worth the extra weight. Titanium is great for ultralight fetishists but has a poor cost-benefit ratio.

Many backpackers prefer the convenience of meals that rehydrate in their packaging. If you go with this scheme, you only need a single pot for boiling water and a pot cozy to keep things warm as they rehydrate. On the other hand, if you prefer making a full-blown meal, you'll need at least one additional pot. The fancier your dining, the more extensive your kitchen requirements will be.

All but the ultralight hard-cores will want a nice insulated cup, a spoon, and possibly a bowl. A simple spice kit can greatly improve meals; a mini grater and some Parmesan cheese can make a huge difference.

Some of us won't be caught dead without good coffee in the morning, preferably fresh ground. While a French press or stovetop espresso maker suits some, cleanup is a hassle. For great taste with easy cleanup and minimal bulk and weight, the best option is a coffee filter.

Backpackers often find themselves in bear country as well as the home of many other critters. Depending on where you travel, precautions are often needed to protect your food from marauders. Some areas require bear canisters, while others permit hanging food (see chapter 6). Shelters in some places have annoying mice or raccoons that are smarter than many people, so elaborate precautions may be necessary.

WATER TREATMENT SYSTEMS

When backpacking, it would be great if we always visited pristine areas that have untainted water sources. However, in many regions it is best to err on the side of caution and treat your drinking water to prevent illness from *Giardia*, *Cryptosporidium* (crypto), and other nasties.

Water treatment can be performed by boiling, filtration, ultraviolet light, or chemical methods. In extreme cases of badly contaminated water, multiple methods may be required, though this is seldom the case when backpacking.

Since boiling kills all potential pathogens, the water used for cooking meals and hot drinks is safe. You may have heard it takes 5 to 10 minutes of boiling, but this is an unnecessary waste of fuel; once water reaches a rolling boil (even at high altitude), all microorganisms are destroyed. Boiled water can be allowed to cool for drinking, but it has a flat, metallic taste.

Water filters have improved in recent years, making them faster, smaller, lighter, and less finicky. Modern pump

Beware! Tempting as it might be to dip your water bottle into a clear mountain stream, it's not worth risking a bout with *Giardia*.
STEPHEN GORMAN

WATER TREATMENT TIPS

Whatever the treatment method, start with the best water source possible. Rather than the outlet of a pond, try using the inlet, where the water is fresher, or out in the middle, where things have had a chance to settle out. Get as near the source as possible, such as where a stream emerges from the ground or snowbank. Be aware of what may be upstream, farms and "wilderness" with grazing livestock in particular.

If there is a lot of sediment in the water, it is a good idea to pre-filter by pouring through a fresh coffee filter. This keeps filters from clogging and helps chemical treatments work faster. Water with a great deal of fine sediment can be left in a container overnight to settle out, but be sure you don't stir it up when decanting the good water.

No matter which methods you use for treating water, they are all for naught if you are not careful about hygiene while on the trail. Good hygiene starts with keeping fingernails short and cleaning your hands after going to the bathroom. Thankfully, this is easy due to the availability of hand sanitizer in small containers. Less-obvious sources of contamination include washing dishes or brushing teeth with contaminated water and even shaking hands with other hikers. Also pay attention that dirty water does not contaminate your treated water.

Ultimately, deciding whether water needs to be treated is a value judgment based on your location and your risk tolerance. Nothing in North American water will kill you if it isn't treated; at worst we are talking about a bad case of gastric distress. However, dehydration can lead to disorientation and even heat stroke, which definitely can kill you—and quickly. So don't be foolish and forgo drinking water from a stream or lake if you or your hiking partner is overheating, even if you have no way to treat the water.

filters offer fast delivery of clean water without any taste issues. The new gravity-feed filters are great for watering larger groups, since they require almost no work. However, most filters are ineffective against viruses, so they should not be relied on in Third World countries. And because freezing can cause filters to crack, they are not recommended in winter.

Once very popular, iodine treatment methods are no longer recommended due to numerous problems, including inefficacy against crypto. The nasty taste can be alleviated by adding vitamin C (such as in sport drinks); however, if this is done too soon, the water is unsafe. Very cold water requires a higher dosage or much longer wait than the standard 30 minutes. Finally, iodine tablets have a short shelf life (three months) once the bottle is opened.

A better alternative is chlorine dioxide treatment, which imparts minimal taste. Though the name sounds similar, this is chemically very

Newer water filters that can convert to gravity-feed (rear) are a good choice for individuals and groups. When supplying water for just one or two people, a water bottle with integrated UV-C light (front) is a very fast and convenient method.
CLYDE SOLES

different from the chlorine found in bleach (not recommended). Chlorine dioxide still takes 15 to 30 minutes, depending on water temperature (4 hours in severe cases), and mixing the liquids is a nuisance. The chlorine dioxide pills work well but are a bit costly; they are a good backup for other methods.

The newest method of water treatment, ultraviolet light, is now a favorite. It only takes 2 minutes to kill the nasties in clear water (longer if it's cloudy), so you can enjoy safe, fresh water when you stop at a stream. The drawback to UV-C is the reliance on batteries, and it only works with a liter at a time, which may be impractical for larger groups.

For a more in-depth discussion of water purification options and techniques, see chapter 6.

A good compass has built-in declination adjustment to compensate for magnetic north, a sighting mirror for accurate readings, and a long baseplate for working on maps. CLYDE SOLES

The best GPS receivers have large color displays, barometric altimeters, and high-quality topographic maps available for download. Be aware that some models with touch screens are virtually unreadable in direct sunlight, rendering them almost useless for backpacking. CLYDE SOLES

ACCESSORIES

Right at the top of your list of essential accessories should be a map and compass. Even certified gearheads with all the gadgets will assure you it's wise to still carry the basic navigation tools, even if you have a smart-phone and Global Positioning System (GPS) receiver. Batteries die, electronics fail, there's no cell signal when you need one. But a good compass and a map of the area will always get you through.

Nobody needs a GPS receiver to go backpacking. These high-tech gadgets are a nice luxury that can help in certain circumstances. Purchasing a GPS unit before you have mastered the art of navigation with map and compass is foolish.

Certainly on overnight trips, a headlamp is essential to help with chores. Even on day trips, it is wise to carry a small headlamp in your pack, since accidents do happen. The most important feature of any headlamp is a locking switch that cannot accidentally turn on inside your pack. Beyond that, it's nice to have a dim broad beam for tasks and a bright narrow beam for spotting distant objects.

A good headlamp for backpacking is compact, rugged, waterproof, and has multiple beam settings. For day excursions, an ultracompact emergency headlamp weighs virtually nothing, takes up almost no space in the pack, and can really save your hide when needed. CLYDE SOLES

While outdoor shops offer an array of multitools, it's hard to beat the venerable Swiss Army knife for backpacking. In some situations, multitools are a good option, especially if you think you may need pliers, but beware of bringing a big one that's overkill and too heavy.

Which knife to carry is a matter of preference. At times, scissors, a small blade, and a miniature screwdriver (inside the corkscrew) all come in handy. Yet the longer locking blade, wood saw, and Phillips-head screwdriver also have their advantages. CLYDE SOLES

KNIFE SHARPENING

A dull knife is almost as bad as no knife at all. Check the sharpness before each trip. The blade should easily slide through a piece of paper. If it doesn't, get to work with a whetstone. When you're in the field and using your knife hard, it can lose an edge quickly. But with a little practice, you can learn to field-sharpen your blade, even without a whetstone. Find a smooth, palm-size stone (river stones work well). Lubricate the stone with spit. Place your blade at about a 15-degree angle to the stone, and apply gentle pressure as you swipe the blade over the stone in a smooth, fluid, arc-like motion. Make about thirty passes, then flip the blade over and do the same on the other side.

Practice sharpening at home on your kitchen knives.
©JPS/LICENSED BY SHUTTERSTOCK.COM

Depending on whom you talk with, trekking poles are either an essential bit of kit or an unnecessary hassle. The pro-pole crowd points to increased support on tricky terrain, greater safety during river crossings, reduced stress on knees, and the option of using the poles for supporting a tent. The anti-pole hikers note the extra energy wasted, the annoying clicking noise, and the irony that ultralight hikers have less need for support.

If you choose to use poles, learn to use the straps properly by inserting your hand from below so that the wrist is supported. Be sure the grip

Trekking poles offer additional support on rocky trails, but some hikers don't think they are worth the extra energy required to carry and use them.
STEPHEN GORMAN

A trekking umbrella is designed to hold its shape in strong wind and is made from silnylon to save weight. Good trekking poles (right) collapse to less than 20 inches long and extend to more than 47 inches; the small trekking basket will not catch on underbrush and provides flotation in soft sand. CLYDE SOLES

is comfortable in bare hands, the strap is padded, and the carbide tips are replaceable. Unless you have money to burn, features like shock absorbers and carbon fiber shafts aren't needed.

While some might consider an umbrella frivolous, there are two climates where they are worth their weight in gold. If you are hiking out in the open on hot days, the shade from an umbrella is far cooler than that offered by a hat. When backpacking in persistent rain without much wind, an umbrella is more comfortable than wearing a hood, keeps you and your gear drier, and lets you hear better.

Sunglasses are essential protection for your eyes from both UV light and wind. Although you can get by with fashion shades meant for driving, the best option for backpacking, particularly if you go above tree line, are models that wrap around the face.

Good outdoor sunglasses can adapt to variable lighting conditions, either by changing the lenses (top) or by using photochromic lenses that darken in bright light. CLYDE SOLES

Take a moment to enjoy the beauty
all around. THINKSTOCK.COM

CHAPTER 2

CLOTHING

While the gear in your pack relates to your comfort in camp, it's the clothes on your back that affect comfort on the trail. Rather than thinking of clothes as individual items, it is better to look at clothing systems for different environmental conditions.

HIKING SHOES AND BOOTS

Where the rubber hits the trail can have a lot to do with a successful backpacking trip. With proper selection, you'll barely notice what is on your feet and will be able to focus on the experience. However, inadequate footwear, improper fit, or ill-suited socks can quickly turn a great hike into huge misery.

Hiking shoes differ from trail runners in the stiffness of the midsole. Although a bit heavier, the stiffer flex provides a more solid platform when walking on rough trails, and it helps prevent bruising the bottom of the feet from stepping on sharp rocks. Trail running shoes tend to be

Trail running shoes (right) are lightweight but offer minimal protection for your feet. Good hiking shoes (left) are a better option for backpacking because they generally offer more support and superior traction. When carrying a heavier pack through rugged terrain, especially if there is mud and snow, good medium-weight backpacking boots (top) are worth the extra weight.
CLYDE SOLES

lighter, which saves energy, and more flexible, which may cause fatigue; their primary advantage is superior breathability and faster drying time after getting wet.

Both hiking and trail running shoes are available with waterproof/breathable linings, but this option costs more, adds weight, makes them hot, and keeps your feet wet if water comes in over the ankles. Don't bother unless you plan to wear gaiters.

Despite what many people think, lightweight hiking boots do not provide any ankle support. These are essentially over-the-ankle shoes that help keep dirt and water away from your socks. Light hikers are a good choice both for day hikes and short backpacking trips, particularly if wet conditions are anticipated. Better models have waterproof/breathable linings and relatively few seams for greater durability.

Medium-weight backpacking boots offer extra protection, support, and durability for more-rugged terrain and heavier loads. These are a good choice for trekking in remote areas, where an injury can have real consequences.

If you are carrying a heavy pack over rugged terrain that may lack trails, heavy-duty backpacking boots are a good choice. Generally made from full-grain leather with few seams, these boots are also suitable for general mountaineering with crampons.

Frequently the footbeds provided with new hiking boots are made from cheap foam that flattens quickly. Many backpackers will benefit from aftermarket footbeds that cradle the foot and distribute pressure more evenly. These can enhance ankle support and alleviate some blister problems, though some combinations can merely move blisters to a different spot.

One item you definitely do not want to skimp on is hiking socks; they have improved greatly in recent years. Good quality socks carefully blend wool and other materials to absorb perspiration and reduce friction. If you have trouble with blisters, try different socks before replacing boots.

A part of the footwear system that is often overlooked, foot ointments can go a long way toward preventing blisters. Rubbed onto your

With lightweight boots and shoes, a single pair of high-quality wool blend socks is the best option. Most backpackers wearing heavier boots are more comfortable with two pairs of socks. The inner pair (top) is a light or synthetic material that wicks moisture away from the foot. The outer pair (bottom) is a heavier wool and synthetic blend, providing moisture absorption and comfort. The two pairs move against each other instead of rubbing against your feet.
STEPHEN GORMAN

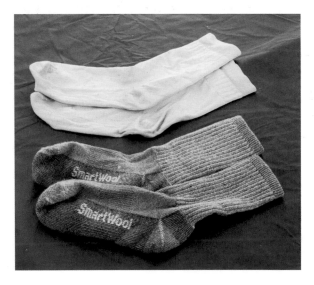

feet, these nongreasy ointments, such as Hydropel, help transport moisture away from the skin and reduce friction.

Knee-length gaiters can be very useful when there is still snow in the backcountry and when bushwhacking while wearing shorts. Select a model with waterproof fabric below the ankle and breathable fabric above. A front opening is more convenient than side or rear, and neoprene or cable instep straps last much longer than string.

HOT WEATHER CLOTHING SYSTEM

Your choice of clothing for hiking in hot weather will depend on the region of the country and the time of year. Your first inclination may be to wear shorts and a short-sleeve shirt, and in many places this may indeed be excellent. However, in areas where tick-borne diseases are a problem, it is wise to wear long pants and a long-sleeve shirt. Similarly, when hiking in the desert during summer months, the extra sun protection of long clothing is prudent.

When selecting shorts for backpacking, examine the waist region for seams and rivets that create pressure points underneath a hip belt. Also be sure there are no rough seams around the inner thigh that will chafe. Somewhat baggy shorts offer good airflow without snagging on brush. Nylon fabric is faster drying and more durable than cotton. Many hikers opt for convertible pants with legs that zip off to become shorts.

While tempting, cotton T-shirts are lousy for backpacking (except in desert climes) because they get soaked with sweat and chafe your skin. For greater comfort, select a loose-fitting T-shirt made from polyester knit, which offers good airflow and fast drying while protecting your shoulders from the sun. Women may also wish to wear a sports bra with mesh ventilation, but check for seams that will chafe or create pressure points under shoulder straps.

In areas where ticks, mosquitoes, and blackflies are a problem, your best option is to wear long clothing, tuck your pants into your socks, wear light colors so you can see

The best option for hiking in hot weather is loose-fitting, long sleeve shirts and pants made of nylon fabric. If it's also bug season, clothing with an insect shield treatment will greatly improve your comfort. Be sure to wear a hat with a full brim to keep sun off your face, neck, and ears (baseball caps don't cut it).
CLYDE SOLES

ticks more easily, and even wear a head net if the bugs are really bad. You might also consider treating your hiking clothes with an insect repellent called permethrin to reduce the need for using bug sprays and lotions on your skin. Pretreated insect repellent clothing lasts about fifty washings before losing efficacy. Or you can purchase permethrin spray and treat your own clothing, which lasts about five washings.

Particularly where Lyme disease is prevalent, be sure to treat your hiking socks (and short gaiters if you wear them) with permethrin too.

CLOTHING NEEDS FOR WARM AND COOL WEATHER

Warm Weather
- technical (non-cotton) T-shirt
- long-sleeve shirt
- shorts
- long pants (Save some pack space and weight by getting a pair of zip-off convertible pants).
- warm jacket (fleece, down, or synthetic puffy)
- rain shell
- rain pants
- socks (two pairs for trips up to a week; a third pair for longer trips)
- undies (whatever minimum you feel comfortable with)
- sunhat

Cool Weather
- long-sleeve base layer
- long john bottoms
- soft-shell pants
- warm mid-layer (fleece, thin down, or synthetic puffy)
- camp coat (big, puffy, warm down or synthetic jacket with hood)
- rain-shell jacket (with hood)
- rain pants
- socks (two pairs for trips up to a week; a third pair for longer trips)
- undies (whatever minimum you feel comfortable with)
- warm hat
- light gloves (for walking)
- warm gloves/mittens (for in camp)
- neck gaiter

Hiking pants, whether convertible or not, should have a gusseted crotch and articulated knees for maximum freedom of movement. Stretch nylon is the best fabric option, though you may also desire mesh side vents for increased airflow. While knit fabrics are a good choice for T-shirts, long-sleeve hiking shirts should be woven synthetic to prevent mosquitoes from biting through the material.

Desert hikers don't have to deal with bugs; instead, they have the oppressive sun. Long clothing is advisable, preferably white, though you may find cotton is cooler than synthetics. These days, some clothing has ratings for sun protection, and it is worthwhile looking for "UPF 50" on the hangtag.

Since wearing long pants reduces ventilation, you may experience chafing of the inner thighs. Synthetic boxer shorts may be one solution because they are longer than briefs and dry quickly. Another possibility is compression undershorts (like bike shorts without the padding), which give a smooth sliding surface. You also might try anti-chafing lubricants, such as Body Glide, to reduce friction.

Hats are also an important component of a hot-weather clothing system. While baseball caps and mesh running hats make a fashion state ment, they also say you don't care about sun protection. Smart hikers wear hats with full brims that protect the ears and neck. Should you be forced to wear mosquito netting to keep bloodsuckers at bay, a full-brim hat increases comfort. In particularly brutal sun, you may even wish to use an umbrella for shade.

COOL WEATHER CLOTHING SYSTEM

When hiking in spring, fall, or at high altitudes, you will need a versatile layering system that can quickly adjust to the conditions. And even though the days may be sweltering in the desert or high mountains, the nights are often downright chilly, so extra layers should be at hand.

For base layers, you will probably find medium-weight long underwear the most useful because it wicks moisture well, provides some but not too much warmth, and works well alone and in combination with other layers. Modern synthetics deliver the best performance because the fabrics dry quickly, are comfortable next to the skin, and the better versions no longer suffer problems with odor retention. Merino wool has made resurgence in recent years because it is relatively warm when wet and naturally odor resistant, and superior processing has eliminated most of the scratchiness.

White, medium-weight synthetic tops keep you cool in the sun and dry quickly. High-quality, medium-weight merino wool underwear (center) is comfortable next to the skin and helps regulate temperature. For the coldest conditions, heavyweight synthetic (left) can be worn over lighter layers. CLYDE SOLES

There are a gazillion options for mid-layer tops that provide some insulation, block wind, and resist moisture. Among the most popular choices is a windshirt with wicking polyester knit lining; this works well on its own and under other layers, since it slides easily. Soft-shell jackets made with stretch woven fabrics provide greater abrasion resistance but

The combination of mid-weight synthetic with a wind shell (left) is superb as both a mid-layer and an outer shell. Stretch soft-shell jackets are great outer layers on cold days when you are active; underarm zippers allow more ventilation when working hard. CLYDE SOLES

are a bit heavier and bulkier in the pack. Though less weather resistant, fleece tops also make great mid-layers due to good warmth and breathability. So far, windproof fleece is unsatisfactory for the backcountry due to weight, bulk, and slow drying time.

For your legs, it's hard to beat a good pair of soft-shell pants: They are rugged, allow great freedom of movement, provide moderate warmth, resist wind, and repel water. Features you want include a thigh pocket, zippered gussets on the lower leg, and instep patches.

When bugs are not a concern, good nylon hiking shorts are a pleasure to wear. Pants made for backpacking (right) are made with rugged, quick-drying fabric and a waist that will not create pressure points underneath a hip belt. In colder weather, stretch soft-shell mountaineering pants (center) provide durability, wind and water resistance, and great freedom of movement. Wind pants with a mid-weight synthetic lining and full-length side zippers (left) can be easily donned over pants or shorts as part of a layering system. CLYDE SOLES

There are lots of choices too for insulating outer layers. As with sleeping bags, down offers maximum warmth with minimum weight and bulk. However, synthetic-insulated tops are also excellent because you can toss them on over wet clothes and stay reasonably warm as things dry. In milder conditions, a vest may be all you need when combined with other layers. But if colder weather is anticipated, you will appreciate a nice sweater or jacket.

A high-quality down vest (right) offers a tremendous warmth-to-weight ratio and takes up little space in the pack. A favorite layer for many alpinists, a synthetic-insulated jacket (center) blocks the wind better than fleece, is more compact when stuffed, and dries very quickly. If conditions are dry, an ultralight down sweater (left) is a remarkably comfortable insulation layer.
CLYDE SOLES

A stocking hat and lightweight gloves play a vital role in staying warm. Although the oft-heard claim that 90 percent of your heat is lost through your head is utter nonsense, a fleece or wool hat does help you

AVOID COTTON

It's great for everyday use, but aside from really dry, sunny environments (like the desert), cotton is a liability in the backcountry for several reasons:

- Once wet, cotton takes forever to dry unless you have strong bright sun. So when you sweat through your T-shirt on a big climb, your pack straps may start to chafe where the cotton stays wet underneath. The same goes for cotton socks.
- Cotton loses its shape over multiple days, so a T-shirt that started off fitting you well will likely be stretched out and flapping after a few sweat-and-cool cycles.
- If you need a little extra warmth, cotton doesn't provide it.
- Cotton is not as durable and tear resistant as other outdoor fabrics.

Bottom line: There are far better fabrics to choose from. Synthetic fabrics (polyesters and nylons) dry in a snap and are very strong for their weight. Polyester shirts wick sweat extremely well, and they don't lose their shape over time. However, synthetic fabrics (especially polyester) tend to get stinky pretty quickly. Wool is another fabric to consider. Today's wool is superfine and soft. It resists odor even after days of use, and it can be toasty warm but still breathable. Wools typically don't dry quite as fast, though, so sweat hogs tend to prefer synthetics.

effectively regulate body temperature. Thin fleece gloves provide just enough warmth without sacrificing dexterity, are reasonably durable, and dry quickly.

LAYERING 101

Staying comfortable in the outdoors is all about layering. The key is to have a system of clothing that you can use in different combinations to stay warm and dry. A basic layering system consists of three parts:

Base layer. Your next-to-skin layer is responsible for wicking sweat away from your body when you're working hard. As discussed in "Avoid Cotton," synthetics and wool are your best option here, as they will wick sweat, dry quickly, and help you maintain a consistent body temperature.

Mid-layer. This is your insulating layer. Depending on the season and the location of your trip, you might choose a very thin fleece, a light wool jacket or sweater, or a puffy insulated jacket (again, avoid cotton; it doesn't insulate well). As for puffies, you have many different types of insulation to choose from: Synthetic fills (like PrimaLoft) are generally less expensive, and they don't absorb water like down can. If a synthetic jacket does get wet, your best bet is to wear it dry. If you're moving, your body heat will dry it fast. Down is the lightest, warmest fill you can buy. It's more expensive, but it packs down extremely well, whereas synthetic fills are generally bulkier to pack. But down—even the new variations, which have been treated for water-resistance—will eventually get wet and lose their loft. When they do, they lose their ability to insulate, and they dry more slowly than synthetics. Treated

Your next-to-skin layer has a big job: Wick sweat quickly away from your skin and dry fast, even while you're working hard. Your mid- and outer layers will vary depending on the weather conditions. THINKSTOCK

down will dry a little faster (and with fewer clumps), but the bottom line is that you want to steer clear of soakings if you're wearing down.

Shell. Your outer layer has two jobs: Cut the wind, and repel precipitation. Look for a hooded hard-shell fabric made of a waterproof/breathable fabric such as Gore-Tex, eVent, or Pertex Shield. Make sure your shell jacket is roomy enough to accommodate all your other layers underneath. If you're a heavy sweater, consider getting a shell with pit zips (venting zippers underneath the arms).

STORM CLOTHING SYSTEM

The level of storm protection you need depends greatly upon where and when you go backpacking. Certainly the needs of those in the Pacific Northwest differ from those in the Rockies. And springtime in New England can be a soggy experience, while fall seldom sees much inclement weather.

In relatively dry climates, storm protection is something brought out infrequently and often put away after the thunderstorm passes; thus lightweight and compactness are important. Often it is used more as a wind shell than a rain shell, so breathability is also a consideration.

In damper climes with high humidity, breathability is a relative term since there is only so much any fabric can do; excellent ventilation is key. Understand that you will get wet in some conditions, even with the very best shells available, because of condensation rather than leaking fabric—plan accordingly. For some trips you may wear the jacket and pants all day long, so you will probably want a bit more durability. Ponchos are only passable in the most benign places where the wind doesn't blow and the temperatures are warm; otherwise, they are a prescription for misery.

A basic windshirt made from ultralight nylon (front) can be a great complement to a heavier rain shell. In chilly weather, a hooded wind shell made with a wind-blocking laminate (upper right) is ideal for high aerobic output. For complete rain protection, a light parka with a waterproof/breathable laminate and no lining (upper center) offers a good compromise of minimum weight and bulk. When durability counts, a mountain shell made with a three-ply waterproof/ breathable fabric (upper left) gives the greatest longevity. CLYDE SOLES

Among the most essential features of a good storm shell is a well-designed hood that allows peripheral vision, keeps glasses dry, and does not channel water inside. Mesh-lined pockets double as vents, but these often must be closed when it's really dumping, so underarm zippers are still desirable. Smarter designs have a pocket that also doubles as a stuff sack.

Storm pants should be simple but not too simple. Forget any storm pants that require removing boots to put on and take off. Full-length side zippers will leak, so they are only recommended for winter use when you need to take pants off while wearing skis or crampons. Because your pack's hip belt tends to push them down, pants need a good belt or waist closure that doesn't create pressure points (e.g., no cord locks).

When hiking in all-day drizzle, you may wish to use a rain hat with a full brim, or an umbrella, instead of your jacket's hood. This allows you to hear much better and helps prevent overheating when working hard.

DRYING WET CLOTHES

When you only have a limited supply of things to wear and they get wet—either from rain, sweat, or an unintended fall into the drink—you need a few tricks up your sleeve for getting them dry fast. The best thing you can do—barring ample sunshine and time—is continue to wear them, as unappealing as that might sound. Keep wet clothes on, and wear your shell gear on top. Your own body heat is your best chance at getting them dry. At night, wear the wet clothes inside your sleeping bag, or lay them out flat against your body. Avoid balling them up at the foot of your sleeping bag or trying to line dry them in your tent. If you do, chances are they'll be just as wet in the morning—and miserably cold to put on again.

Franconia Ridge, White Mountain
National Forest, New Hampshire.
THINKSTOCK.COM

CHAPTER 3

TRIP PLANNING

Whether for an overnight trip or a multi-week journey, you will reap the greatest rewards by preparing for your adventure. Remember the five Ps: Proper Planning Prevents Poor Performance.

Trip preparation involves deciding who will be joining you, where you will go, and when you will go. This will allow you to fine-tune your gear and food selection, develop a realistic timeline, and anticipate potential problems.

Partnering up is easy if your soul mate also enjoys backpacking and has a similar level of fitness. But it gets more complicated if you have different visions about goals and degrees of comfort. Do everyone a favor and sort out potential issues ahead of time. Unrealistic expectations have led to many a nightmarish trip.

Once you have your partner(s) lined up, or decide to go it alone, pull out the guidebooks (or go to backpacker.com/destinations) and pick a trail. You'll quickly learn that not all miles are created equal, so judging by distance alone can leave you coming up short. In addition to trail descriptions, better guidebooks will include time estimates, elevation gain and loss, and warnings about less-obvious hazards. If you are going into less-traveled areas, you may have to glean this information from topo maps or even Google Earth.

Don't scoff at the value of advance research. For example, if you go to the Bugaboos in British Columbia and don't know about the voracious porcupines that like to eat the radiator hoses on cars, your great trip can end on a huge sour note. You're also in for a rude awakening if you think you can just show up and get a permit for the Mount Whitney Trail in summer without a reservation.

It is also wise to note contact information for ranger offices, permit requirements, and emergency numbers. Many areas have specific rules about traveling in bear country, and what is fine in one area may not be allowed in others.

Find out when hunting season starts and ends. If you are out on the trails during this time, it is wise to add some blaze orange to your clothing

Topographical map.
THINKSTOCK.COM

or pack. Avoid wearing white, because a glimpse through the trees can resemble the flash of a deer's tail.

Part of your research should include prevailing weather patterns for your destination, especially if it's several states away. It helps to know that a snowstorm is a real possibility in August when hiking in Colorado's high country. As your departure date gets closer, start following the weather on the Internet. These days, "surprise" storms are exceedingly rare, and getting caught unprepared is foolish.

Pick realistic goals, and save the ambitious projects for when you have the experience and fitness to pull them off. Especially before doing a mega-trip, it is wise to do a couple of mini shakedown trips to evaluate your gear, your partners, and your own readiness. A big trip may quickly be cut short by a pair of ill-fitting boots or participants who bite off more than they can chew.

Some teams will divide communal gear among themselves for equal weight distribution (for example, one person carrying the tent body; another, the poles and fly). A better method is for one to carry the complete tent and the other to carry the complete kitchen; if they somehow get separated, each can survive the night reasonably well off.

Splitting group weight evenly is also unfair if one person has significantly less lean muscle mass than the rest of the group (women have more body fat than men, so total weight is inaccurate). To avoid "domestic moments," the stronger person should shoulder more group gear and the heavier pack.

Take time in town to evaluate your team's abilities so you can choose a trip that will be appropriate for all.
DAVE ANDERSON

One ultimate truth of backpacking: The fitter you are, the more enjoyable the experience. If you are heading off on a multiday trip and are badly out of shape compared to other people in the group, it's likely to be an unpleasant experience. It's far better to arrive in camp pleasantly tired than feeling like you just survived a death march. Give yourself a few months with a proper conditioning program before any major excursions.

BEFORE YOU GO: PLANNING AHEAD

The first step in planning ahead is choosing a trip that is appropriate for your skill level. Too often people get into trouble because they underestimate the challenge of their route or overestimate their individual capabilities. Be honest with yourself and with your teammates. If you haven't hiked more than a mile in your life, planning to cover 20 in two days on your first trip out is unrealistic.

Self-Assessment

To help evaluate the appropriateness of your objective, each member of your team should consider the following questions:

- What kind of physical condition are you in? Do you work out? If so, for how long? Have you hiked with a pack on? What kind of mileage have you hiked in a day?
- Have you done a trip of this sort before? If so, what, if anything, is different about this particular plan? If not, do you have any

A little training will help you enjoy your trip more and may prevent accidents due to fatigue. DAVE ANDERSON

relevant experience that might help you evaluate your potential performance?

- What skills will the trip demand? How do you rate your competency at these skills? Do you need further training?
- Does anyone on the trip have first-aid training?
- Once everyone on your trip has evaluated him- or herself, you are ready to pool your data and make a plan.

Physical Conditioning

Wilderness trips can be casual—you may ride horses into the mountains and lounge around for five days while a cook prepares meals for you—or you can plan to hike 20 miles or more a day to traverse an entire range. You need to be realistic about how the demands of the trip you are considering align with the reality of your physical ability. Twenty minutes on the treadmill three times a week doesn't really equate well with hiking uphill for 5 hours with 35 pounds on your back.

If you have the time to train for your trip (you'll need a few weeks to really harden your body), do. Your best bet is to load up a backpack and go hiking. Start slowly and build up time and distance as your body gets used to the weight and motion. If you do not have access to a place to take day hikes, load up a pack and get on the stair climber at your local gym. People may look at you strangely, but there's nothing like training specifically for an activity to ensure that you'll be in shape when you begin the trip.

Many outing clubs and wilderness adventure schools offer classes on basic outdoor skills.
DAVE ANDERSON

What does physical conditioning have to do with outdoor survival? A lot, really. If you are out of shape, you are more likely to get injured or become sick. Tired people fall, make bad decisions, stop paying attention to their surroundings, and end up disoriented and lost. Also, if you are miserable, you'll have a lousy time, so why go into the mountains attempting something that is way over your head? Be realistic. Choose an objective that is appropriate for you and for your team.

Experience

Do your research and make sure you know what kind of hazards you may encounter during your trip. Be honest about your experience. It is appropriate to push yourself—you never develop your skills if you don't try something new every now and then—but it is stupid to put yourself in a situation for which you have no training or knowledge. For a basic backpacking trip, the skills required are rudimentary: You must be able to keep yourself warm, dry, fed, and found. Depending on your route, you should include more-advanced skills, such as being able to cross rivers and read maps, or specialized techniques for travel over rock, snow, or ice.

If you are a novice to the outdoors and uncomfortable learning on your own, consider taking a class or finding someone to come along on your trip who is more experienced. Practice skills at home, hire a guide, join a club. There are all sorts of ways to gain skills without bumbling your way blindly into a bad situation.

Team Composition

Before you head out on your trip, sit down with your companions to talk about what you want from the experience. Shared values and desires are critical to ensuring that your team is well functioning and that you have a good time out there. You should be aligned in terms of how hard you want to work, how much risk you are willing to accept, and what you want to achieve. Dysfunctional teams make mistakes and tend to fall apart, which leads to discord and fragmentation.

Choose an Appropriate Trip

With the information you have gathered, you are now prepared to choose a trip that is appropriate for your skill level, your physical conditioning, and your personal goals and objectives. As mentioned above, information

on trips can be garnered from any number of places: Guidebooks, magazines, the Internet, local outing clubs, guides and outfitters, and outdoor shops are all great places to find out about trips of all levels of difficulty, distance, length, and location.

EQUIPMENT PLANNING

Many backcountry emergencies result from people being poorly equipped to meet conditions. Backpackers succumb to hypothermia because they fail to bring appropriate clothing. Day hikers forget their maps and end up lost. Proper equipment is critical to navigating through and living comfortably in the outdoors. Proper equipment is also essential to dealing with emergencies.

Coming Up with an Equipment List

It can be daunting to pack for your first wilderness adventure. You want to make sure you have enough—but not too much—gear, because you don't want to carry 60 pounds on your back just to make sure you are ready for any and every potential need. Try to carry gear that can serve multiple functions: A water bottle can be your coffee cup; a bandanna can be a washcloth, hair band, or sunshade. Make detailed lists, and note what you do and do not use so that on future trips you can fine-tune the packing.

Many backpackers like to divide their gear lists into personal stuff and group gear. Personal equipment includes clothes, toiletries, sleeping stuff, and so forth. Group gear is everything you will share: shelters, cooking equipment, first-aid supplies, and technical tools such as a climbing rack.

Your gear will be dictated by the following considerations:

1. Length of trip
2. Elevation, season, weather
3. Specific goals (climbing, skiing, fishing, birding, etc.)

BASIC GEAR LIST

Personal Gear

- Upper body layers (base layer, insulating layer(s), and one T-shirt made from polyester or wool; save cotton for trips in hot, dry climates)
- Lower body layers (base layer, insulating layer, and one optional pair of shorts made from polyester or wool)
- Raincoat and pants (can be used as wind gear in winter conditions)
- Breathable wind gear (top and bottom)
- Warm hat, sunhat
- Gloves or mittens, socks
- Hiking shoes, camp shoes (optional)
- Headlamp, lighter, and pocketknife/multitool
- Eating utensils (bowl, spoon, water bottle, lighter)
- Sleeping bag and pad
- Toiletries, bug repellent, sunscreen
- Backpack
- Water treatment (filter, halogens, etc.)

Group Gear

- Cooking gear (stove, 1–2 pots, channel-lock pliers, water container, spatula or serving spoon, frying pan [optional])
- Repair kit
- Shelter (tent or fly to hold all participants)
- Spade for digging catholes, toilet paper, trash bag
- First-aid kit
- Hand sanitizer or soap
- Maps, compass, GPS (optional)
- Communication device (cell or satellite phone, SPOT tracking devices, etc.)

Emergency Gear

In many books you'll see a list of ten essentials, or emergency gear you should have on your person at all times. If you are carrying a full backpack and are prepared to be out for a few days, there is no need to carry extra emergency gear. You should have everything you require to be comfortable available in your backpack. But there is one item many experienced outdoorspeople advocate carrying separately: a lighter in a plastic bag. With a lighter in your pocket, you can start a fire to stay warm if something happens; for example, if you get lost going to the bathroom near camp or your pack falls in the river and floats downstream. In these kinds of situations, your lighter turns into essential emergency gear.

For day hikes into the mountains, or when you leave your camp for a few hours, it's a good idea to carry a few essentials in a small pack just in case the weather changes or you are out longer than anticipated. These include:

A hat provides a lot of warmth for very little weight. DAVE ANDERSON

> Extra layer
> Warm hat
> Rain jacket
> Water and water-treatment capability
> Pocketknife
> Snack
> First-aid kit
> Lighter

Just remember, carrying emergency gear does not prevent emergencies. Your best weapons in the outdoors are your preparation, common sense, and ability to think clearly under pressure. With these things, you can survive almost anything.

Know Your Gear

Search-and-rescue professionals are constantly going out to look for lost people who are carrying maps and GPS receivers but don't know how to use them. It doesn't help to have all the right gear in your backpack if you can't operate it. Take time to learn how to use your equipment before you leave home: Light your stove, set up your tent, practice using your GPS in conjunction with a map. If necessary, seek training to ensure your competency.

You should also avoid going out on long trips to isolated places with untried gear. Make sure the equipment you bring along does what it is supposed to do. If you haven't used a particular brand of tent or stove,

ask around or read reviews on the Internet to ensure that you've chosen a model that will work for your purposes.

If you are using old gear, pull it out of storage and check to make sure it is in good repair before leaving. Carry a repair kit so you have the tools you need to fix your gear if something breaks down—if your stove gets clogged or a tent is torn in a windstorm, for instance.

PLANNING A ROUTE

Most backcountry travelers usually—wisely—stick to trails or established routes on their initial forays into the wilderness. But even if you plan to be on a trail all day, look carefully at the map before you set off. It's all too easy to blast through a trail junction and end up miles off track if you aren't paying attention and haven't identified some key landmarks to keep track of your progress. Here we present some basics of route planning and navigation. For a complete discussion of navigation techniques, see chapter 5.

The first step is to pinpoint your starting location. Now, using a stick or some kind of pointer, trace your planned route carefully, making note of key features you will pass on the way. These features can help keep you on track just as a handrail on a staircase helps guide you. A backcountry handrail may be a river that you will be following for several miles; or you may be contouring around a peak, so the slope angling off to one side will be your handrail. If you find yourself with a river on your right side when it should be on your left, or if you are traveling upstream when you were intending to go down, you know something is wrong.

A landing, on the other hand, is a point you can tick off as you go by, just as landings on a staircase indicate the passage of floors. Say you notice that you will cross a trail junction a few miles after you begin hiking. You know you have hit your landing when you come to that point.

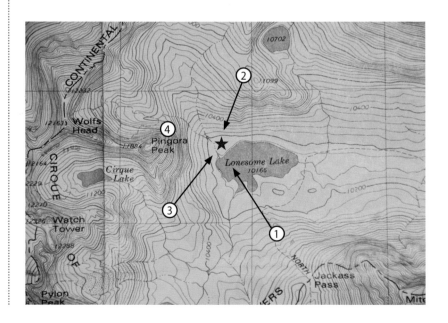

This campsite—identified by the red star on the map—can be pinpointed by four key characteristics: (1) its location at the northwestern end of Lonesome Lake; (2) in a relatively flat, open meadow; (3) near the main inlet to the lake. (4) The campsite is east of Pingora Peak. DAVE ANDERSON

A river crossing or the top of a pass are other landings that are helpful in keeping track of your progress.

Make note of these handrails and landings before you set out. Anticipate when you should reach a specific spot (see next page), and observe the terrain as you hike, checking off handrails and landings as you pass them. Keep track of your time as you travel, and notice when you come upon specific features. If you thought you would reach a river crossing an hour or two after leaving camp, and you find yourself 4 hours out without any sign of water, you probably need to reevaluate your position to make sure you have not gone astray.

It is a good idea to hike with a map in your hand or in an easily accessible pocket. This allows you to consult the map readily, especially if you find the land isn't fitting into the picture you had created before you set out. Such discrepancies may reflect a failure of your imagination, or they may be warning signs that you have lost track of the appropriate trail. For detailed advice on what to do if you become lost, see chapter 10.

Measuring Distance

You can eyeball distances roughly on a map, but for a real sense of how far you have to go and how long it will take to travel that distance, you need to be a bit more methodical in your measurements. An easy trick is to take a piece of parachute cord or string and lay it against the graphic

Use a piece of string to follow the twists and turns in the trail when measuring distance. DAVE ANDERSON

CALCULATING TRAVEL TIME

Place one end of your measuring string at your starting location and hold it in place. Use the cord to trace your path, taking care to follow the bends and twists in the trail. Once you've reached your destination, count up the miles your route entails.

Most hikers average 2 to 3 miles per hour on a trail. Your pace slows down considerably if you have a lot of elevation gain during the day, however. So before you jump to the conclusion that a 6-hour trip down the trail is going to take you 2 hours, make sure you look at the elevation gain the route entails.

The best way to calculate elevation gain is to follow your route, counting the contour lines you will cross. You don't really need to count elevation loss, as traveling downhill usually does not slow you down. And losing elevation does not negate elevation gain, so just because you climb 1,000 feet and then lose 1,000 feet does not mean your net gain is zero. You still need to factor in how that 1,000-foot elevation gain is going to affect your travel time to come up with an accurate sense of when you can expect to reach camp.

So count up the contour lines along your route and come up with a total number. For example, over the course of the day, you will gain a total of 2,200 feet. In general, a gain of 1,000 feet equates to approximately 1 extra mile of travel. So in this scenario you should estimate an additional 2.2 miles of travel time. If your linear mileage was 6 miles, plus an extra 2.2 miles for elevation gain, you will travel the equivalent of 8.2 miles, which should take at least 2.5 hours total to travel. You'll want to build in some cushion time for rest breaks, lunch, or scenic side trips, so in reality you'll probably want to allow yourself at least 4 hours to travel the distance.

scale diagram at the bottom of your map. Mark off miles along the cord with a permanent marker. Now you have a flexible measuring stick that makes calculating distances easy.

Anticipating Hazards

Even if you plan to stay on trails, wilderness travel involves some potential hazards. In the mountains you can anticipate trails crossing boulder fields or fording rivers. High-elevation passes are notorious for lightning in the afternoon, and marshy areas in early spring may mean slow going through mud and bogs.

Look closely at your route, and make note of potential hazards you may encounter. For example, say you are on a trip in the Wind River Mountains of Wyoming in early June. The sales clerk at the outdoor store in a nearby town says snow line is just above 10,000 feet, but the days are warming, and things are melting fast. Your prospective line of travel for the day involves an 11,000-foot pass, with a steep descent on a north-facing slope. You then plan to drop down along a river that drains five major valleys. The trail fords the river above a small canyon.

Your map is not going to give you a precise picture of what conditions you will find as you travel, but you can make some fairly accurate guesses

Snow-covered boulders are notorious for hiding so-called "elephant traps," or places where the snow is rotten and will not support the weight of a hiker, resulting in potentially dangerous falls.
DAVE ANDERSON

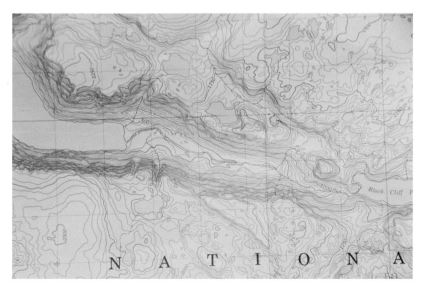

In early season when mountain snows are melting rapidly, rivers that drain large areas like this one can be difficult or impossible to cross.
DAVE ANDERSON

based on elevation, aspect, and weather. (You can also view the route in 3-D on Google Earth to get a better idea of the terrain. However, the ease of doing this is limited by the fact that many trails aren't shown.) First, when viewing the map and anticipating the route, you know you can expect to run into snow on the pass, since snow line is at 10,000 feet. Many passes in the Wind Rivers are bouldery, and late-season snow in boulders can be tricky. Therefore, you should anticipate postholing and slow going in places. The steep descent on a north-facing slope is almost certainly going to be snow covered in early June, and you may need an ice ax to descend safely.

The river is likely to be swollen with snowmelt if the days have been warm and it drains a large area. You may find it difficult or impossible to ford the stream, and the canyon downstream is an added danger if you happen to fall during the crossing.

Depending on your experience level and equipment, you may decide your route is not feasible at this time of year and you need to find an alternative destination. (As mentioned, see chapter 5 for a complete discussion of navigation techniques.)

CONTINGENCY PLANS: PLANNING FOR THE WORST

Competent wilderness travelers are constantly asking themselves "what if" when traveling through the backcountry, but the questioning should begin at home. Emergency planning ensures that you are prepared for

In the continental United States, you can be confident that all rivers eventually will take you to civilization if you follow them downstream, but it may take you a while to get there. DAVE ANDERSON

the unexpected, that people know where and when to look for you, and that your actions are rational and predictable in spite of the emotional trauma associated with any kind of emergency situation.

Here are the steps you need to take before you leave home:

a. Research outside resources.

- Where is the nearest telephone, or do cell phones work where you are traveling? Will you carry a cell phone or other emergency communication device (satellite phone or personal locator beacon)?
- What agency do you contact for help in an emergency situation (National Park Service, local sheriff's department, Bureau of Land Management, USDA Forest Service, and so on)?
- What are the logical "escape routes" out of the wilderness? (Do the rivers flow out to civilization? Can you reasonably follow them?)
- Are there any locations where you may be able to find help, such as an outfitter camp, a ranger cabin, or a popular destination where you are likely to encounter other campers?

b. Create a detailed itinerary.

- Write out your trip plan, with camping spots, dates, and travel routes identified. Include possible alternatives, potential obstacles, and contingency plans in case you are unable to complete your desired route.
- Identify an approximate end time when you expect to be home, as well as a second "freak" time—a time when you want people to start looking for you.
- Explain what your action plan is should an emergency occur.
- Outline the equipment and resources you and your team have available.
- Leave a copy of the itinerary with a trusted friend.

c. Check in with land management agencies.

- Secure permits for camping (if needed).
- Investigate potential hazards or obstacles that could affect your plan (bridges out, landslides, high water, and so forth).
- Consider leaving an itinerary with the permitting agency.

Hikers sometimes leave their itinerary in their car at the trailhead (top), but it's a debatable practice because it can invite thieves. Some wilderness permits (bottom) are in high demand; apply early.

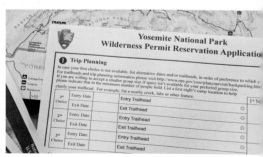

d. Look into weather conditions.
- Check into long-term forecasts for the area you are traveling.
- Gather information on potential weather extremes.

Regardless of how well you plan your trip, there may come a time when factors beyond your control result in an extreme situation requiring survival skills. For a complete discussion of outdoor survival techniques, see chapter 10.

MEAL PLANNING

Since food is one of the heaviest stuff sacks in your pack, the temptation may be to cut back when planning meals—potentially a big mistake. Insufficient calories will leave you sluggish and tired, which can contribute to accidents and possibly even put you in a dangerous situation. A starvation diet results in muscle loss too, so it's a poor method for losing body fat.

Many factors affect your caloric needs, including weight, metabolism, and difficulty of the hike. For a ballpark estimate of daily requirement when backpacking in the mountains, multiply your weight in pounds times 22. Thus a person weighing 120 pounds needs about 2,640 calories, while a 200-pounder needs 4,400 calories. On easy days, you can do well with less, but on long, hard days even that amount will leave you hungry.

Most of the freeze-dried meals sold in outdoor shops that supposedly have "two servings" barely have enough calories for a single hungry hiker (dinners often allow just 300 to 400 calories per person). To make matters worse, they are expensive, the flavors are bland, and the texture is best described as lumpy mush. On the plus side, they are fast and easy.

Fortunately there are many good options for trail foods from small specialty companies (e.g., Packit Gourmet) that combine freeze-dried and dehydrated foods to produce superior recipes. You can also do well by shopping at supermarkets and natural grocers for "instant" meals. And many backpackers prepare meals at home by drying foods in a dehydrator or oven.

Freeze-dried food is the lightest option out there for backpackers, but it can also be the most expensive.
STEPHEN GORMAN

On shorter trips, where weight may be of less concern, hydrated foods in sturdy foil packages (such as tuna and Indian meals) are a great way to supplement instant rice, couscous, or pasta. You can boost the calories and flavor of many meals by adding nuts, hard cheese, or salami; these all keep for a week or more on the trail. Also, bring some dried herbs in small bags and individual packets of hot sauce and honey to make the bland more interesting.

You can reduce weight and bulk, plus simplify life considerably, by repackaging meals into zip-lock bags before leaving home. It helps tremendously at the end of a long day to just pull out a meal with all the pertinent information (water required, cook time) on the outside and get 'er done.

The most convenient backpacking meals are packaged in food-grade plastic bags (either prepackaged or do-it-yourself freezer bags); simply add boiling water, wrap the meal with insulation, and wait. When ready, just eat out of the bag. These one-bag meals save fuel since there is no simmering, no pots to clean, and extra hot water can be used for drinks.

If you don't mind a little after-dinner cleanup, there are also many excellent one-pot meal possibilities; this is often the best option with groups. Rather than simmering the entire time, save fuel by boiling water, adding your ingredients, then shutting off the stove and waiting a bit longer than normal. For tender food, start rehydrating with cold water as soon as you get to camp, then set up your tent and attend to other chores before cooking.

SAMPLE QUESTIONNAIRE FOR GROUP FOOD PLANNING

Do you have any dietary restrictions?
Are there any foods you will not eat?
Name some of your favorite types of food.
Do you like to cook or bake, or would you rather just boil water?
How important is variety to you?
What do you like to eat on the trail while hiking?
How much do you eat?

Another option is to do a hybrid meal where the instant rice or couscous rehydrates in a freezer bag while you cook up a sauce with the yummy protein and fats. This doesn't work with pasta unless it has been precooked.

There is a lot to be said for making the first dinner of your backpacking trip an amazing one. It's easy to keep many vegetables fresh for a day, and you can even freeze something like a steak and carry it wrapped inside your sleeping bag. This sets a great tone for the rest of your trip and, if there are leftovers, makes for a good breakfast too.

Since you want to break camp and get on the trail quickly in the morning, breakfasts should be fast and easy. Don't bother with things like pancakes; instead opt for oatmeal and granola. However, don't deny yourself good coffee or tea, since that helps with your hydration and bowel movements.

When backpacking with a small group (two to four people), it is best to eat communally, but find out about likes, dislikes, and allergies ahead of time. Larger groups should break up into cook teams. It is also a good idea to make one person (preferably the most skilled) the designated cook; his or her tent gets pitched by the others.

Lunches and snacks tend to be individual affairs, with some sharing. There is no need to eat energy bars or gels, since real food is just as effective and a lot tastier. Make your own trail mix by going to stores with bulk bins and picking the things you like. Tortillas are the best sandwich bread, since they hold up well on the trail and can be used for a wide range of options.

For much more detailed information on backcountry cooking and food options, see chapter 7.

PLANNING AND PACKING YOUR BACKPACK

When packing your backpack before hitting the trail, the little things can add up to make a big difference later. If you start out with a good organization system, life in the backcountry will be simpler and more pleasant. For example, it helps to keep cook gear together so you aren't always looking for a lighter. And there is no point in pulling out your sleeping bag until the tent is set up.

Rather than put all your food in one big bag, it is better to divide it into smaller sacks for breakfast (and morning drinks), midday (lunch, snacks, and drink mixes), and dinner. This makes it easy to always have trail food handy, since it can be atop everything else.

The next step of pack planning is eliminating redundancy. Whenever possible, you want to carry gear that serves multiple functions. Think: Less is more. Pay attention to what you use—and especially what you don't use—on trips and figure out what can be eliminated.

Instead of carrying large bottles of sunscreen and bug repellent, take just what you need in small vials. Food can often be repackaged to reduce garbage; be sure to bring the cooking instructions. Don't take the entire guidebook; photocopy the relevant pages and you'll save weight and bulk, and the book will last longer. One pair of extra socks is good, but two is excessive for most trips. Spare underwear, sleeping bag liners, and emergency blankets are just deadweight.

When deciding what to cut, think twice about eliminating insulation and food. While ultralight fanatics and alpinists like to cut things to the bone, this can be a roll of the dice with serious consequences—pull it off and the admirers rave; when things go wrong, they howl about unpreparedness. Seldom will an extra fleece sweater and bit of food slow you down significantly; if they do, blame your physical fitness and not the gear.

Keep snacks handy in accessible pockets on your pack or clothes.
THINKSTOCK.COM

Similarly, a first-aid and repair kit is something you will hopefully never need. But reducing it too much, or leaving it behind, can mean the difference between minor inconvenience and an aborted trip.

It really helps to have things you will need during the day near the top of your pack. Better yet, carry snacks in hip belt pockets and have your water bottle located so you can reach it without removing your pack.

After all that planning, it's time to load up your pack. As a rule of thumb, you want the heaviest items (generally food and water) in the center of your pack and close to your back for greatest load transfer to the hips and stability. Most people carry the sleeping bag inside the bottom of the pack with the tent just above. It is an exceptionally bad idea to carry tent poles on the outside of the pack—they will get lost. After the tent goes food and kitchen gear; if using a gas stove, keep the fuel below your food in case of leaks. Clothing goes on top of the pack so you have quick access.

Jesup Path, Acadia National
Park, Maine THINKSTOCK.COM

CHAPTER 4

ON THE TRAIL

You've planned, you've packed, and you've arrived at the trailhead; now it's time to start walking. But before you head out, go through a checklist of the safety precautions you should have already taken. Did you tell someone where you are going, what trails you are taking, and when you expect to return? Don't count on being able to call 911 on your cell phone or even get a satellite signal with an emergency locator. Take the extra time to inform a friend or family member of your plans if you haven't already.

It is wise to get an early start so you have plenty of time for the day's agenda. This is especially important in the Rockies, where afternoon thunderstorms often dash above-tree-line plans. Sometimes you may even wish to sleep at the trailhead if it is permitted.

Start out for your hike well fed and hydrated, since this is "free" weight and may even save you from having to carry lunch. Also take the time to adjust your socks so there are no wrinkles and lace your boots up so they are snug in all the right places.

When putting on your pack, it is best to lift it by the grab handle between the shoulder straps. If the pack is heavy, slide it up so the bottom rests on the top of your thigh, then bend down and tuck one arm through a shoulder strap and stand up all the way. Hunch your shoulders to raise the pack up a bit, fasten the hip belt, and adjust the buckle so the belt is snug. Often you will want to fiddle with the shoulder and stabilizer straps a bit so that there are no pressure points.

HIKING TECHNIQUE

Once you begin hiking, maintain a strong, steady pace. At the end of the day, you will be less tired if you avoid intervals of hiking hard followed by catching your breath. Don't bother with techniques such as "rest steps" or "pressure breathing" unless you're at high elevation, climbing steeply. Just find a pace that you can keep up all day long and stick with it.

Rest and drink at stream crossings. THINKSTOCK.COM

It is generally better to take frequent short breaks instead of occasional long stops. You'll find it is hard to get going after setting your pack down and allowing your muscles to cool. Use those short breaks to look around, eat some snacks, sip some water, and take some photos. As soon as you feel a chill, get going again. Many backpackers have rued their decision to "tough it out" when they felt a hot spot on their feet. What could have been a simple 5-minute stop to treat an impending blister instead becomes days of pain dealing with a full-blown raw spot.

You might be able to walk and chew gum at the same time. But don't try to hike and read a map, or hike and drink from a bottle, or hike and take a photo. Far too many accidents have occurred when a moment's inattention caused a stumble or even walking off the trail! You should never be in such a hurry that you can't stop for a moment—leave that attitude in the city. Heck, even smell the roses.

Another good time to stop is at stream crossings. These can be an opportunity to rehydrate and refill your water bottles or bladders. On hot days, there is special pleasure in a quick soak of your feet. Even just submerging your wrists can help cool your body temperature.

The art of navigating in the backcountry revolves around never getting lost in the first place. Sounds blindingly obvious, but it's remarkable how many people cannot point to their location on a map once they leave the trailhead. Many seem to trudge along oblivious to the surroundings and barely cognizant of trail markings.

Smart backpackers keep a mental map of their approximate position as they hike. They confirm their location whenever they get to a trail junction or notable landmark. And they frequently look behind them because they know going in the reverse direction can look amazingly different. Unless you are going off-trail through deep forest or above tree line in a whiteout, it isn't that hard to stay found. For more on navigation, see chapter 5.

Keep an eye on time too so that you know well in advance if you are falling behind schedule. It is infinitely better to reach your campsite with an hour or two of daylight left. If it becomes apparent that you won't reach your destination when hoped, it may be better to start looking for an alternative camp.

HIKING ETIQUETTE

How your group interacts can be harmonious if everyone has a positive attitude and reasonable expectations. Or the group can devolve to discord and bickering when people become selfish and unyielding. Trust us, the former is better.

There is often a tendency for the fittest hikers to go charging up the trail, leaving the rest of the group far behind. Aside from the greater risk of people getting lost, this can create resentment that dampens the trip for everyone. A smarter course of action is to load the speed demons up with more weight and hike at the pace of the slowest person. That way everyone gets a workout and arrives together.

With larger groups, it is a good idea to designate a lead person on the trail (not necessarily the group leader) and a sweep. The lead should keep at least one other person within sight. When you get to a trail junction, everyone waits until the sweep is visible and clearly knows the proper direction.

You have two basic choices when you encounter other trail users: You can be pleasant or you can be a jerk. Be the former and say "howdy" or comment on the weather (or at least offer a friendly smile). Just don't be the loud jerk who has long, unwelcome conversations, shouts to make echoes, or otherwise pollutes the wilderness with noise.

When you encounter other hikers on the trail, the uphill hiker has the right-of-way. If you are heading down, be polite and step aside unless they decide to take a breather. Before moving off-trail, though, do a quick check for poison ivy and sound footing (bad form to go splat while getting out of the way). If you come upon a slower party from behind, ask permission to pass, and then quickly do so on the left.

It is generally best for larger groups to yield to smaller groups, but this too can depend on the situation. Don't clog the trail by hiking two abreast either, unless there is plenty of room to pass.

Mountain bikers on designated trails have as much right to be there as you do. In theory, bikers are always supposed to yield to hikers; however, they have to pass you at some point. So anticipate this and be prepared to step aside when it's convenient. Since mountain bikes have a hard time getting started again on uphills, it is best to step out of their way before they reach you. If you prefer not to share the trail with bikes, do your homework and choose a path where they aren't allowed.

If you encounter pack animals, either going up- or downhill, always give the animal the right-of-way. When you step aside for horses, try to go on the downhill side of the trail because they will be less likely to bolt. However, yaks have a fondness for knocking hikers off trails, so go uphill of those beasts.

HIKING IN THE RAIN

There is no such thing as staying dry while backpacking all day in the heavy rain! One way or another, you will get wet. The good news is that you can be perfectly comfortable even when a bit damp if you plan for it.

When working hard while carrying a pack in high humidity, you are going to sweat. This is compounded by condensation that can form inside outer shells when warm, moist air hits cold fabric. Waterproof/breathable fabrics are a huge help, but even the best of them can only do so much. Opening vents isn't a perfect solution either, since water has a way of finding its way inside.

The trick to enjoying rainy weather is making the most of your gear. Dress with quick-drying layers next to your skin and perhaps a lightweight mid-layer. The key is to generate warmth from hiking so you don't need a lot of insulation. Depending on the temperature and terrain—and your schedule—you may want to moderate your pace to minimize sweating, or increase it to boost warmth. Unless in a driving downpour, keep your vents open and use a rain hat or an umbrella instead of a hood.

Since rocks and roots can be treacherously slick when wet, using hiking poles is an especially good idea in the rain. Adjust them relatively short, though, so water doesn't run down your sleeves. When there are puddles in the trail, it is best to walk through them because walking around does more damage.

Lightning storms should be taken very seriously, especially when there is less than 30 seconds between the flash and the thunder. Get down off an exposed ridge or summit immediately. Try to seek shelter among a low stand of trees—never the highest tree in the area—and keep the group spread out at least 100 feet apart. If you can't find trees, look for low ground among boulders and cower in a crouching position.

For more information on weather and outdoor hazards, see chapter 8.

BATTLING BUGS

Biting bugs have always been a nuisance. But in this age of West Nile fever (mosquitoes) and Lyme disease (ticks), both seriously debilitating conditions, preventing bug bites has taken on a new urgency.

DEET, the old standby, is still the best bug repellent on the market; it lasts for about 4 hours, although the 30 percent strength is all you need. So far, none of the herbal repellents have proven effective for more than an hour or two. When conditions are especially bad, a mosquito-proof head net worn over a wide-brim hat and long-sleeve clothing treated with permethrin are your best option.

When the ticks are bad in summer, wear a long-sleeve shirt and long pants with gaiters or the legs tucked into your socks. Lighter-colored clothing makes it easier to spot ticks and will be cooler in the sun. Hike in the center of the trail, and avoid tall grass and bushes. If you hike with a dog, be sure it has protection against ticks as well.

STREAM CROSSINGS

Crossing raging creeks and swollen rivers is arguably the most dangerous part of backpacking. Never go into rushing water that is over your thighs! The force is far greater than you can imagine.

Scout upstream and down for the safest crossing spot. Typically this is a wider spot in the creek where the current is slower. But be certain there are no immediate downstream hazards such as a waterfall or a strainer (fallen tree).

Do not attempt to cross barefoot; the cold water makes it easy to injure your feet without knowing it until too late. Either wear the sandals you brought for the occasion or wear your trail shoes or boots. Remove long pants to reduce water drag on your legs, unfasten the sternum strap on your pack, and keep the hip belt secure so you don't lose your balance.

It is generally best for one person to cross at a time while using a pair of trekking poles (a single pole is far inferior here). Cross sideways to the current, taking small steps, and move slightly downstream toward the opposite bank. Always keep three solid points of contact and use the poles to probe your way.

Other members of your group should be deployed downstream, ready to render assistance, but don't make the mistake of getting dragged in during a rescue attempt. If you have a rope, it should be used as a throw line; never tied around the waist. Hand lines can be misleadingly dangerous and are best

The safest way to cross a stream is usually one person at a time while using a pair of trekking poles.
STEPHEN GORMAN

avoided. Crossing as a group is a complex undertaking; there's strength in numbers, but don't be tempted to take unnecessary risks just because you have support.

If you do get swept off your feet, never try to stand up! This can result in a trapped foot and drowning. Instead, float on your back with your feet pointed downstream and work your way to shore. For a more complete discussion of stream-crossing techniques and moving water hazards, see chapter 8.

HIKING IN HIGH, COLD MOUNTAINS

Backpacking above 10,000 feet presents a few challenges that can take a little getting used to . . . not the least of which is the thin air. You can also anticipate colder nights, snow at any time of year, and some issues when cooking.

Sadly, for those coming from sea level, there are no shortcuts to acclimatizing. The best you can hope for is to alleviate some of the symptoms of altitude maladies with aspirin or ibuprofen. Those who suffer greatly may wish to use acetazolamide (Diamox), a prescription medication that helps relieve symptoms. However, taking Diamox does not speed the body's adjustment to altitude.

Slow down your normal pace when hiking at high elevation. STEPHEN GORMAN

When you reach altitude, slow your normal pace down or you will soon find yourself gasping for breath. Going too high too fast is what makes backpackers feel like they got run over by a train. Take your time, drink lots of fluids, and eat plenty of carbohydrates. Even if you've had mountain sickness in the past, it doesn't mean you will always get it. Unfortunately, the reverse is also true.

Because there is less atmosphere, the sun is much more intense, so you must be extra careful to wear sun protection. The glare off snow also requires greater eye protection than offered by standard sunglasses.

When hiking in spring and early summer, you are likely to encounter deep snow in many places. Though you probably do not need insulated boots, you will likely need knee-high gaiters since you will be postholing. If it's a big snow year, you may even want to bring a pair of small snowshoes.

Early in the season, snowfields that need to be crossed often cover trails. You might be able to get away with just using your hiking poles for short sections, but a slip can send you rapidly sliding into rocks. This is a time when it can be well worth carrying a pair of lightweight crampons, such as Kahtoolas, for security on icy slopes. You may even want hiking poles with a self-arrest grip or an ice axe, which can also be used for chopping steps.

Although butane stoves perform better at higher altitude, this can be offset by decreased performance in the cold. Modern butane stoves with a preheat coil or pressure regulator are the most convenient. But if you are relying on melting snow for water for a group, you may wish to carry a reliable blowtorch-style white gas stove.

Regardless of the stove model, don't count on a Piezo Ignitor or refillable lighter to work at high altitude. Simply carry a Bic disposable lighter and keep it warm in your pocket. When cooking on snow, you will need a melt-proof stove platform for your stove (such as a thin piece of wood or foil-wrapped cardboard).

Anticipate that it will take longer for water to boil. And due to the lower boiling temperature of water (193°F at 10,000 feet instead of 212°F at sea level), it will take longer for foods to cook or rehydrate. Fast-cooking starches (such as ramen, orzo, couscous, and instant rice) are a better option than spaghetti or normal rice.

Trekking poles are useful when crossing soft snowfields in the midday sun like this, but an ice ax and even crampons may be desired on hard, icy slopes.
STEPHEN GORMAN

Since nausea is fairly common for people with mountain sickness, carry some bland foods like oatmeal, soups, and crackers. Once your body adjusts, you can handle spicy foods again and may even crave fatty foods. Bring plenty of tea, instant cider, and hot chocolate to encourage hydrating at breakfast and dinner.

To prevent water from freezing at night, it is standard practice to bring a water bottle inside the sleeping bag; be certain that it will not leak. And to avoid having to crawl out of the tent at night, many campers carry a pee bottle; be certain it can't be mistaken for a water bottle during the night. For more on the hazards of hiking in high, cold mountains, see chapter 8.

HIKING IN HOT DESERTS

In contrast to the mountains, backpacking in the desert presents a different set of challenges . . . not the least of which is the heat. Of course water is scarce, and the nights can be surprisingly chilly. But desert hiking has its own rewards and should not be missed.

The best time to visit most deserts is in spring and fall; summers are just too brutally hot, and winters can be bitter. Far too many hikers underestimate how dangerous it is to work hard in hot weather. When the air temperature is above 95°F, radiation, one of your primary mechanisms for reducing core temperature, is lost. This only leaves you with evaporation, and that too will soon be lost if you don't carry a lot of water.

For most times of the year when backpacking in the desert, you need a minimum of 5 liters of water per person per day; that is 11 pounds in your

Don't be afraid of snakes when hiking in the desert, but do watch where you step. STEPHEN GORMAN

pack. Unless you plan your trips around guaranteed water supplies or bury caches ahead of time, you will be limited to how long you can stay out.

In very hot weather, choose loose-fitting, light-colored clothing that has long sleeves. Many desert hikers prefer cotton because it absorbs water and evaporates more slowly than synthetics. Definitely wear a hat with a full, wide brim, not just a baseball cap.

Avoid hiking in the hottest part of the day (mid-afternoon), go at a slow pace, rest frequently, and take sips of water every 15 minutes. During the day, be sure to drink fluids with electrolytes to replace what is lost in sweat. Due to the risk of heat exhaustion and heat stroke, which can sneak up with little warning, always hike with a partner so you can monitor each other's condition.

Contrary to popular belief, you pretty much have to work at getting bitten by a rattlesnake. Aside from the generous warning they provide, they don't tend to be aggressive unless provoked. Watch where you step, don't make them mad, and you'll be fine. Ignore those rules and you're on the way to the ER, in a slow, controlled manner; getting bit may hurt like heck, but adults won't die if they receive proper treatment. Don't bother carrying snakebite kits, and ignore cut-and-suck folklore—none of that works and actually causes more problems.

Avoid brushing against cactus, or you may spend an hour plucking out needles. It is wise to carry a multitool with needle-nosed pliers, as well as splinter tweezers, for this unpleasant task.

When making camp, do not pitch your tent in an arroyo (dry creek bed) if there is even a hint of rain in the distance. A storm that is miles away can send a flash flood roaring down. Backpacking through slot canyons can be very dangerous in spring and summer, when storms are most common.

After you select a campsite, get everything ready, but leave your sleeping bag stuffed to prevent sharing your bag with a scorpion. Some backpackers carry an ultraviolet flashlight to spot scorpions at night. For more information on hiking in extreme temperatures, see chapter 8.

HIKING IN BEAR COUNTRY

North America has about half a million bears, mostly black bears. Yet in our recorded history, bears have killed fewer than fifty people, an average of less than one person per year. For each recorded fatality caused by bears (all species), we have approximately 8 caused by spiders, 13 by snakes, 34 by domestic dogs, 90 by bees and wasps, and 190 by lightning.

In the United States alone, domestic dogs bite about 2 percent of the population every year, about 5 million people, and kill around twenty-five people per year. Even Western national parks with large grizzly bear populations average less than one bear-caused fatality per year, despite the fact that millions of tourists travel through the entrance stations annually.

So, statistically speaking, walking the streets of a big city is more hazardous than walking the trails of bear country.

Nonetheless, bears are dangerous. Hopefully, however, with the distribution of more information on how to safely hike and camp in bear country, fewer and fewer bears will make the front page and more and more people will be able to enjoy bear country.

That's our side of the story. There's also the bears' side.

Carelessness can kill not only you or the next person coming down the trail, but also a bear. Most bear attacks, including nonfatal encounters, result in dead bears. Worse, many surprise encounters involve mother bears with cubs, and in far too many cases, both the mother bear and cubs are "removed from the population," which means euthanized or, arguably worse, imprisoned for life without parole in a zoo, research lab, or drive-through wildlife park.

When bears lose their fear of humankind, wildlife managers have little choice but to remove them. In certain circumstances, usually our fault, a bear can gradually become more conditioned to human food or garbage. Once a bear picks up this nasty habit, it's the start of a slow, but virtually guaranteed, death march. Hence the saying, "A fed bear is a dead bear." The bear might avoid its fate for years, but sooner or later it crosses the line and authorities take it out.

Here's the bottom line: Bear encounters obviously pose a threat to human safety, but they also pose a threat to bear safety—not just the safety of individual bears, but of the entire population. This side of the story doesn't make many headlines, but it's another reason we should take every precaution to avoid an encounter. Too many bear encounters could even lead to a movement to rid the forests of bears.

Therefore, the information included here has two goals: to save you and to save a bear.

Note: This section deals primarily with hiking in bear country. For more information on camping and food storage when backpacking in bear country, see chapter 6.

Minimizing Risk in Bear Country

The first step of any hike in bear country is an attitude adjustment. Nothing guarantees total safety. Hiking in bear country adds a small additional risk to your trip. However, that risk can be minimized by adhering to this age-old piece of advice: Be prepared. And being prepared doesn't only mean having the right equipment. It also means having the right knowledge, which, again, is your best defense.

Don't Let Fear Ruin Your Trip

Don't be the hiker who describes his or her recent backpacking vacation like this: "I didn't see a single bear, but I heard hundreds of them at night while lying sleepless in my tent." You can—and should—thoroughly enjoy your trip to bear country. Don't let the fear of bears ruin your vacation. This fear can accompany you every step of the way. It can constantly lurk in the back of your mind, preventing you from enjoying the wildest and most beautiful places left on Earth. Even worse, some bear experts think bears might actually be able to sense your fear.

Being prepared and knowledgeable gives you confidence. It allows you to fight back the fear that can haunt you throughout your stay in bear country. You won't—nor should you—forget about bears and the basic rules of safety, but proper preparation allows you to keep the fear of bears at bay and let enjoyment rule the day.

Be aware of bears and know how to avoid encounters, but don't let fear ruin your trip into bear country.
THINKSTOCK.COM

Risks are Relative

Although human-bear encounters make for sensational news, the actual risk of being attacked by a bear is statistically extremely low. Dogs and bees are much more dangerous, and you're more likely to get in an accident on the drive to the trailhead than get hurt by a bear. So be prepared and hike and camp responsibly, but don't overreact to the threat of bears.

Five Basic Rules of Hiking Safely in Bear Country

Nobody likes surprises, and bears dislike them too. The majority of bear maulings occur when a hiker surprises a bear. Therefore, it's vital to do everything possible to avoid these surprise meetings, starting with "The Basic Five":

- Be alert.
- Hike in a group and stay together.
- Stay on the trail.
- Avoid hiking at sunrise and sunset.
- Make noise.

If you follow these five rules, your chances of encountering a bear on the trail narrow to the slimmest possible margin.

No Substitute for Alertness

As you hike, watch ahead and to the sides. Don't fall into the all-too-common habit of fixating on the trail a few feet ahead. It's especially easy to do this when dragging a heavy pack up a long hill or when carefully watching your step on a rocky or eroded trail.

Using your knowledge of bear habitat and habits, be especially alert in areas most likely to be frequented by bears, such as in avalanche chutes or berry patches, along streams, through stands of whitebark pine, and in salmon-spawning areas.

Watch carefully for bear sign and be especially watchful (and noisy) if you see any. If you notice a track or scat but it doesn't look fresh, pretend it's fresh. The area is obviously frequented by bears.

Watch the Wind

The wind can be a friend or foe. The direction and strength of the wind can make a significant difference in your chances of encountering a bear.

When the wind blows at your back, you're much safer since your smell travels ahead of you, alerting any bear on or near the trail ahead.

Conversely, when the wind blows in your face, your chances of a surprise meeting with a bear increase because a bear can't smell you coming, so make more noise and be more alert.

A strong wind can also be noisy and limit a bear's ability to hear you coming. If a bear can't smell or hear you coming, the chances of an encounter significantly increase, so watch the wind.

Safety in Numbers

There have been very few instances in which a large group has had a serious encounter with a bear. Instead, a large percentage of hikers mauled by bears were hiking alone or with one other person. Large groups naturally make more noise and put out more smell and probably appear more threatening to bears. In addition, if you're hiking alone and get injured, there's nobody to go for help. For these reasons, some national parks recommend parties of four or more hikers when going into bear country.

If a large party splits up, it becomes two or more small parties or a group of solo hikers, and the advantage is lost. So stay together. If you're on a family hike, keep the kids from running ahead. If you're in a large group, keep the stronger members from going ahead or weaker members from lagging behind. The best way to prevent this natural separation is to ask one of the slowest members to lead. This keeps everybody together.

Hike in groups in bear country. THINKSTOCK.COM

People Are Supposed to Be on Trails

Although bears use trails, they don't often use them midday when hikers commonly use them. Through generations of associating trails with people, bears probably expect to find hikers on trails, especially during the middle of the day. On infrequently used trails, however, it may be more likely to find a bear using the trail or bedded down near the trail.

On the other hand, bears probably don't expect to find hikers off trails. Bears rarely settle down in a day bed right along a well-used trail. However, if you wander around in thickets off the trail, you might stumble into an occupied day bed or cross paths with a traveling bear.

Sleeping Late Has Its Rewards

Bears—and most other wildlife—usually aren't active during the middle of the day, especially on hot summer days. Many wild animals, including bears, are most active around dawn and dusk. Therefore, hiking early or late increases your chances of seeing wildlife, including bears. Likewise, hiking in the middle of a hot day reduces the chances of an encounter.

Sometimes It's OK to Be Loud and Obnoxious

Perhaps the best way to avoid an encounter is to make sure the bear knows you're there, so make lots of noise. However, the best type of noise is a source of debate.

One theory supports metallic noise—such as bear bells chiming, an aluminum fly rod case or metal-tipped walking stick clanging on trailside rocks, or pebbles rattling in a can—as the best. Metallic noise doesn't occur in nature, so it must come from humans, the theory goes, and is less likely to be muffled by natural conditions than human voices.

Other bear experts, however, think that human voices or loud clapping rather than metallic noise are more likely to alert bears of your presence. One recent research project in Alaska found that bears more or less ignored both metallic noise (bear bells) and human voices unless these sounds were unusually loud, but were alerted immediately by the sound of snapping sticks and bear-like growls. Loud clapping tends to sound like twigs breaking and has been effective in alerting bears.

All bear experts recommend making noise, but you have to make the decision on what type of noise. One way to make the decision easier is to check at the local ranger station, which often gives out specific recommendations.

Sometimes It's *Not* OK to Be Loud and Obnoxious

While planning your noisemaking, be sure to discuss respect for other hikers—or as some experts call it, "appropriate noise." Hikers hike to get away from "noise pollution," so keep in mind that some conditions warrant silence to better enjoy wild nature. For example, if you're closely following another group of hikers up the trail, you can forgo noisemaking. The same goes in places where there's no chance of seeing a bear, such as open stretches of trail through tundra or alpine meadows or trails gouged out of cliff faces, where you can see a long distance up the trail. You can safely remain quiet and enjoy the wilderness in these situations and then yell or clap loudly when you approach a thicket or brushy ravine. Also, please preserve everybody's wilderness experience by not making loud noises in camp.

Getting too close to a bear to take pictures is a bad idea. Use a long lens instead. THINKSTOCK.COM

You Don't Need a Better View

If you see a bear, don't try to get closer for a better look. The bear might interpret this as an act of aggression and charge.

Use a Longer Lens Instead

A high percentage of people mauled by bears are photographers. That's because they're purposely being quiet, hoping to see wildlife. In some cases they try to get closer to a bear for a better photo. Such behavior is counter to all rules for traveling safely in bear country—and threatens the bear too, which is often killed after being involved in a serious encounter.

Trail Runners Beware

Many avid runners like to get off paved roads and running tracks and onto backcountry trails. But running on trails in bear country can be seriously hazardous to your health.

Most runners avoid running during the heat of the day. Instead they run early or late in the day, when bears are most active. Runners rarely make enough noise when running, and they might even sound like a wild animal (i.e., bear food) running on a trail.

Experienced trail runners know that you tend to get closer to wildlife running than you do walking. Some people think that's because you cover distances faster than expected by wildlife. Other people think it's because you tend to be quieter when running. Whatever the reason, running on trails obviously increases your chances of surprising a bear.

The best advice is to avoid running in bear country, but if you're a hopelessly addicted runner and can't resist trying a scenic trail in bear country, at least strap a bell on your fanny pack, take bear pepper spray, and run during the heat of the day.

Leave Night to the Bears

Like running on trails, hiking at night can be very risky. Bears are often more active after dark, and you're less likely to see them until it's too late. If you get caught out at night, be sure to make lots of noise.

Dead Meat

If you see or smell an animal carcass when hiking in bear country, immediately vacate the area. Don't let your curiosity keep you near the carcass a second longer than you need to recognize this as an extremely dangerous situation.

Bears commonly hang around a carcass, guarding it and feeding on it for days until it's consumed. Your presence could easily be interpreted as a threat to the bear's food supply, and a vicious attack could be imminent.

If you see a carcass ahead of you on the trail, don't go any closer. Instead, abandon your hike and return to the trailhead. If the carcass is between you and the trailhead, take a long detour around it, upwind from the carcass, making lots of noise along the way. Be sure to report the carcass to the local ranger or game warden. This tip might prompt a temporary trail closure or special warnings but might also prevent injury to other hikers and the death of a bear. In some cases, rangers will go in and drag the carcass away from the trail, but usually they will temporarily close the area.

Cubs are cute, but stay away!
THINKSTOCK.COM

Cute, Cuddly, and Lethal

The same advice for approaching carcasses goes for bear cubs. If you see one, don't go even an inch closer. The cub might seem abandoned, but it most likely is not. Mother is nearby, and female bears fiercely defend their young.

Side Trips

Many backpackers like to take a side trip during a long day to see a special place or enjoy a few hours without the heavy pack. If you do this, be sure to hang your pack out of reach of bears in much the same manner as you would hang your food at night. If you don't take the time to do this, you might end up with, at the least, a destroyed backpack or, at the worst, an encounter with a bear defending the food reward it found in your pack. You could also be doing a great disservice to future backpackers by conditioning a bear to look for food in backpacks. Once again, the result would be a dead bear.

As a fringe benefit, you won't have holes chewed in your pack by rodents.

Regulations for Your Safety (and the Bears')

Nobody likes rules and regulations. However, national parks and forests have a few that you must follow. These rules aren't meant to suck the freedom out of your trip. They're meant to help bring you back safely—and to keep bears wild and alive.

When you get a backcountry camping permit in a national park, you get a list of these rules. In some cases they're printed right on your permit. In national forests you might not need a permit, but you can check with the local ranger for any special regulations. In both national parks and national forests, carefully read the notices on the information boards at trailheads.

Do You Want to See Bears?

Now you know how to be safer while hiking: Walk up the trail constantly clanging two metal pans together. It works every time. You won't see a bear, but you'll hate your "wilderness experience." You left the city to get away from loud noise.

Yes, you can be very, very safe, but how safe do you want to be and still be able to enjoy your trip? It's a balancing act. First, be knowledgeable and then decide how far you want to go. Everybody has to make his or her own personal choice.

Here's another conflict. If you do everything recommended to avoid bear encounters, it might work *too* well. You most likely won't see any bears—or deer or moose or eagles or any other wildlife. Again, you make the choice. If you want to be as safe as possible, follow these rules

- Knowledge is the best defense.
- There is no substitute for alertness.
- Hike with a large group, and stay together.
- Don't hike alone in bear country.
- Stay on the trail.
- Hike in the middle of the day.
- Make lots of noise.
- Never approach a bear.
- Cubs are deadly.
- Stay away from carcasses.
- Know and adhere to regulations.

religiously. If you want to see wildlife, including bears, only make noise when necessary and don't use bear bells. You are, of course, increasing your chances of an encounter instead of decreasing them.

Bear Pepper Spray

In recent years bear pepper spray, which stings the eyes and hampers breathing, has earned more and more respect from experts. Many people have escaped uninjured by using bear spray to turn away a charging bear. Now most park rangers recommend it and carry it themselves when in bear country. In no recorded case has bear spray made a bear more aggressive or harmed the bear. In fact, getting sprayed might make a bear more wary of humans.

Even though bear spray can help erase that deep-seated fear that can ruin a wilderness adventure, it has a downside. Bear spray, like firearms, can create a false sense of security. Having bear spray mounted on your belt or pack strap doesn't mean you can skip the precautions outlined here.

Poor handling of food and garbage can get you (or other campers who follow you) into much more trouble than bear spray can solve. Canned pepper definitely does not make you bear-proof. Instead of being a cure-all, bear spray is merely your next-to-last line of defense. If it doesn't turn away the bear, your only remaining options are playing dead or physical resistance.

Here, point by point, are tips for using bear spray:

- Be sure you buy something called "Bear Spray" or "Bear Pepper Spray." Some products labeled "Pepper Spray" are not meant for use on bears.
- Before you leave the trailhead, read the directions on the bear spray container or packaging. If you're uncertain about how to operate the spray, buy an extra canister, test-fire it, and discard it. Then hit the trail with a new full canister. (You can also get inexpensive test canisters from some companies to familiarize yourself with operating the spray.)
- If you test-fire the canister, don't do it into the wind—it can drift back and give you the personal experience of what a bear feels like when sprayed.
- Don't test-fire bear spray in bear country, where the lingering smell might actually attract bears.
- Make sure you carry bear spray in an instantly accessible place. If you need it, you might only have 1 or 2 seconds to get ready to use it.
- All members of your party should carry bear spray at all times and keep it instantly accessible. Don't forget it when going into the woods for a nature call or leaving camp to go fishing or climbing.
- Keep bear spray close by when cooking. It won't do you much good 100 yards away in your pack if a bear, attracted by food smells, suddenly comes into camp.
- Don't spray it on yourself, your hiking partners, around camp, or on equipment. This might attract bears.
- Carry a large canister, 225 grams or more.
- Use a bear spray with a high level of active ingredient, 1 to 2 percent capsaicin.
- Make sure your bear spray is a fogger, not a stream pattern.
- Don't go for the lowest price; get a high-quality product.
- Remember the limited range of the spray, usually 20 to 30 feet.

Bear spray won't do you any good if it's stuffed away in your pack. Carry it in a holster on your pack belt so it is instantly accessible and can be used without even removing it from the holster. JOHN BURBIDGE

- Don't let your bear spray get extremely cold or hot. Don't leave it in a hot vehicle all day. It could explode.
- Only use bear spray to deter charging or attacking bears, not on any other bear you see.
- Airlines prohibit taking bear spray on planes, so you might have to buy it after you've reached your destination.
- In some cases you might have trouble getting your bear spray across the US-Canada border, but recently Canada has started allowing travelers to cross with EPA-approved bear spray. Most major brands are EPA-approved.

Encounters: What to Do?

The threat of having a close encounter with a bear is like the threat of having a heart attack. If you practice preventive health care, stay physically fit, and watch your diet, you're much less likely to have heart problems. Likewise, if you follow the safety guidelines in this chapter, you're much less likely to have a close encounter with a bear. With both heart attacks and bear attacks, preventing a problem is so much better than dealing with the problem.

An encounter is a situation where you may be at risk. In many cases, it's what happens when you don't follow all the recommendations discussed thus far. An encounter could be surprising a bear on or off the trail. It could be a bear coming into camp. It could also be a predatory attack.

If you're uncertain about what to do in case of an encounter, you aren't alone. Even bear experts disagree on how to react to various kinds of encounters. Every encounter is different; every person is different; every bear is different. Consequently, there's no checklist for what to do. Nonetheless, your reaction to an encounter can definitely affect your chances of coming away uninjured.

HAVE A REHEARSAL

Not many recommendations apply to all bear encounters, but one does: Cool heads prevail. Panic is your greatest enemy. To help avoid panic, do rehearsals before you hit the trail. Go through hypothetical situations, and decide what each member of the group should do. This rehearsal builds self-confidence.

Defensive or Offensive?

The most recent recommendations from bear scientists and managers divide all encounters into two categories—defensive and offensive. Defensive encounters are situations in which you suddenly come upon a bear and the bear is most likely as surprised as you are. Offensive encounters are situations in which a bear intentionally moves toward you. Most likely, but not always, the offensive bear is bluffing or simply curious instead of being truly aggressive or predatory.

Previously, bear managers had different recommendations for black bears and grizzly bears, but now, in most cases, they lump all bears together and split them up as defensive or offensive bears. In other words, note the behavior, not the species.

How to Play Dead

Bear experts used to recommend playing dead by curling up in the cannonball position, but most now recommend lying flat on your stomach, legs separated, hands clasped behind your neck, elbows extended. This position gives your vital organs as much protection as possible and makes it hard for the bear to turn you over. While playing dead, remain silent and leave your pack on to further protect your body. If the bear turns you over, quickly roll back onto your stomach.

Playing dead: If you're wearing a backpack, leave it on

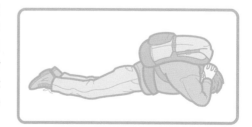

If You See a Bear at a Distance

First and most important, don't move toward the bear while you enjoy this rare and beautiful sight. If the bear is a long distance away from the trail, enjoy your wildlife-viewing experience and continue down the trail. If the bear is uncomfortably close to the trail ahead but is acting naturally and not moving toward you, slowly back down the trail about 0.25 mile, keeping an eye on the bear until out of sight. Wait a few minutes and then hike back up the trail, making lots of loud noise. If the bear is still near the trail ahead and still acting naturally, take a big detour around the bear, upwind if possible, so the bear can get your scent. Stay out of sight, if possible, but make lots of noise to ensure the bear knows you're there. Then, quickly (walk, don't run) leave the area.

If You See a Bear from Camp

If the bear is at a distance, get your bear spray out and make lots of noise to scare it away. If there's still time before nightfall, break camp and move to another campsite. Seeing a bear circling a camp during the day might mean it will come into camp at night.

If the bear is close to camp, move to the base of the escape tree you previously scouted out. Take noisemakers and bear spray with you. If the bear comes closer, climb the tree. Take the food with you, if possible, so the bear doesn't get a food reward. If you don't have a good escape tree or time to climb it, stand together to look bigger and more threatening to the bear; everyone should have bear spray ready to fire. If the bear comes dangerously close, spray it.

If You See a Bear at Close Range

Most important, don't panic or run wildly or scream. Running or other sudden movements might cause the bear to charge. As long as you stay coolheaded and under control, you have an excellent chance of leaving the encounter with only vivid memories, not injuries. If you act like prey, you can become prey.

The first thing to do is nothing. Make no sudden moves or sounds. Stand still. Be quiet. Slowly take your bear spray from its holster and remove the safety clip. Keep your backpack on. Look around for cubs. Then, carefully assess the situation.

Watch for aggressive behavior, such as laid-back ears, hackles up on the back of its neck, head rapidly swinging from side to side, threatening *woofs*, or feet slapping on the ground. If the bear mashes its teeth together making a loud *pop*, it's very agitated and likely to charge. If the bear stands on its hind feet and puts its snout up, it isn't a sign of aggression. The bear is trying to get your scent or get a better look to figure out what you are.

Any bear that moves toward you should be considered offensive or aggressive. This or any other aggressive behavior is your cue that the bear wants you out of its turf, so back away slowly, talking quietly in a monotone. Avoid sudden movements. Don't turn your back on the bear; instead turn sideways to the bear if you can. Be nonthreatening and submissive. Avoid direct eye contact with the bear. As you carefully retreat, slowly move your arms up and down—like doing jumping jacks without jumping. You can drop something on the trail (clothing, walking stick, etc.) to distract the bear, but not anything with food in it. You don't want to give the bear a food reward for chasing you.

If you decide to climb a tree, make sure you can reach the tree and get 15 feet up it before the bear can get there. Running toward the tree could easily prompt the bear to chase you. Remember, bears can sprint at up to 35 miles per hour. In several documented encounters, people have underestimated a bear's speed and been mauled as they tried to reach or climb a tree. Also, bears sometimes climb trees. Trees are not guaranteed safe unless they're too thin, with weak branches, for the bear to climb.

If a Bear Charges You
It's easy to say and hard to do, but, again, don't panic. Many bear charges are bluffs. Point your bear spray at the bear and stand your ground. Sometimes a bear will make several bluff charges. Don't spray the bear unless you're sure the bear isn't bluffing and is within range (i.e., less than 30 feet). If the bear stops after a bluff charge, slowly wave your arms, talk softly, and slowly back away. Again, you can drop something without food in it to distract the bear. If the bear doesn't stop, spray it.

If the Bear Makes Physical Contact
If the bear charges and makes physical contact with you, it's important to think "offensive or defensive bear." If you surprised the bear and it charges you suddenly out of nowhere, it's probably a defensive bear threatened by you unexpectedly appearing nearby—or it might be defending its cubs

A close range bear.
THINKSTOCK.COM

or food cache. Act submissive and play dead, unless the bear becomes predatory, which is your cue to fight back with everything you can.

Even if a defensive bear roughs you up, don't fight back. Remain flat and silent. Don't look at the bear. If the bear moves away, be patient and continue to play dead until you're sure it has left the area. Then immediately (no running!) move out of the area. If the bear continues to maul you while you're playing dead, you know it isn't a defensive bear. It's probably an offensive bear, so give up the game and use whatever physical resistance you can muster as a last resort.

If you know the bear has purposely moved toward you, getting closer and closer until it has made physical contact with you, consider it an offensive bear. When attacked by an offensive bear, don't play dead or act submissive. If you can't escape up a tree or into a vehicle or building, fight back with all your might and with whatever weapons you can find. It might seem futile to face an opponent many times faster and stronger than you are, but you might be surprised what you can do in a life-threatening circumstance. If you see one of your companions in this situation, intervene on his or her behalf.

If a Bear Comes into Camp during Daylight

A bear coming into camp is not the same type of bear that you surprise on the trail. This bear has chosen to approach you and is definitely an offensive bear. It could be a bear that has become conditioned to human food and garbage, possibly by people who camped there before you. This bear is more dangerous because it has stopped trying to avoid an encounter. The bear might not intend to attack. More likely, it's looking for another food reward. Try to prevent the bear from getting it. Allowing the bear to get more food only makes it more dangerous for you and the next campers.

Stay calm. Avoid direct eye contact. Stay together in a close group to look bigger and more threatening. Talk softly, and slowly retreat. If you have to abandon the camp and sacrifice your camping gear, do it. Return to the trailhead and immediately report the encounter to a ranger.

A bear that enters camp during the day is a dangerous bear.
THINKSTOCK.COM

If the bear moves toward you, react in the same way you would if it approached you on the trail.

If a Bear Comes into Camp at Night

Get the bear spray ready and use your flashlight to verify that it's a bear. It might be a campground deer or one of your hiking partners answering a nature call.

If it's a bear and you have time to get to your escape tree, do it, but don't leave the tent if you aren't sure you have time to get up the tree. If the bear is hanging around the cooking area because of the food smell, make lots of noise and try to scare the bear away.

If a Bear Enters Your Tent

This is the worst possible situation, but fortunately it very rarely happens.

A night attack comes from a predatory bear. Don't act like prey. Don't lie still in your sleeping bag. Don't play dead. Don't run or scream, but don't act passive. If you can't escape to a vehicle or building or up a tree, fight back with everything you have. Use the bear spray. Make loud noise. Shine your flashlight in the bear's eyes. Temporarily blind the bear with the flash on your camera. Whack it on the nose with your flashlight or walking stick. Use whatever physical resistance you can. Some backpackers like to keep a knife handy inside the tent when camping in areas with high concentrations of bears, not to fight off the bear but to slit a hole in the tent wall to escape through.

Be Realistic, Not Fearful

After reading a few pages about how to deal with encounters, it might be harder to overcome the fear of bears, but be realistic. If you practice the methods outlined in this chapter and given to you at the local ranger station, you have only the slightest chance of ever having an encounter. And even if you do, you have a good chance of coming away uninjured.

If bears wanted to prey on humans, it would be easy for them. Bears could easily kill hundreds of people per year, but then of course there wouldn't be any bears because we would kill them all. Obviously, 99-plus percent of bears want to stay away from people. Keep this in mind as you prepare for—and then enjoy—your backpacking trip in bear country.

Maroon Bells, Colorado. THINKSTOCK.COM

CHAPTER 5
NAVIGATION

Before you go into the mountains, try this: Pull out all the maps for the area where you are heading, lay them across the floor, and dream. The intricate twisting brown contour lines, white snow patches and bright blue lakes, the trails or lack of trails winding through the landscape—all are enough to get your adrenaline going. Try to identify potential routes that will take you away from the main thoroughfares, over obscure passes and into places that seem off the beaten track. Some backpackers spend hours perusing the possibilities, conjuring up images of what they might see if they were there: Cliffs, rivers, glaciers, forests—that information and more is laid out in front of you on a topographic map.

If you've driven a car, you have undoubtedly used highway maps. These maps also show roads, trails, rivers, lakes, and other relevant features, but they give no indication of the topography you may encounter. Road maps just show you a flat world, which is fine for driving; you don't really need to know whether you are going uphill or down when your automobile is doing all the work. But once you lace up your boots, throw on a backpack, and start walking, every up and down makes a difference. You want—really, need—to know what the landscape looks like before you set off to cross it on foot. For this kind of navigation, you need a topographic map.

Topographic maps create a two-dimensional picture of a three-dimensional world. With a little practice, topographical maps give you a sense of the place you are going and the things you will encounter en route. You can use a map to predict travel times, to anticipate challenges or obstacles, to pick out camping spots or rendezvous points, to choose a fishing hole or a cliff to climb, or just to excite your imagination about the infinite possibilities for adventure represented on the page.

Backcountry navigation requires more than just the ability to use navigational tools. You also need to develop your sense of direction. People who have lived or traveled in a given area for an extended period of time

Take time to look around and orient yourself to the landscape. You'll start to recognize macro features and general trends in the topography that help you develop your internal sense of direction. DAVE ANDERSON

Look at your map frequently to develop an accurate sense of scale and to keep track of your whereabouts. DAVE ANDERSON

learn to recognize key signs that help clue them in to where they are: The mountains trend north–south, for instance, or most streams flow in an easterly direction to empty into one major river. Such clues can help you recognize the cardinal directions—north, south, east, and west—before you pull out your map and compass.

The sun can also be helpful in orienting yourself to your surround-

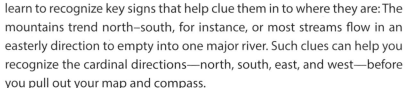

ings. If it is late afternoon and you are walking into its glare, you know right away you are heading west. But the fact is that if you've been paying attention to the lay of the land as you hike, you are unlikely to be completely disoriented when it comes time to bring out the map to figure out where you are and where you are going.

For most backpackers who stick to well-marked trails, topographic maps are all you really need to navigate the wilderness, but there are other tools—a compass, an altimeter, a GPS—that can fine-tune your navigational skills and allow you to pinpoint your position with a degree of precision that may be critical at certain times, such as when following a bearing to paddle to an unseen island or when telling a pilot exactly where you are located.

Like so many things in life, trailside navigation is an art, not a science. You need to master the tools and learn the language, but ultimately good backcountry travelers develop an eye that allows them to see the landscape from the lines on the map. This chapter is the first step in helping you develop your own navigational eye.

SPECIFIC NAVIGATION TOOLS

In this chapter we will introduce the basic, critical tools you need for navigating in the wilderness. These tools include, first and foremost, a topographic map.

Most backcountry travelers should also carry a compass. Compasses contain a magnetic needle that automatically points to magnetic north, allowing you to orient yourself in the event you become confused about your whereabouts. You can use a compass to align your map to the landscape. Or you can shoot a bearing—either a visual bearing off the land or a bearing from your map—that will lead you to your destination. Both skills will be explained in the following sections.

We will also discuss the use of altimeters for navigation. Altimeters indicate elevation, which can be helpful when you know you are somewhere on a slope or pass but can't pinpoint your location from the landforms around you. Having an elevation point can allow you to home in on your precise position.

Finally we will introduce readers to a GPS receiver, which uses satellites to identify your location and allows you to outline a path on your map or overland. GPS receivers are a great way to locate precise points, such as a rendezvous spot or a trailhead, where accuracy is critical

You can have an intellectual understanding of these tools but still be lost in the mountains if you don't know how to use them in the field. Orienting a map from the landscape or following a compass bearing takes practice and skill. This chapter includes basic steps and exercises to allow you to teach yourself these skills and give you the confidence to venture out into the wilderness on your own.

TOPOGRAPHIC MAPS

All maps depict a portion of the Earth's surface graphically. What makes topographic maps different from a regular road map is that they show topography, or the shape of the land. Landforms—mountains, valleys, ridges, and hills—are depicted through the use of contour lines, or lines that connect equal points of elevation. To visualize what a contour line represents, take a rock and submerge part of it in a cup of water. The line

Dip a rock halfway in water to depict a contour interval.
DAVE ANDERSON

Keep your topo map dry in the backcountry. Water-resistant paper helps; waterproof coating and map cases are also available.
DAVE ANDERSON

that marks the break between wet and dry is a contour interval, or a point of equal elevation on that rock.

The gold standard for American topographic maps is United States Geological Survey (USGS) maps. The USGS took over the mapping of the United States in 1879 and has been its primary mapping agency ever since.

The best-known USGS maps are the 1:24,000-scale topographic maps, also known as 7.5-minute quadrangles; 7.5-minute maps have been made for all forty-eight contiguous states and Hawaii. In Alaska 7.5-minute maps are only available for areas around Anchorage, Fairbanks, and Prudhoe Bay. The rest of the state is covered by 15-minute maps and contain less detail because of their smaller scale.

The 7.5-minute mapping program was completed in 1992 and has subsequently been replaced by the National Map program, a collaborative effort between the USGS and a variety of governmental and private partners to deliver geographic information through the Internet as downloadable data. However, paper copies of 7.5-minute quads remain available and are one of the most useful types of maps for backcountry travelers because of their great detail and accuracy.

Here we will focus on understanding USGS 7.5-minute maps. At the end of this section, we'll introduce other types of topographic maps you may encounter in your travels. The map-reading principles you use are the same, regardless of the brand or scale of your map.

Information in the Margins

The information in the margins of your map is critical background data. Here's where you'll find the map's name, location, scale, date of issue, and other relevant information. Most hiking trips are going to take you across more than one 7.5-minute quadrangle, so you'll need to know what other maps are in the area in order to make sure your entire trip is covered. Scale and contour intervals are invaluable to understanding how far you can travel and what kind of terrain you should expect to encounter en route. In some areas where the land is flat and featureless, contour intervals can be as low as 10 feet, while in other mountainous regions you may find maps with 80-foot or greater contour intervals. That can make a big difference if your intended path takes you over forty contour lines in the course of a day. On a map with 80-foot contours, that means you'll be climbing 3,200 feet, while on one with 10-foot contours, you'll only go up 400.

WHAT'S IN THE MAP MARGINS?

Start by looking at the margins of your map to locate several key pieces of information; specifically, the map's name and scale; its latitude, longitude, and UTM location; the names of adjoining maps; and the date. On this map the **name** is Aspen, Colo. (a) and the **date** is 1960 (b), with photo revisions made in 1987. The **scale** of the map is 1:24,000 (c), which means 1 inch on the map represents 24,000 inches on the ground. Below this number there is a **graphic scale** (d). For 7.5-minute maps, 1 inch on the map equals 2,000 feet, which translates to 2.6 inches on the map equating to 1 mile on the ground. The **contour interval** (e), or the distance in elevation between contour lines, is 40 feet. Below the contour interval you'll find the datum used for the map (f). This map uses the National Geodetic Vertical Datum. **Latitude and longitude** (g) can be found in the map corners. For example, in the lower right-hand corner of this map, you'll find the latitude Is 106° 45' west, while latitude is 39° 7' 30" north. Intermediate lat/long marks are found both up the side and along the bottom of the map. (h) The UTM zone and grid for this map is also found in the map corners. The **adjacent map**, "New York Peak" (i), lies immediately to the southeast of this map, while the "Hayden Peak" (j) quad is due south.

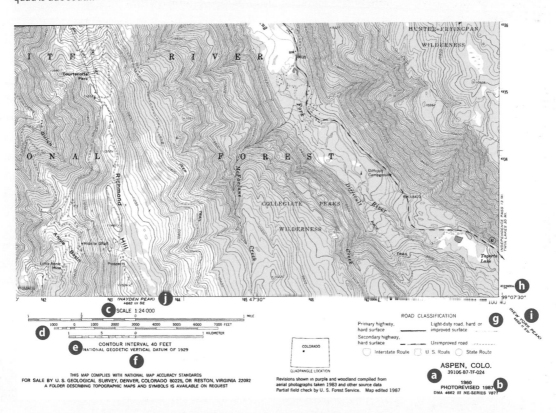

Date

The date on a map is also a vital piece of information. For example, Aspen, Colorado, has changed dramatically since 1960, when the map in the illustration on the previous page was first made. Most of these changes are man-made rather than natural; you don't really expect a mountain to alter its shape in fifty years, but trails get rerouted, new buildings appear, and bridges may come and go, so it's important to know how old the map is before you rely too heavily on ephemeral data to pinpoint your location or choose a route.

The Aspen map was photo revised in 1987, which means some changes will be shown in purple, but 1987 was still more than twenty years ago, so you are likely to encounter other modifications on the ground that do not appear even in the revised version. The bottom line is this: If the map is more than ten years old, be wary of man-made features or any other variations that could have taken place in the intervening years.

Declination Diagram

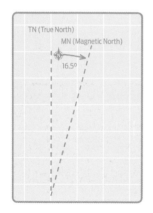

On all maps the top points north. Compasses, however, actually point to magnetic north, which varies from a few degrees up to 30 degrees off from true north. The specific angle of this variation is determined by your location; therefore, it will be different for different maps. You'll find a graphic representation of this difference in the margin at the bottom of your map. This is called the declination diagram. The line topped by a star points to true north, the one topped by "MN" points to magnetic north, and a third line, capped by "GN," points to Grid North. We will discuss these features in more detail in the compass navigation section.

Color

Cartographers have been using color to provide information on maps for hundreds of years. You may encounter some variations in the specific hues found on different maps, but in general basic color designations haven't changed much since the 1400s.

- **Black:** Indicates man-made features such as buildings, roads, surveyed benchmarks, and labels for towns, peaks, rivers, etc.
- **Red:** Used for more prominent man-made features such as surveys, boundaries, and major highways.
- **Brown:** Used for contour lines to identify relief features and for elevation markers.

- **Blue:** Identifies hydrological features such as lakes, rivers, swamps, and ponds. A dashed blue line enclosing a white area indicates permanent snowfields or glaciers.
- **Green:** Indicates vegetation with military significance (most topographic maps were originally created for military purposes). This means vegetation that can hide or encumber troop movements, such as forests, orchards, or scrub.
- **Other:** Occasionally other colors may be used to show special information, such as purple for photo revisions. These colors are usually explained in the marginal information.

Common Symbols

Topographic maps are remarkably intuitive once you've played around with them a bit. A curved line with small hatch marks radiating off the top looks like a grass hummock and is. These symbols are used for indicating swampy areas. Buildings are black squares; a black square with a cross represents a church. Still, it is helpful to familiarize yourself with some of the more common symbols shown here so you can interpret your map with more accuracy and precision.

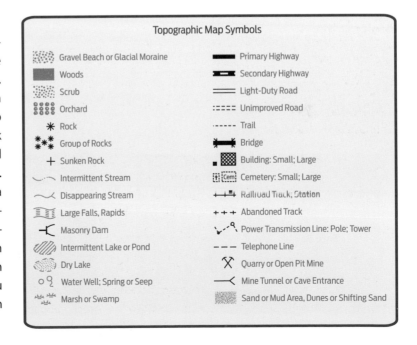

Topographic Map Symbols

Symbol	Description	Symbol	Description
	Gravel Beach or Glacial Moraine		Primary Highway
	Woods		Secondary Highway
	Scrub		Light-Duty Road
	Orchard		Unimproved Road
	Rock		Trail
	Group of Rocks		Bridge
	Sunken Rock		Building: Small; Large
	Intermittent Stream		Cemetery: Small; Large
	Disappearing Stream		Railroad Track; Station
	Large Falls, Rapids		Abandoned Track
	Masonry Dam		Power Transmission Line: Pole; Tower
	Intermittent Lake or Pond		Telephone Line
	Dry Lake		Quarry or Open Pit Mine
	Water Well; Spring or Seep		Mine Tunnel or Cave Entrance
	Marsh or Swamp		Sand or Mud Area, Dunes or Shifting Sand

Using Your Map: Contour Lines

As we've explained before, contour lines connect equal points of elevation. That's a simple enough definition, but learning to actually interpret these lines—that is, to translate the wiggles on your map into a mountain or valley—takes some skill.

Get out a map and look at the contour lines. Without much effort, you can pick out steep terrain where the lines get crammed together and flat terrain where big blank spaces appear. Every fifth contour line will be darker than the intermediate lines and is known as an **index contour.** The elevation of the index contours appears printed along each line at regular intervals. On many 7.5-minute USGS maps, the contour interval is 40 feet, with index contours occurring every 200 feet.

Occasionally, on maps representing flat terrain, the cartographer may include supplementary contour lines, which are represented as dashed brown lines. These lines indicate one-half the contour interval, or 20 feet if the contour interval is 40.

KNUCKLE MOUNTAIN

One of the best ways to understand contours is to use your hand as a mountain. Make a fist. Take a marker or pen and carefully trace a line that stays level around each individual knuckle. Make these lines at regular intervals; say, 0.25 inch apart. Don't let the line dip down between fingers, or climb up over finger bones. You'll find you must angle up into the "valley" between your fingers to stay level (forming a V that points uphill) and then must move out over the "ridges" represented by each finger (forming a V that points downhill). Once you've drawn a series of lines at various elevations, flatten your hand. Now you will see the topographic map of your hand: a two-dimensional representation of your three-dimensional fist.

Recognizing Landforms

Probably the best way to learn to recognize landforms is to take a map, go outside where you have an expansive view, and pick out landmarks. This exercise helps you develop a sense of the map's scale and an eye for how physical features appear when transcribed into contour lines.

First pick out a nearby mountain or hill and describe its shape. Does it have a steeper side? Are there cliffs visible? Do you see valleys where streams run off? Is it a flat-topped mountain, or does the peak have a distinctive pyramid shape at the summit? Do forests blanket its sides?

Now find the mountain on your map and look at how these characteristics are depicted. You'll notice ridges have distinctive V shapes that point downhill. Summits appear as closed circles; cliffs may have disappearing lines where the rock is overhanging.

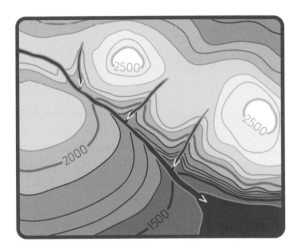

Here you can see a fairly steep-sided river valley. If you had looked at this landscape before consulting your map, you'd probably have decided that the best walking route was on the southern side of the river, on the open slope. The map reinforces this viewpoint, showing little room along the riverbanks for hiking, while the southern slope is gradual and should allow easy travel.

This illustration shows how the contour lines depict features in the land. Steep slopes have lines close together, circles represent mountaintops, passes between peaks are depicted by the pinching of lines, and valleys are represented by kinks or Vs in the contour lines that point uphill.

Now look at a valley. Does the valley have a river or stream in the bottom? Can you see where the stream meanders through flat meadows? Or is it pinched in and flowing straight down through a steep-sided canyon? Do any side streams flow in? Are there trees or swampy areas?

After you have described the valley, look at it on the map. You'll notice that the contour lines for big, wide-bottomed glacial valleys fold back in a gentle U shape that points uphill, while in steep-sided canyons the contour lines wrap back around themselves tightly into narrow Vs.

To ensure you know exactly where you are, take the time to describe at least five land features surrounding your location before you consult your map.

- Proximity to water
- Slope angle
- Tree cover
- Aspect
- Major landforms (peaks, drainages, meadows, etc.)

If you can subsequently identify each of those features on your map, you can be fairly confident you've pinpointed your location correctly.

For a discussion of how to plan your route using a topo map, see the trip planning information in chapter 3.

Common Map-Reading Mistakes

The most common mistake all map readers make at some point in their career is the trap of wishful thinking. We've all been there: You're beat, your feet hurt, your pack is getting heavier by the minute, and with a little creative imagination, you can convince yourself that you really have hiked 5 miles and are now standing smack in the middle of your predetermined destination. You know the lakeshore doesn't seem exactly right, and you thought the hill on the south side of the lake was going to be steeper, but it has to be right. After all, you were only traveling 5

TRICKS FOR AVOIDING COMMON MAP-READING ERRORS

- Check your map frequently.
- Note the time you pass specific handrails or landings. Recalculate your arrival time if you are moving slower or faster than anticipated.
- Observe the landscape before you pull out your map. Describe things verbally.
- Have five identifying landforms in mind before you begin trying to find your location on the map.
- Don't dismiss an obvious conflict.

FOLDING YOUR MAP

Lay your map on a flat surface, and fold it in half lengthwise with the printed side facing in. Now fold these halves back on themselves so the printed side now faces out. The map should now be folded into fourths lengthwise. Find the map name. Now bend the folded map in half again so the name is hidden on the inside. Fold the two ends back on themselves, ending up with a small square with the map name facing out.

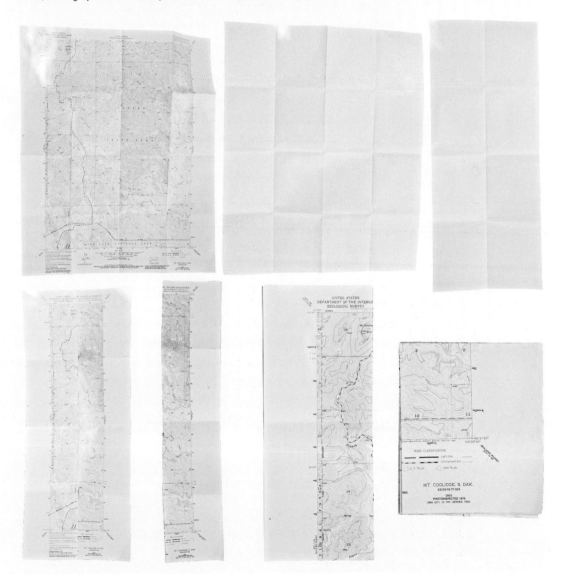

miles today and it's been 6 hours since you left camp. It doesn't matter that you all decided to nap at lunch for 2 hours or that scouting the river crossing took longer than you thought it would take. You still should have covered 5 miles by now.

If you recognize these thought patterns, you are not alone. It's easy to convince yourself you are where you want to be and not that difficult to reinterpret the landscape around you to fit the place you want to be on the map. We've all overestimated how quickly we are traveling and convinced ourselves that we've covered the distance, when in reality we still have a mile or two to go.

Finally, many novice—or out-of-practice—map readers have an inaccurate sense of scale and really can't tell how large a hill or meadow should be from its representation on the map. Look at big, obvious features first and then focus down on the more-detailed features. Don't dismiss contradictory evidence. It's highly unlikely mountains have moved or the sun is setting in the east just because you want to be at your camp. You are just not reading the map correctly.

Other Types of Maps

In addition to smaller-scale USGS maps (such as 15-minute maps), you can now buy commercial topographic maps—hiking maps—for many popular destinations across the country. These maps are often made on waterproof paper and cover a larger area than a 7.5-minute map, thereby allowing you to carry fewer maps to cover your trip. However, they are often smaller scale, such as 1:48,000, which means 1 inch on the map equals 48,000 inches on the ground, or twice as many inches as a 7.5-minute map. Many of these maps have shaded landforms that help the peaks and valleys pop out. This shading is not critical, but it can help you visualize dimensions and depth quite effectively.

WATERPROOFING YOUR MAP

Many commercial maps are printed on tear-proof, waterproof paper, which is a great feature. If yours is not, or if you printed it on regular computer paper, consider painting it (both sides) with a waterproofing agent, such as Aquaseal Map Seal. Always pack your map in a gallon-size zip-lock bag as an extra precaution.

Also, you can now buy software mapping programs for your computer that allow you to customize your maps. Some outdoor retail stores have these programs, allowing you to purchase customized maps without having to replace your own with the software or a large printer.

COMPASSES

A compass is simply a device that indicates direction. A floating needle within the compass points to magnetic north, allowing you to orient yourself and your map to the surrounding landscape. This information is particularly useful when visibility is obscured either by weather or trees.

Boxing the Needle

The first step in using your compass is to orient it so that it is pointing to magnetic north and the bezel is aligned correctly. To do this, you need to box the needle, or "put the guard in the guardhouse" (the guard being the red north-seeking arrow). Hold the compass in the palm of your hand, and rotate the bezel until north lines up with the direction of travel arrow on the base plate. Now, keeping the compass level, turn your body until the red north-seeking arrow is "boxed" in by the north-indicating arrow printed on the bottom of the compass housing. Your compass is now oriented to your present location.

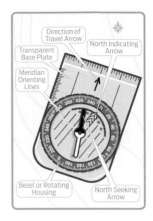

A basic, functional compass needs to have a bezel or rotating housing with an external ring printed with a compass rose indicating degrees and the cardinal directions: north, south, east, and west. Within the bezel you need a north-seeking arrow that floats in a fluid-filled capsule and a north-indicating arrow printed on the bottom. The base plate of the compass should be clear and have a direction-of-travel arrow printed on its surface.

Boxing the needle.
DAVE ANDERSON

Declination

The difference between true north at the top of your map and north as indicated by your compass needle is known as declination and reflects the angle between magnetic north and true north at your specific location. Declination diagrams are found along the bottom margin of your map.

To align your compass with true north, shift the bezel to the right or left of north the number of degrees indicated in the declination diagram. If you are in the Rocky Mountains, this means magnetic north is east of true north. The angle varies, but for the sake of an example, let's say magnetic north is east of true north by 10 degrees. To adjust your compass, turn the dial to the left or west of north by 10 degrees, or to 350 degrees. You then box the needle. Your direction-of-travel arrow will now be pointing toward true north.

Here's another way to orient your map. Box your needle, then align the edge of the compass with the arrow pointing toward magnetic north in the map's declination diagram (pictured). DAVE ANDERSON

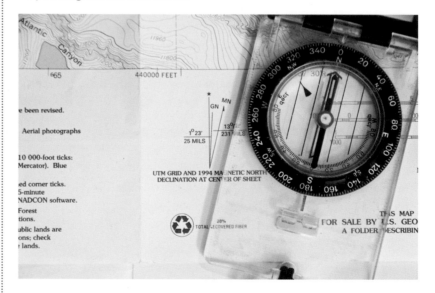

Orienting Your Map

To orient your map with a compass, follow these basic steps:
1. Set the compass dial to account for declination, as described above.
2. Align the edge of the compass base plate with the printed edge of your map.
3. Rotate the map and compass until the needle is boxed.
4. Your map is now oriented precisely to true north.

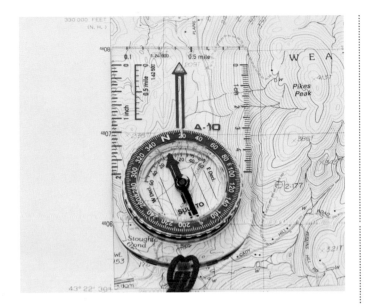

Orienting your map.
DAVE ANDERSON

Taking a bearing between location and destination (red Xs). DAVE ANDERSON

Taking a Bearing from Your Map

Sometimes it can be difficult to navigate without using your compass; for example, hiking through dense forests or across flat mesa tops where the land is relatively featureless and visibility may be obscured. Crossing open water in a boat or traveling in fog can be challenging without some way to keep track of your direction of travel; it will also test your ability to follow your course using landmarks alone. In these situations it can be very helpful to know how to shoot and follow a bearing.

The first step in shooting a bearing is to orient your map to true north. Then draw a line between your location and your desired destination. Now place the edge of your compass base plate along the line and turn the bezel until you have boxed the needle. The number on the bezel dial that lines up with your direction of travel arrow is your bearing.

To follow this bearing, keep the dial set with your bearing lined up with the direction-of-travel arrow. Now, holding your compass at waist level,

Taking a bearing from the land. DAVE ANDERSON

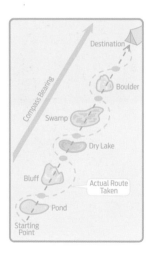

rotate your body until the needle is boxed. Your direction-of-travel arrow is now pointing toward your destination. Most likely, however, your path will be blocked by obstacles, making it impossible for you to just walk forward in a straight line all the way to your intended destination. So to allow for easier travel, pick out a landmark—one as distant as possible—along your projected line of travel, walk to that landmark, and repeat. You can use trees, rocks, even people sent ahead to stand along the path if nothing else will serve.

You can take a bearing from the land simply by pointing your compass at a landmark and boxing the needle. Again, the number that lines up with the direction of travel arrow will be your bearing. But if you can see your landmark, you probably don't need to take a bearing to reach it. Shooting a bearing off the land is usually most useful when you want to figure out your exact location on the map through triangulation.

Simple Triangulation

There are times when you know roughly where you are but can't pinpoint your location exactly because the land is fairly featureless close by. This may happen in the middle of a glacier or during a crossing of a lake. In this case you can triangulate—or use the intersection of two bearings shot from distant landmarks—to home in on your location.

Start by orienting your map. Then choose two known, visible locations such as a mountain or obvious low pass. Shoot a bearing off this landmark. Keeping the needle boxed, lower your compass onto the map, placing the edge of the base plate through the center of the landmark you just sighted. Draw a line along the edge of the compass through the landmark extending toward you. Your location is on this line somewhere.

Now pick a second landmark and repeat the process. The two lines should intersect at your location.

You can also use linear landmarks—say a river or ridge—as one of your triangulation lines. Then you just need to shoot one bearing off a known landmark. The intersection of that bearing and the river or ridge where you are traveling will be your location.

ALTIMETERS

Altimeters measure barometric pressure and translate that information into an elevation reading. As you climb up in elevation, the barometric pressure falls and the altimeter reflects the change, calculating your elevation as you go. If you have a general sense of where you are on the map—say, you know you are midway up Mount Baker—an altimeter reading allows you to pinpoint your elevation. Once you locate the contour line for that specific elevation on the map, you know where you are.

Altimeters vary in their reliability and precision. Many people have watches that calculate elevation, as well as pace, distance, even heart rates. These watches work fairly well, but they can be sensitive to weather changes, which also cause the barometric pressure to rise and fall. You may need to recalibrate your altimeter to match your current location,

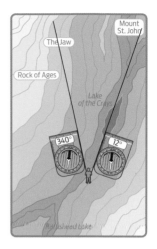

Use two landmarks to triangulate to home in on your location.

Altimeter. DAVE ANDERSON

If your altimeter shows a rise in elevation when you haven't even left camp, it's likely a low-pressure system is moving your way.
DAVE ANDERSON

and you may also want to bring along extra batteries to ensure it works when you need it. Mechanical altimeters are more reliable but less durable than electric ones.

In general, altimeters are not necessary for most backcountry travelers, so don't feel compelled to go out and buy one unless you are planning to be at high elevations where accuracy is vital. If you happen to own a watch with an altimeter built in, you can play around with it and use it to fine-tune your navigation. If your watch shows a rise in elevation and you haven't even left camp, you can guess a low-pressure system is moving your way and the weather is probably going to deteriorate.

DIVIDING THE WORLD: LATITUDE AND LONGITUDE

Since people began exploring and mapping the world, they have worked to devise systems for codifying locations—grids for dividing the Earth into uniform pieces. The ancient Greek geographer Ptolemy created his own grid system, listing coordinates for places throughout the known world, but it wasn't until the Middle Ages that one system—latitude and longitude—was adopted universally.

In the 1940s the US Army Corps of Engineers developed another grid system—Universal Transverse Mercator (UTM)—that relied on uniform squares and was based on the number 10, which makes calculations simpler than latitude/longitude, which is based on 60 divisions per unit. UTM has become commonly used today in conjunction with GPS receivers.

Lines of latitude run parallel to the equator. Lines of longitude run north–south and intersect at the poles.

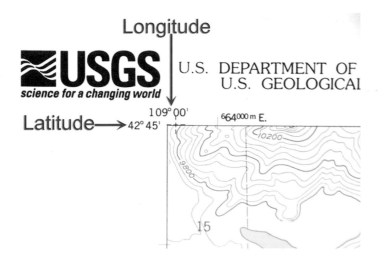

Longitude

USGS
science for a changing world

U.S. DEPARTMENT OF
U.S. GEOLOGICAl

Latitude

109° 00'
42° 45'

664000 m E.

Latitude/longitude was the first universal grid system used for dividing up the Earth and is still used by pilots, sailors, and many GPS users. However, it is more cumbersome than UTM and is therefore becoming less useful for backcountry travelers. Still, it is helpful to understand the basics of lat/long.

Anyone who has spun a globe around has seen the lines of latitude and longitude dividing up the Earth.

Latitude lines ascend and descend from the equator in horizontal bands starting with 0° at the equator and ending at 90° at the poles. To help you remember, think of latitude lines as the horizontal rungs of a ladder (ladder-tude). These lines help identify your position north to south.

Longitude lines—also known as meridians—radiate out east and west for 180° from the Prime Meridian, which runs through Greenwich, England. The meridians meet in the middle of the Pacific Ocean at the International Date Line. Longitude is used to locate your position east to west.

Latitude and longitude lines are measured in degrees, minutes, and seconds. One degree equals 60 minutes; 1 minute equals 60 seconds.

Latitude lines are evenly spaced; therefore, degrees of latitude represent a constant distance regardless of your location. Longitude is trickier because the north–south lines bend to meet at the poles; as a result, a degree of longitude represents a varying distance on the ground, depending on your latitude. The farther north you are, the more severe the effect on latitude.

Plotting Your Location Using Latitude/Longitude

Measurements of latitude appear in the left and right margins of USGS maps; measurements of longitude appear on the top and the bottom. Black tick marks along the borders of the map indicate 2.5-minute intervals, and black crosses appear within the map where lat/long lines intersect. To help make it easier to identify your location using lat/long, you can use a straightedge to connect these marks and create a grid on your map.

Universal Transverse Mercator (UTM)

What is UTM?

The UTM grid system divides the world into sixty zones that run north–south. These lines are intersected by latitude lines, creating a numbered grid with each square representing 1 square kilometer. Because the UTM grid is based on uniform squares and uses base-10 math, it is simpler to use with a GPS than latitude/longitude.

On USGS maps the UTM coordinates are located in the upper-left and bottom-right corners. They appear like this: 664000mE and 4734000mN and are expressed as the "easting" and "northing" values. The digits that represent thousands of meters and tens of thousands of meters are enlarged to help you quickly locate which kilometer reference line to use.

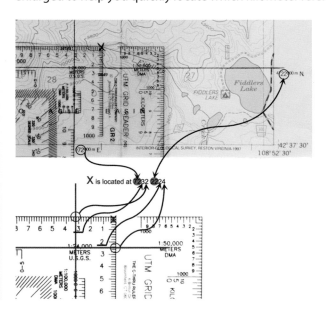

Use a UTM grid reader to help pinpoint locations.

UTM is rapidly replacing lat/long for travelers seeking precision and ease in their navigation because it provides a constant distance between all points on any USGS map, whereas lat/long varies depending on your latitude.

Reading UTM Coordinates

In order to read and plot UTM coordinates accurately, it helps either to have a UTM grid reader (see page 100) or to have the grid drawn on your map. Some USGS maps come with the UTM grid printed on them, but most do not. Using a straightedge, you can draw the grid yourself by connecting the UTM ticks printed in blue along the borders.

Datum

The datum or dated map data set for your map must be included when using UTM. This information appears in the block of text at the lower left-hand corner of USGS maps and may be the North American Datum 1927, the National Geodetic Vertical Datum of 1929, the North American Datum 1983, or the World Geodetic System 1984. Online mapping tools such as Google Maps commonly use the World Geodetic Systems 1984 (WGS 84), so WGS 84 is becoming the most commonly used reference. Entering the wrong datum for the map you are using is the most common GPS error. For example, a WGS 84 coordinate taken from Google Earth or a website and manually entered into a GPS set to NAD 27 datum can be off by close to a mile. Match your datums. Datum mix-ups can also cause confusion if you are trying to give information on your location to a pilot or rescue team.

GLOBAL POSITIONING SYSTEM (GPS)

GPS uses satellite signals to pinpoint your location wherever you may be. Today's pocket-size receivers can tell you where you are to within 10 feet in a matter of seconds. Many units on the market today are capable of storing hundreds of locations in their memory, can calculate both the distances you've hiked and your average hiking speed, and can even point you in the direction you want to go. It's a great tool but requires some skill to use and should not be considered a replacement for good map-reading skills.

Each GPS unit (and now smartphones with navigation apps) will function somewhat differently, so you'll have to read the manual and do some practice "hikes" around the house to get the hang of it. That said, there are some basic concepts related to GPS receivers that we will discuss here.

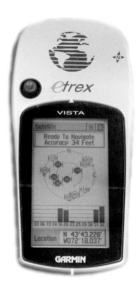

A handheld GPS unit.
DAVE ANDERSON

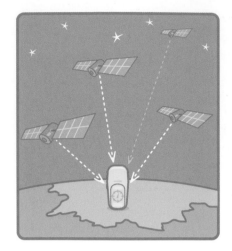

How a GPS Works

The US Department of Defense launched the first GPS satellites in 1978. Today GPS technology is not limited to the military, and the system is used for mapping and surveying; to navigate automobiles, ships, airplanes, and boats; and in mining, forestry, agriculture, and many other fields. The first handheld GPS receivers were introduced in 1989, and backcountry travelers quickly adopted the technology to aid in backcountry navigation.

GPS receivers pick up signals from a network of twenty-four satellites circling the earth twice a day. Most units will acquire signals from at least three satellites within 3 minutes of being turned on. This is known as getting a position fix. For your GPS to work well, it must operate in 3-D mode, which requires signals from a minimum of four satellites. In most places this is not a problem; however, tight canyons and dense forest canopy may cause enough interference to block the signals. If you have fewer than four signals, your receiver will be functioning in 2-D mode, which is less accurate. In fact, readings may be off by as much as a mile in 2-D, so it is important for you to know what mode you are in before you begin plotting your position.

The receiver measures the signals it receives and basically triangulates the messages to calculate your position. Each position fix is displayed in either UTM coordinates or in latitude/longitude.

Entering Waypoints

Waypoints are representations of points on the Earth that are stored in your GPS's memory. By guiding you from waypoint to waypoint, your receiver can aid in route finding. Entering waypoints creates a route description or record of the places you've visited. Waypoints can be stored in two ways: by entering the coordinates manually or by pushing a sequence of buttons to record a snapshot of your physical location in the receiver's memory.

This information is valuable for a variety of purposes. A friend may give you waypoints for a rendezvous spot, a hidden campsite, or perhaps a secret fishing hole. You can give waypoints to a pilot coming in to pick you up or take out an injured hiker. You can also enter the waypoints into your GPS and then push the "Go To" function. This brings up an arrow that directs you to that point.

When recording a waypoint, hold the GPS unit level out in front of you.
DAVE ANDERSON

Remember that the GPS does not recognize hazardous terrain, so the Go To arrow may take you right to the edge of a cliff or an impassable canyon. If you are forced to turn off the direct linear route by such an obstacle, the GPS will adjust and correct your line.

If you make a habit of recording waypoints while traveling, your GPS will enable you to retrace your route—linking the points you passed before—even if you are in complete darkness or a blinding blizzard. Entering your waypoints does not require plotting or entering numbers but merely pressing a sequence of buttons under the waypoint menu in your receiver.

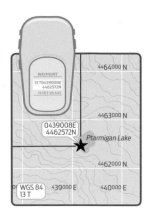

Waypoint.

So Why Plot Coordinates?

If the GPS can do it all, why bother learning how to plot coordinates? The answer is so that you can interface with your map.

You need to know how to plot either UTM or latitude/longitude coordinates on your map to interpret the readings you are receiving from your GPS and find your location in the physical world around you. Furthermore, GPS receivers aren't good route finders: They won't tell you the best way to get from point A to point B, and they can't identify a nice place to camp or a good peak to climb.

To travel effectively in the backcountry, you should rely on your map first and foremost and use your GPS to enhance your precision and communicate your location to others.

Common Errors or Problems

A GPS receiver's accuracy can be affected by "multipath interference."

Multipath interference happens when a signal bounces off an object such as a cliff or a building on its way to your receiver. It's hard to tell if this has affected your reading, so to be on the safe side, stay away from cliffs when taking a position fix in the backcountry.

Probably your biggest potential problem is going to be battery power. Low battery power can cause GPSs to malfunction, so bring lots of spares if you plan to use your receiver frequently. Make sure you know whether your receiver is waterproof. If it is not, carry the unit in a plastic bag to keep moisture out. Finally, protect your transceiver from extreme temperatures, both hot and cold. Again, such conditions may affect the GPS's ability to function, and it may give you inaccurate readings or perhaps fail to work at all.

NATURAL NAVIGATION METHODS (NO MAP, COMPASS, OR GPS)

What happens if your GPS batteries die, you lost your map, and/or you neglected to pack a compass? Keep your cool and use these skills, which you should practice every chance you get, whether you're driving in the car, walking the dog in the park, or on a hike.

If you have a compass, it's easy to find north. The arrow always finds north for you. But there are ways to find north even without a compass. Some are complicated, involving sticks in the sand and watch faces, math, and geometry. If you're just trying to get home, stick to the simple ways: watching the sun and stars.

In the Northern Hemisphere, the sun rises in the east to southeast and sets in the west to southwest. (***Note:*** The exact direction of the rising and setting sun varies slightly during the course of the year as the sun takes a higher or lower path across the sky, depending on the season.) Use this information to orient your map, or at least maintain a consistent course as you navigate through the terrain. If you keep going straight, you will eventually hit a road. Remember this comforting thought: In the Lower 48, you are never more than 40 miles from a road; likely less than 10.

It's also possible to navigate using the stars, as long as the weather cooperates. You can get all fancy here if you happen to be an astronomy

Everyone can spot the Big Dipper, right? This simplified image shows the approximate relationship of the North Star (the biggest, uppermost star here) to the Big Dipper. THINKSTOCK.COM

pro, or you can simply learn to locate the North Star. The Big Dipper is the most widely recognized constellation. Find it. Imagine a line connecting the two front stars that form the dipper, and follow that trajectory upward. The first bright star you hit is the North Star. Mark that direction on the ground (with a stick or rock pile); when the sun rises, use that information to verify north.

For more on the subject of being lost and tactics for outdoor survival, see chapter 10.

Lake Jocassee Gorges, Upstate Mountain, South Carolina. THINKSTOCK.COM

View of Waimea Canyon at sunrise,
Kauai, Hawaii. THINKSTOCK.COM

Point Reyes, California.
THINKSTOCK.COM

CHAPTER 6
IN CAMP

Rolling into camp, your first thoughts are probably to relax before dealing with chores. A better course of action is to drop your pack, perhaps toss on a warm layer, and deal with some of the necessities before you cool down. It's oh so much better to relax when you know you can really relax.

LEAVE NO TRACE

Before getting into the basics of setting up camp, it's important to take a moment to learn the seven principles of Leave No Trace camping and hiking. The Leave No Trace program has established a set of basic principles designed to help guide people on ways to minimize their impact on wildlands. The goal of the program, which was started in 1994, is to allow people to enjoy the wilderness without loving it to death.

The seven principles* are:
- Plan ahead and prepare.
- Travel and camp on durable surfaces.
- Dispose of waste properly.
- Leave what you find.
- Minimize campfire impacts.
- Respect wildlife.
- Be considerate of other visitors.

*© LEAVE NO TRACE CENTER FOR OUTDOOR ETHICS; LNT.ORG

CHOOSING A CAMPSITE

Typically, the first major chore is preparing your night haven. If possible, you want a site that isn't too far from the water that you will need for cooking but no closer than 200 feet. Sometimes a great view is wonderful, but those spots are often brutal in a storm. And camping near the trail is a bad idea because a tent is an eyesore for others and people will tramp past at ungodly hours.

When evaluating potential tent sites, look for a flat spot that will not become a lake if it rains; compacted soil in heavily used sites are prone to flooding. Digging a trench around your tent to divert runoff is absolutely forbidden—it is ineffective, and those scars last for many years. Check overhead for "widow makers" (i.e., dead trees and branches that may fall in the wind) in forests. Though tempting, don't camp in creek beds, particularly in the desert, because a flash flood can ruin your night. Look for shelter from wind, or, if bugs are bad, you may prefer a breezy site to minimize flying pests.

Once you've found the spot, clear out any rocks and branches that will poke holes in your tent. Pitch your tent, inflate your pad, and pull out your sleeping bag to loft up. This is a good time to change into warm, dry clothes for the evening.

At this point, you may wish to fetch enough water for dinner and breakfast, decide where to locate your kitchen, and rig your food-hanging system. It is wise to put a good distance between your sleeping bag and all things that smell tasty to critters. Cooking in one place, washing dishes in another, and hanging your food in yet another can decrease the likelihood of nighttime disturbances.

After dinner, you will need to hang your food and tidy up the campsite (see the upcoming section on camping in bear country). Make sure that important things are protected against rain during the night. Have your headlamp and any other necessities (stocking hat, eyeglasses, etc.) laid out where you can reach them during the night. It helps to establish a routine so you can find things easily.

Choosing a Kitchen Site

The lore of backpacking is filled with tales of dinners ruined by pots tipping over due to unstable stoves. Do yourself a favor and take the time to locate a good spot for setting up your kitchen. Ideally you can find a large flat rock for your stove—bonus if it's on a ledge that you can hang your legs off while cooking—but you may need to clear a bit of ground of flammable leaves.

The two most important factors for speeding cooking and saving fuel are using a windscreen and keeping a lid on the pot. Other ways to conserve include heating items by placing them on the lid of the cooking pot and using a pot cozy (or wrapping with a towel) to keep a pot warm while the food hydrates.

Backpackers are frequently warned to never cook inside a tent. But the reality is that there are times when cooking outside is not an option. If you must cook under shelter, do it in the vestibule and far enough away from walls and sleeping bags to prevent melting. Always keep at least one large vent open, and cook with extreme caution. If you are in grizzly country and anticipate rain, a separate cook fly is worth carrying.

When cooking, you may need to stir frequently to prevent burning because many stoves concentrate the heat (better pots help). Also, tall, skinny pots need more stirring for even heating of the food.

After dinner it is wise to clean dirty pots, bowls, and cups before things set up. Hot or warm water is best, but even cold water will suffice if used with biodegradable soap. Never wash dishes directly in a stream or pond! Always carry them 200 feet away and then broadcast the dishwater over a wide area. This applies to bathing too, if you feel the need.

For a complete discussion on choosing the best kitchen site as well as techniques for campsite cooking, see chapter 7.

WATER PURIFICATION

When in the backcountry, staying hydrated should always be at the forefront of your mind. Hikers should drink between three and five quarts per day, depending on the temperature, the altitude, and your level of exertion. All backcountry water should be treated in some fashion (with chemicals, a filtering device, or by boiling), but if you don't have the means to treat your water, drink anyway. You're more likely to die of dehydration than you are of a stomach bug (which will likely hit long after you get home, anyway).

Water Filtration Gear

At the bare minimum, always have a water bottle with you, even on the shortest of hikes. Bottles are tough to improvise (unless you find someone else's garbage), and the importance of staying hydrated cannot be overstated.

Bottle. It doesn't matter what type you bring, as long as you bring something. Even a convenience store bottle that once held Evian will last for a long time with care. Gatorade bottles (32-ounce) are among the lightest you can get, and they're sturdy enough to last for an entire season (or more).

Multnomah Falls, Columbia River Gorge, Oregon.
THINKSTOCK.COM

Pot. If you're on a multiday trip, you probably have some sort of metal cook pot in your pack, which is a critical instrument for collecting and treating water (as well as countless other tasks).

Zip-lock plastic bag (1-gallon size). These are useful for holding water and making water through transpiration (see below). They weigh nothing, so always pack one or two.

Chemical tablets or drops. These ultralight tablets or drops will turn even the nastiest water potable. But they won't change the taste or appearance of gross water, and they take from 30 minutes up to 3 hours to work properly. Recommended: MSR Aquatabs (cascadedesigns.com) or Aquamira Water Treatment Drops (aquamira.com)

Pump filters. Like the other types of filters mentioned below, pumps reliably remove sediment and pathogens. Your muscle power creates the suction that pulls the water through an intake hose, pushes it through the filter element, and spits it out clean on the other side. Pump filters are usually the heaviest and bulkiest treatment method, and they require some maintenance to prevent clogging. If you pack a filter, be sure you know how to maintain it in the field (see "Filter TLC").

Bottle filters. These handy units are a snap to use. Just unscrew the top, dip the bottle in the water, replace the cap, and suck or squeeze (depending on the model) the water through an integrated filter element inside. They're fairly light and compact, but the filters themselves tend to

(Top row, left to right): cook pot, Aquamira Water Treatment Drops, Platypus GravityWorks; (Bottom row, left to right): MSR HyperFlow, Sawyer Squeeze Filter, Nalgene Wide-Mouth Bottle, Aquamira Frontier Filter, SteriPen Freedom.
KRISTIN HOSTETTER

clog more often than pump filters, making suction difficult; diligent cleaning is a must. Recommended: Sawyer Squeeze Water Filter (sawyer.com)

Straw filters. These affordable, ultralight slurpers are great to pack as a backup. They are essentially just straws with integrated in-line filters, ideal for sucking water from shallow puddles in places where water is scarce. You just lie down on your belly next to a puddle or stream, place one end of the straw in the water, and suck. You won't get copious amounts, but you will get enough to keep you going. Recommended: Aquamira Frontier Filter (aquamira.com)

Gravity filters. Ideal for large groups working from a base camp, gravity filters consist of two bladders connected by a hose with an in-line filter. Just hang a bag of untreated water from a tree and let gravity do its thing. Water will drip through the filter into the "clean" bag while you perform other chores. Recommended: Platypus GravityWorks (cascadedesigns.com)

UV wands. Light, packable, and superfast, UV devices rely on battery power and UV rays to neutralize pathogens. Just dip the wand in the water, press a button, swirl for about 90 seconds, and guzzle away.

FILTERING SMARTS

Follow these tips to get the best results with any filtering device.

- **Look for calm, clear pools.** To preserve the life of your filter, avoid pumping or gathering water from roiling rivers where sediment is flowing.
- **Let water settle.** If you're forced to use sediment-infused water, let it settle in a big pot or waterproof stuff sack before filtering.
- **Adjust the intake hose float.** Pump filters have little buoys on the end of the intake hose. Adjust yours so that the intake pre-filter floats in the water rather than resting on the bottom, where it will suck debris into the filter and clog it.
- **Don't overuse it.** There's no need to filter water you'll be boiling for dinner. Boiling is a foolproof sterilizer.
- **Keep it cozy.** In cold weather, water inside the filter element can freeze up, making pumping difficult or impossible. Wrap your filter in a zip-lock bag and tuck it into your sleeping bag on cold nights.
- **Be gentle.** Big drops or sharp impact can damage the filter element (especially ceramic), so be careful, and be sure to pack it in a protected place inside your pack.

The Boil Method

Long before fancy filters or UV-zappers were invented, boiling was the only foolproof water treatment method, and it still works just as well today. Heating water to boiling obliterates anything living in your water, but the method does have some drawbacks. You need a stove (with plenty of fuel) or a good hot fire and a vessel to contain the water. Plus, you need patience. It can take up to 10 minutes to boil water (depending on the heat source and the conditions), and then you need to let it cool—unless you want to parboil your tongue.

UV treatments don't work well in murky water with lots of sediment (let water sit for 30 minutes or so before treating). And be sure to pack a wide-mouth bottle that's compatible with the wand. Recommended: SteriPen Freedom (steripen.com)

Filter TLC

Here are a few tricks for keeping your filter working properly in the field.

If you have a ceramic filter element, known for its durability and longevity (as well as its hefty weight), you can remove the filter element and scrub it with one of those green kitchen scrubby sponges to remove any sediment that has built up on the outer surface. Once a year or so, sterilize the filter by dropping it into a pot of boiling water for about 5 minutes. (**Note:** Check your owner's manual before doing this; some companies do not recommend it. And be sure to remove any O-rings around the filter, which can get deformed and damaged by high heat.)

Glass-fiber filters rely on an intricate network of folds—and the vast surface area they provide—to trap micro-cooties. When your glass-fiber filter becomes difficult to pump, remove the element and swish it aggressively in clean water to release any sediment caught in the folds.

Most filters can also be **backflushed** when you start to notice pumping resistance. Backflushing is easy and quick; it entails running the water backward through the filter to free any built-up gunk. Check your owner's manual to learn how to backflush your particular device.

FIRES

Campfires are part of our camping traditions. People love to gather around the glow of the flames late into the evening, sharing stories and the coziness the warmth creates. Fires are also destructive. Neglected campfires are one of the leading causes of wildfires in the United States, and campfires can leave behind unsightly scars and impacts in popular wilderness areas. You've seen them: trash-filled fire rings located right next to the edge of a lake or stream and blackened rock overhangs along the base of cliffs. The impacts are ugly and unnecessary. With a little knowledge and skill, you can enjoy a fire without causing lasting scars.

When Are Campfires Appropriate?

Campfires are really only appropriate in places that have an adequate wood supply and where they are permitted by the managing agency.

Fires can provide warmth and a cheery place to gather. THINKSTOCK.COM

There's no need to chop down trees or strip off branches to provide wood for a fire. If that's your only option, fires are not appropriate. DAVE ANDERSON

In the first case you'll have to use your judgment; in the second the rules are pretty clear. When the sign at the trailhead says No Fires, it means no fires. You'll get a ticket if you are found with a campfire in these areas.

How much wood is adequate? If you see dead sticks lying around in abundance, there's enough wood. If you have to search for a long time to find some sticks or are tempted to strip dead limbs off standing trees, there's not enough wood around to support a fire.

Safety Considerations

Think before you start your fire. What's the weather doing? Is it windy? Is the forest dry from hot dry weather or years of drought? Are there a lot of dead trees from beetle kill? Is there a chance your fire could get out of control? If you have answered yes to any of these questions, you should probably reevaluate the safety of building a fire. Your best bet is to save your campfire for calm, cool nights in places where the forests are moist and the ground damp.

If you decide you are safe, make sure you have a container of water nearby to use in case the fire gets out of control.

Fire pans are a good option for low-impact fires.
DAVE ANDERSON

Low Impact Fires

The best place to build a fire is in a preexisting fire ring. Here the impacts have already occurred, so your fire will not add to the problem.

If you cannot find a fire pit and are still interested in a fire, you can make a platform from mineral soil (dirt that contains little or no organic material) to hold your fire. Mound fires like these are easy to dismantle when you are done and leave no trace of your passing. Fire pans are also useful if you plan on building lots of fires. Mini backyard barbecue grills, aluminum roasting pans, or metal oil-drain pans make good fire pans. You can punch holes in the corners of the pan and use string to attach it to your backpack. Fire pans should be lined with mineral soil or propped up on small rocks to avoid scorching the ground underneath.

Use an existing fire ring when possible.
DAVE ANDERSON

Cooking on Fires

Cooking on fires can be fun, although dirty. You'll probably want to pack a stuff sack to carry your blackened pots in to avoid turning everything in your backpack black. Some people carry a lightweight grill to use over a fire, but unless you plan to cook on fires most of the time, that's an extravagance you can live without.

In lieu of a grill, you have two options. You can create a pseudo grill by making a tripod for your pot from three equal-size rocks. Make sure the rocks are stable so that the pan doesn't tip over when you sneeze or make

FIRE-STARTING GEAR

The good news is that fire-starting gear is practically weightless, yet it can save your bacon in a dire situation. On every trip, always pack at least two—preferably three—methods of creating fire. A disposable lighter is an absolute must. Make sure it works and has plenty of fuel. For your second source, you've got several choices:

Waterproof matches. The best ones are dipped in wax or some other material to make them burn longer and come in a watertight case with a striking surface. Recommended: UCO Stormproof Match Kit (industrial rev.com)

Magnesium block. Magnesium takes a spark very easily but can be tricky to use; in real-world conditions, those tiny shavings tend to blow around. You must shave the spine of the magnesium block until you have a small pile (nickel-size, at least) of material nestled into your dry tinder; then hit it with a spark (from flint or a ferro rod). Recommended: Coghlan's Magnesium Fire Starter (coghlans.com)

Fire-starting gear takes many shapes. Pack at least two methods of creating a flame (preferably three). Clockwise from top left: UCO Stormproof Match Kit, Coghlan's Magnesium Fire Starter, BiC lighter, County Comm Peanut Lighter, Soto Pocket Torch, Light My Fire Swedish FireSteel 2.0, Spyderco Manix2 steel knife.
KRISTIN HOSTETTER

Bic lighter. The old standby; bring a couple.

Peanut lighter. These refillable lighters are—you guessed it—peanut-size and, thanks to a rubber O-ring around the cap, totally waterproof. Despite the lighter's diminutive size, the lighter fluid seems to last forever. Recommended: County Comm Peanut Lighter (countycomm.com)

Flint. Flint is a hard sedimentary rock. When struck with steel, it will throw a spark. But the flint sparks have a relatively low temperature, so it's tough to ignite anything but char cloth.

Steel or carbon steel knife. Use your blade to create a spark with ferro or flint. *Tip:* Always use the thicker, blunt back of the blade for sparking so that it doesn't wear down your cutting edge.

Ferro rod. Also known as ferrocerium, fire steel, misch metal, or metal matches, a ferro rod is a man-made, pencil-thin stick of hardened rare earth metals and iron. It's the stuff used in cigarette lighters. When scraped with steel (like your knife blade), it showers tons of tiny hot sparks onto a well-prepared tinder pile and produces fire. Ferro rods are often mistakenly called "flint" (see above), but they differ from flint in that they are man-made and generally a bit easier to use than a natural flint. Recommended: Light My Fire Swedish FireSteel 2.0 (lightmyfire.com)

Torch lighter. Like mini blowtorches, these devices produce a hot, directed flame that makes fire-starting easy. Recommended: Soto Pocket Torch (sotooutdoors.com)

MOUND FIRE HOW-TO

Step 1: Gather a stuff sack full of mineral soil. What is mineral soil? It's dirt that contains little or no organic material. You can find mineral soil under the roots of fallen trees and on beaches, sandbars, and dry washes.

Step 2: Place a tarp or ground cloth over the surface where you plan to build your fire. Good fire sites include large rock slabs or non-vegetated dirt. Build a mound from your mineral soil approximately 2 feet across and 6 to 8 inches thick (you may need to make several trips to gather enough soil for your mound). You may also want to tuck the tarp under the soil to prevent rogue coals from burning a hole in it.

Step 3: Build your fire using small-diameter wood (in general, only use wood you can break easily with your hands—about wrist-size in diameter). Make sure you gather dead and downed wood from a number of different locations to avoid depleting one area. Rotting wood provides vital nutrients to the soil, so leave some behind.

Step 4: Enjoy your fire.

Step 5: Cleanup starts with burning all your wood down to ash. Scatter any unburned wood you may have gathered to help camouflage the site. Your ashes should be cool to the touch before you dispose of them. If they are still warm, douse them with water. Scatter the ashes far and wide, again to hide evidence of your fire. Gather up your mineral soil in the tarp and return it to its source. Camouflage the area by scattering duff and sticks and fluffing up trampled grass. Voilà! Your fireplace has disappeared.

DAVE ANDERSON PHOTOS

a minor adjustment to the setup. This method keeps your pot up above the heat source and allows you to replenish the fire as you cook if it becomes necessary. You can also create a bed of coals and place your pot directly on the hot coals. The only disadvantage to this technique is that you can't add more heat without removing your pot. Many backpackers find the direct-coal method best suited for baking, when they want a low, steady heat source. Boiling water this way seems to take forever.

Use rocks to get your pot up above the fire. DAVE ANDERSON

BREAKING CAMP

Come dawn, start motivating and resist the urge to sleep in (assuming you are moving camp—if not, by all means sleep in!). Get dressed right away for the day's hike, with your sweater or jacket over top to fight off the chill. Coffee drinkers will want to get their brew going as soon as possible, and the rest of the group would be wise to humor their addiction. Retrieve your food bag and start heating a pot of water on the stove.

While water is heating for drinks and hot cereal, stuff your sleeping bag, roll up the sleeping pad, and stow away things you won't need during the day. By this time the water is probably boiling, so go enjoy breakfast.

Once breakfast is finished, clean up and pack away the kitchen and food. Take down your tent and return the area to a natural state. Police the entire campsite for micro-trash.

Before you hit the trail, it will be time for your morning toilet break; that 2 pounds of food you consumed the day before is now 1 pound of feces. Some heavily used parks are requiring backpackers to carry out everything—yes, everything—and will provide bags for that purpose. Everywhere else you will need to dig a cathole about 6 to 8 inches deep and 6 inches in diameter. You can use a stick or tent stake, but it does help to carry a small trowel for this purpose.

The site should be at least 200 feet from water and out of sight of trails; a bit of privacy is nice when taking a bio break. Do yourself a favor and make sure there is no poison ivy, poison oak, stinging nettles, or cactus in the vicinity! Be sure to bury everything and restore the site to natural.

As a more durable yet comfortable alternative to toilet paper, you might try thick half-size paper towels. Burning and burying toilet paper or paper towels is no longer recommended because neither method works

well, and "trekker prayer flags" often result as animals scatter unsanitary paper that takes years to break down. Carry two freezer bags to collect used toilet paper and tampons, then dispose of them when you reach the trailhead.

CAMPING IN BEAR COUNTRY

The more popular the backpacking destination, the bigger the problem with mice, ravens, raccoons, and bears. Many of the shelters on the East Coast are equipped with "mouse mobiles," which are strings with inverted empty cans to prevent rodents from reaching the goodies (like a squirrel guard on a bird feeder). Leave your pack unguarded with food inside, and you may find a hole chewed in it.

While those small animals are a nuisance, bears are a wildland resident that deserves more attention. Staying overnight in bear country is not dangerous, but it adds a slight additional risk to your trip. The main differences between day trips into bear country and camping in bear country are more food, cooking, and garbage. Plus, you're in bear country at a time when bears are commonly most active. Once again, however, following a few basic rules greatly minimizes this risk.

Selecting a Campsite in Bear Country

Since bears and people often like the same places, selecting a good campsite is a key decision.

Bears are exciting to see in the backcountry, but you definitely don't want them getting into your food stash.
STEPHEN GORMAN

GET SOME LOCAL KNOWLEDGE

Most national parks require backpackers to have a backcountry camping permit. One reason for this system is safety. If a bear has been raiding camps in one area in the park, rangers probably won't allow any overnight camping there.

Backcountry campsite reservation systems also provide an opportunity to discuss the bear situation with a knowledgeable ranger. After you select a campsite, ask the ranger about bear activity in the area. In most parks, you get a brochure or can watch a short video on camping in bear country.

Land managers for many national forests and other public lands don't require permits or designate campsites, but It's always wise to stop in at the local ranger station and ask about bear activity before heading for the trailhead.

Sometimes you have little to say about where you camp. If you're backpacking in a national park, regulations probably require that you stay in a precisely located campsite reserved in advance. The National Park Service (NPS) considers the bear situation when designating campsites, and discussing it with a ranger might prompt you to choose one site over another.

In most national forests and some national parks, you can camp anywhere. Regulations might require you to camp certain distances from water or trails, but you aren't confined to a specific campsite.

When You Get to Your Campsite

When you find your campsite, immediately think bears. Look around for bear sign. If you see fresh sign, move on to another site with no sign of bear activity. If you see a bear in or near the campsite, don't camp there—even if you're in a national park and you have reserved this campsite. If you have time before nightfall, return to the trailhead and report the incident to a ranger. If it's getting late, you have little choice but to camp at an undesignated site and report it to the ranger after you finish the hike. Safety always prevails over regulations. Don't get yourself in a situation where you have to hike or set up camp in the dark.

Being careful not to camp in a site frequented by bears is perhaps the most important precaution you can take. Unfortunately, people who cause a bear to become conditioned to human food or garbage are rarely the people who suffer the consequences of their misdeeds. The person who is injured usually comes along later and unknowingly camps in the same site where a bear has become accustomed to getting human food.

Look for signs of previous campers. If you find food scraps, litter, or other signs that the previous campers didn't use proper bear-country camping techniques, consider choosing a different campsite.

It's very important to plan your hike so you aren't setting up camp a half hour before nightfall, which doesn't leave time to move to another campsite if necessary. If you set up camp in the dark, you have little chance to check around for bear sign or evidence of previous campers.

Key Features of a Good Campsite

A key feature of any good campsite in bear country is a place to store food. Most designated sites in national parks and in some national forests have a food storage device such as a "bear pole" or metal bear-resistant box. And in some places you're required to use a bear canister. However, in most national forests and other public lands, even in some national parks, you're on your own, so scout the campsite for trees where you can hang your food and garbage. You need a tree at least 100 yards from your tent with a large branch, or two trees close enough to suspend your food between them on a rope. You can also use a tree that has partially fallen and is still leaning securely on other trees. In any case, the trees must be tall enough to get the food at least 10 feet off the ground and 4 feet from the tree trunk.

Choose a campsite away from popular fishing areas such as along salmon-spawning streams or lake inlets. If previous campers fished close to camp, they may have left dead fish or fish entrails around camp, and the smell of fish definitely attracts bears. If you have fish for dinner, clean them at least 200 yards from camp and dispose of the entrails by throwing them into deep water.

Avoid camping along trails, streams, or lakeshores, which often serve as travel corridors for bears. Since bears like to travel and remain concealed in trees, camp in an open area. If possible, set your tent near an "escape tree" that you can climb in case a bear comes into camp, and make a mental note of its location so you can find it at night. Pick a tree that's not too easy to climb; you don't want it to be easy for the bear.

Setting Up Camp

Once you've found a good campsite, take the next crucial step of correctly setting up camp, which isn't as simple as it sounds. Some camping traditions can increase the chances of a bear entering your camp.

You probably have seen photos of picturesque camping scenes with a family just outside the tent entrance sitting around the fire cooking dinner. Forget this. Except in extreme circumstances when survival is on the line and you cannot leave your shelter, the sleeping area and the cooking area must be separated.

Set up the tent at least 100 yards upwind from the cooking area. Also, if possible, pitch the tent uphill from the cooking area. Since night breezes in the mountains usually blow downhill, the wind will carry food smells away from the sleeping area instead of over it.

Spreading out the camp might create some extra walking and inconvenience, but if a bear comes into your camp, it's likely to go straight for the smell of food—where you've been cooking and eating. Obviously, you don't want to be sleeping there. Concentrate all food smells in the cooking area, and keep them away from your sleeping area.

Hang or store food as close to the cooking area as possible. In many designated campsites, rangers have strategically placed the bear pole or metal food locker near designated cooking areas. This practice helps concentrate all food smells in one place far away from the sleeping area.

Get in the habit of separating cooking-area and other fragrant items from sleeping-area items in your backpack. Then, while setting up camp, you can conveniently separate articles into two piles.

For large parties, set up tents in the most secure areas and space them out linearly. Put the most experienced people at each end of the line of tents. Hikers who plan to stay up most of the night listening for bears get the inside spots.

Storing Food and Garbage

If the campsite doesn't have an established food storage device (bear pole or metal box), be sure to set one up or at least locate one before it gets dark. Storing food after darkness falls isn't just difficult—it also makes it easier to forget some juicy morsel on the ground. Store food in

A model campsite for camping in bear country locates the sleeping area at least 100 yards upwind and uphill of the cooking and food storage areas.

airtight, waterproof bags to lessen the amount of food odor circulating throughout the forest. For double protection, put food and garbage in zip-lock bags and then seal them tightly in a larger plastic bag.

Even better, use a portable bear-resistant food storage container (BRFC), which some national parks require. This gives your double-bagged food and garbage triple protection. To be extra careful, hang the BRFC or put it in the group bear box, but at least be sure to leave it near the cooking area at night and nowhere near the tents.

In addition to storing food and garbage properly, try hard to keep food odors off your pack; but if you fail, you can put the food bag and garbage inside and hang the pack.

Store scented items such as toothpaste, sunscreen, bug dope, and water bottles (especially if used for juice, lemonade, or fitness drinks) along with food and garbage.

"Free Sleeping" Invites Disaster

A few national park visitors have been known to have a particularly bad habit called "free sleeping." In an attempt to save money or when all the campgrounds are full, some visitors simply pull off the road in an undesignated camping area and pitch a tent or, even worse, just throw a sleeping bag out on the ground. Besides violating park regulations, this can be very dangerous. The free sleeper might be saving a few dollars, but he or she might also be unknowingly camping in an area heavily used by bears.

Bears can sleep anywhere they want—but *you* shouldn't. Especially in certain national parks, "free sleeping" can put campers in areas heavily used by bears.
THINKSTOCK.COM

Food Storage

Use zip-lock bags to keep food smells to a minimum and keep food odors off your pack, clothing, and other gear. Also, pack a special bag (sturdy and waterproof) for hanging and storing food. You can get drybags at most outdoor retailers, but you can get by with a trash compactor bag. Regular garbage bags are too flimsy and can break and leave your food spread on the ground. Even when using a BRFC, keep food in zip-lock bags.

If not using a BRFC, you also need 100 feet of nylon cord for hanging food and garbage. You don't need a heavy climbing rope; go light instead. Parachute cord will usually suffice unless you plan to hang large quantities of food, garbage, and gear, which could be the case on a long backpacking excursion with a large group.

You can also buy a small pulley system to make hoisting a heavy load easier. Again, you can usually get by without this extra weight in your pack unless you have a massive load to hang.

Getting the Food up There

People get hurt hanging food and garbage, so be careful.

The classic method is tying a rock or piece of wood to the end of your rope and tossing it over the branch and then attaching the rope to the bag or backpack and hoisting it up 10 feet or more. If the load gets too heavy, wrap the rope around a small tree or branch for leverage. To make this easier, take a small ditty bag and permanently attach at least 50 feet of nylon cord to it. Then, when you're at camp, instead of trying to tie a rock on the end of your rope, put rocks or sand in the small bag, close it, and toss it over the branch or bear pole.

Use gloves to avoid rope burn. Don't let the rock or wood come down on your head. (It happens!) And don't let anybody stand under the bag until you're sure it's securely in place. (**Note:** Be careful not to leave your rope behind the next morning. Once you've untied your food, slowly pull your rope over the branch. Don't jerk it. If the rope gets stuck and you can't climb the tree, you'll have to leave it behind.)

What to Hang

Hang everything that has any food smell. This includes cooking gear, eating utensils, water bottles, bags used to keep food in your pack, garbage, and even clothes with food smells on them. If you spilled something on your clothes, change into other clothes for sleeping and hang those

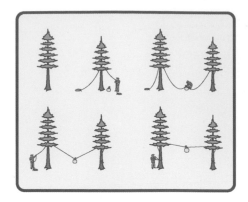

Steps for hanging food and garbage between two trees.

Steps for hanging food and garbage over a tree branch.

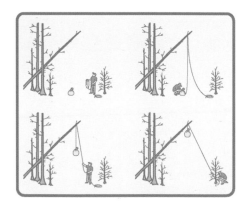

Steps for hanging food and garbage over a leaning tree.

smelly clothes with the food and garbage. If you take them into the tent, you aren't separating your sleeping area from food smells. Also hang scented non-food items like toothpaste, bug dope, and sunscreen.

Hanging food at night isn't the only storage issue. During the day, make sure you place food correctly in your pack. Use airtight packages as much as possible. Store food in the containers it came in or, once opened, in zip-lock bags. This keeps food smells out of your pack and off your other camping gear and clothes.

What to Keep in Your Tent

You can't be too careful about keeping food smells out of the tent. If a bear has become accustomed to foraging for food at that campsite, it's vital for your protection to keep all food smells out of the tent. This often includes your pack, which is hard to keep odor-free, and the clothes you used for cooking and eating. Usually, take only valuables (such as cameras and binoculars), clothing, and sleeping gear into the tent—and of course bear spray. Keep a flashlight handy to identify animals that come into camp.

The Campfire

Regulations prohibit campfires in many areas, but if you're in a place where fires are allowed and in line with LNT principles, and conditions are safe, treat yourself. Besides adding to the nightly entertainment, a campfire can make your camp safer from bears.

The campfire provides the best possible way to get rid of food smells—as long as food scraps and garbage are totally burned away to ashes. Build a small but hot fire and burn everything that smells of food—garbage, leftovers, fish entrails, everything. If you brought food in cans or other incombustible containers, you can put them in the fire too, but you must pack them out after the food smell is burned away. You can even dump extra water from cooking or dishwater on the edge of the fire to erase the smell.

In the crowded wilderness of today, campfires are rarely

in line with the principles of zero-impact camping. However, if you decide bear safety outweighs the zero-impact ethics, be sure you have the fire hot enough to completely burn everything. If you leave partially burned food scraps in the fire, you're setting up a dangerous situation for the next camper who uses that campsite.

Before leaving camp the next morning, dig out the fire pit and pack out anything that hasn't totally burned, even if you believe it no longer carries food smells. For example, many foods like dried soup or hot chocolate

TYPES OF FOOD

Don't get paranoid about the types of food you bring. All food has some smell, and you can make your trip much less enjoyable by fretting too much over food.

Perhaps the safest option is freeze-dried food. It has very little smell, and it comes in convenient envelopes that allow you to cook it by merely adding boiling water, so you don't have cooking pans to wash or store. However, freeze-dried food is expensive. Many campers don't use it—and still safely enjoy bear country.

Dry, prepackaged meals (often pasta- or rice-based) offer a more-affordable alternative to freeze-dried foods. Take your favorite high-energy snack, and don't worry about it.

What food you bring is much less critical than how you handle it, cook it, and store it. A packet or can of tuna, for example, might put out a smell, but if you eat all of it in one meal, don't spill it on the ground or your clothes, and store the can in an airtight bag later, it can be quite safe.

come in foil packages that might seem like they'd burn but they really don't. Pack out the scorched foil and cans (now with very minor food smells). Also pack out foil and cans left behind by other campers.

Burning leftovers in campfires is not allowed in some national forests and national parks, so check local regulations before heading for the trailhead. In most cases you'll find the best advice listed prominently on the trailhead information board: "Pack it in; pack it out."

How to Cook

The overriding philosophy of cooking in bear country is to create as little odor as possible. Keep it simple. Use as few pans and dishes as possible.

If you can have a campfire and decide to cook fish, try cooking in aluminum foil envelopes instead of frying or roasting the fish over an open flame. Then, after removing the cooked fish, quickly burn the fish scraps off the foil. Using foil also means you don't have to wash a pan.

Manage fuel for your backpacking stove carefully. Fuel can be a strong bear attractant. Use a funnel and no-spill container when refilling stoves.

Try hard not to cook too much food so you don't have to deal with leftovers. If you end up with extra food, you have only two choices: Burn it or carry it out. Definitely do not bury it or throw it in a lake or leave it anywhere in bear country. A bear can find and dig up any food or garbage buried in the backcountry.

Taking Out the Garbage

As noted above, in bear country you have only two choices for dealing with garbage: Burn it or carry it out. Plan ahead and prepare for garbage handling. Bring along zip-lock bags to store garbage, and generate as little garbage as possible by removing and discarding excess packaging at home.

Washing Dishes in Bear Country

This is a sticky problem with only one easy solution: If you don't dirty dishes, you don't have to wash them. Try to minimize food smell by using as few dishes and pans as possible—or, better yet, none at all. If you use the principles of zero-impact camping, you're probably doing as much as you can to reduce food smell from dishes.

If you brought paper towels, use one to carefully remove food scraps from pans and dishes before washing them. When you wash dishes, you'll

Bears are attracted to garbage no matter where it is, so make sure you pack out everything you pack in—and leave a clean camp.
PHOTO COURTESY OF USDA FOREST SERVICE

have much less food smell. Burn dirty towels or store them in zip-lock bags with other garbage. Put pans and dishes in zip-lock bags before putting them back in your pack.

If you end up with food scraps in the dishwater, drain out the scraps and store them in zip-lock bags with other garbage, or burn them. You can bring a lightweight screen to filter out food scraps from dishwater, but be sure to store the screen with the food and garbage. If you don't have a screen, use your bandana. If you have a campfire, pour the dishwater around the edge of the fire. If you don't have a fire, take the dishwater at least 100 yards downwind and downhill from camp and pour it on the ground. Don't put dishwater or food scraps in a lake or stream.

Don't put it off. Do dishes immediately after eating to minimize food smells.

Finally, although this possibly runs counter to accepted rules of cleanliness for many people, you can skip washing dishes altogether on the last night of your trip. Instead, simply use the paper towels to clean the dirty dishes as much as possible and then wash them at home. Pack dirty dishes in airtight bags before putting them in your pack.

Storing Dog and Horse Food

It's usually unwise to take dogs into bear country, and it's prohibited in most national parks. If you do it anyway, treat the dog food like human food. Store it in airtight bags and hang it at night.

Although horses probably don't increase your risk of encountering a bear, the large amount of food necessary for horses can become a major bear attractant. Again, treat horse food as carefully as you do human food. Horse pellets are like candy bars to bears.

Storing Food When Camping above Timberline or Tree Line

Camping above timberline or north of the tree line makes food storage difficult, so avoid it when possible. If you must camp in alpine or tundra areas, use a BRFC and store it at least 200 yards downwind and downhill from your sleeping area at night.

One last option is a portable electric fence, a fairly new innovation for backpackers. It can weigh less than 4 pounds, so if you know you'll be camping in a bear-dense area without good food-storage options, you might want to consider taking one along.

Where permitted, using a waterproof stuff sack and a throw bag (right) is a popular option for stowing food overnight. In areas where rodents and birds are the main threat to food, a steel mesh bag (front) is a reasonably light method for keeping critters at bay. Some parks require the use of bear canisters (left); check regulations online. A lighter alternative to bear canisters is to use a durable bag made of high molecular polyethylene (HMPE) (rear) that bears cannot rip open. However, not all parks allow them. CLYDE SOLES

The Interagency Grizzly Bear Committee (IGBC) conducts a thorough testing program for many types of bear-resistant products such as BRFCs, electric fences, hanging devices, coolers, panniers, and garbage cans. Before you go shopping, check out the IGBC website (igbconline.org) for a list of approved products so that you know you're buying an IGBC-approved product. Otherwise you might buy something that isn't really bear resistant.

Attractants and Repellents

Nobody really knows everything that attracts or repels bears, but everybody agrees on one thing: The smell of human food and garbage definitely attracts bears. If you don't want to attract bears, be extremely careful with food and garbage.

Bear experts also agree on two more things: Bears have a supersensitive sense of smell, and they're curious. Given these two facts, it seems best to avoid anything that might prompt a bear to investigate. Try to blend into the natural environment instead of standing out from it. This means avoiding things like brightly colored tents, backpacks, and clothing; camping in highly visible sites such as ridgelines or above timberline; making animal-like sounds; or using any kind of strong scent—all of which might excite a bear's curiosity.

VEHICLE CAMPING IN BEAR COUNTRY

Don't believe that vehicle campgrounds offer added security from bears. In some cases the reverse might be true.

If you're sleeping in a tent, there isn't much difference between backcountry camping and camping in a vehicle campground. Be equally careful with food and garbage.

One advantage of a vehicle campground is easier food storage. Except in a few national parks, where land managers discourage car storage because black bears have become adept at breaking into vehicles, keep food and garbage in airtight containers, and then stow them in your vehicle at night or when not in use. Keep all food smells out of the tent.

One disadvantage of vehicle campgrounds is the small size of the campsite. You can't effectively separate your sleeping area from your cooking area.

When evaluating a vehicle campsite (no different than a backcountry site), look around for bear sign; If you see any, go to another campsite. If you see a culvert trap in the area, it usually means rangers are trying to remove problem bears—a good tip-off to go elsewhere.

Some recent research has indicated, for example, that bears might be attracted to bright colors, such as the yellow used in some backpacking tents and jackets, but ignore or barely notice dull, earth-tone colors, especially camouflage. At the same time, let's be realistic. There's no need to throw away your yellow tent; instead, be careful not to display it prominently on a ridgeline where a bear can see it from a mile away. Don't present bears with a "visual cue" they simply can't ignore and, therefore, must approach to investigate.

THE BEAR ESSENTIALS: CAMPING IN BEAR COUNTRY

- Select a safe campsite.
- Camp below timberline.
- Separate cooking and sleeping areas.
- Sleep in a tent.
- Keep food odors out of the tent and packs.
- Don't sleep in the same clothes used for cooking.
- Cook the right amount of food, and eat it all.
- Store food and garbage out of the reach of bears.
- Leave the campsite cleaner than you found it.

Delicate Arch in Arches
National Park, Utah.
THINKSTOCK.COM

Researchers also have discovered that bears show interest in many strong scents, such as citronella (an ingredient in some insect repellents), fruity shampoos and lip balms, fuel for backpacking stoves, and human urine and feces. There needs to be more research, but in the meantime, it seems prudent to try to minimize the scents associated with being human. (And don't relieve yourself too close to camp.)

If scientists could come up with the right scent, sound, or color to keep bears out of our camps, there would be a collective sigh of relief, but until that happens, don't take chances. Avoid bright colors, unusual or loud sounds, and strong smells. Obviously, hikers and campers aren't currently using anything that actively attracts bears; if they were, there would be many more encounters.

Do Somebody You Don't Know a Big Favor

Report all bear sightings to a ranger after your trip. This might not help you, but it could save another camper's life—and a bear's life too. If rangers get enough reports to spot a pattern, they'll manage the area accordingly and not unknowingly allow camping in a potentially hazardous area.

Final Thoughts on Camping in Bear Country

Camping in bear country can be a lot safer than driving to the trailhead, as long as you know what you're doing. Knowledge is the best defense against bears, and that means avoiding an encounter in the first place. Outdoorspeople who know about bears have already taken the vital first step. They know what kind of equipment to bring, how to set up camp, when and where to hike and be more careful, and which bear and human behaviors increase the chances of an encounter.

Lunch break with a view.
THINKSTOCK.COM

CHAPTER 7
CAMP COOKING

Food in the backcountry serves many functions: It gives you energy to accomplish your goals; it warms you up and gets you going when things are difficult; and it serves as a gathering point, a social focus for your expedition. You build up quite an appetite in the wilderness, and almost everything tastes good, including cheesy ramen soup at 4 a.m. You might not ever eat such a concoction in town, but out in the mountains, before a big hike or peak climb, it can really hit the spot.

Preparing food in the wilderness can be as simple as heating water for ramen or as elaborate as baking bread. The complexity depends upon your desires, goals, and motivation, so before you head into the mountains, ask yourself—and your expedition mates—a few basic questions:

1. What's your goal for the trip?
2. Do you all like to cook, or would you rather be climbing or fishing?
3. Does anyone have any special dietary needs?
4. How much can you carry?

People go camping for all sorts of reasons. Some like to hike long miles, climb peaks, move camp often, and carry the minimum amount of gear. Others prefer to head to a destination and base camp, spending their days wandering nearby looking at birds, fishing, reading, and cooking. Some people travel with pack animals and bring everything from two-burner stoves and Dutch ovens to coolers along with them; others don't even bother to bring a stove. Where you fit in this spectrum is going to determine the type of food and equipment you will bring with you on your backpacking trip.

The critical thing is to make sure that everyone on your trip has some input into the food selection. All of us know that hungry people are cranky people, and the last thing you want is to spend your entire wilderness adventure listening to your tent mate whine about the food, especially if you were the one who came up with the menu. We also tend

If your goal is to move
quickly with a light pack,
you'll probably opt for a
basic menu. DAVE ANDERSON

to make stupid decisions when we are hungry, so it's imperative that you have both enough food and food that is palatable to everyone to ensure you have a group of happy campers.

If you've been left with the task of planning the food for your trip, ask your teammates to fill out a questionnaire, expounding on their likes and dislikes. This will give you the information you need to come up with a plan that is acceptable for all. (A sample questionnaire is included with the trip planning information in chapter 3.)

CHOOSING THE BEST KITCHEN SITE

Have you ever noticed how most house parties end up with everyone crowded into the kitchen? The same is true in the backcountry. The minute someone lights the stove and starts to prepare a meal, people begin to congregate for social hour, to have a hot drink, or to help out with the cooking. Because of this, you want to make sure you choose a durable, Leave No Trace location to site your kitchen. Note that when it comes to siting your kitchen, the main LNT principle that comes into play is camping on durable surfaces. We'll consider proper waste disposal and campfires later in this chapter.

What Is a Durable Surface?

Durable surfaces include rock, snow, established trails and campsites, gravel bars, beaches, and dry grasses. In popular camping areas, your best bet for a minimum-impact campsite is to use a preexisting one. That way you don't create new and unnecessary impacts. Stick within the confines of the site to avoid making it bigger; this means focusing your activities on places where the vegetation is already worn away and using existing trails to go to water or to your tents.

In a pristine area that has not seen a lot of use, you'll need to find naturally hardened sites for your camp kitchen. Look for large rock slabs or a gravely area, or try to find spots under trees where the vegetation is sparse or nonexistent. Avoid places where impacts from previous campers are just starting to be evident. Usually these places will recover if left alone.

Most public land managers require campsites to be 200 feet from water sources. This helps prevent water contamination and keeps you out of sight of other campers who may be spending the night in the vicinity. It also lessens the chance you'll disturb wildlife coming for water during the night. Carry a container to transport water so you don't have to go back and forth to fill up as you prepare your meal.

In bear country it is necessary to site your kitchen at least 200 feet from your sleeping area (see chapter 6 for more information on camping

in bear country). You don't need to go to that extreme if you're not in bear country; just a few feet will help reduce traffic in the tent area and cut down on impacts. Bring all your cook gear and food into the kitchen area so you don't have to get up and move back and forth all the time looking for the butter or that extra pound of pasta you need to finish the meal.

Now you are ready to start cooking.

SANITATION AND DISH WASHING

Hand Washing

First things first. Camping is about getting dirty and maybe a little smellier than normal, but it's not about being unhygienic. Dirty hands spread disease in the backcountry as much as they do in town, so, just as at home, always wash your hands before handling food. Carry a small container of liquid soap. (This tends to be a little easier to manage in the backcountry. Hard soap gathers dirt and pine needles and gets yucky without a soap container, which just adds weight to your pack.) Wash your hands 200 yards from water sources to avoid contamination. Scrub for 15 seconds or more to ensure you've cleaned them thoroughly; make sure you've cleaned your nails as well.

Dish Washing

Although washing the dishes will be the last thing you do after cooking, we'll cover the technique here to get it out of the way (a good principle to apply when washing dishes—just get 'em done!).

The best way to make cleanup easy is to eat everything in your pot. That's where accuracy in your menu planning helps. The most experienced outdoorspeople know how to pack enough, but not too much, food to keep everyone happy and healthy for the duration of their trip. That said, you are going to have to clean your pots at some point, so here are a few tips to guide you.

Dispose of Waste Properly

Leftovers, food scraps, even washing water need to be disposed of properly to avoid attracting animals to your campsite. Your motivation here is twofold: Number one, you don't want to wake up to a bear—or even

a less-dangerous but annoying mouse—pawing around your kitchen. Number two, animals that become habituated to humans often end up dying. Either they are killed because they are dangerous—as in the case of many bears—or they become sick or malnourished. Either way you look at it, your best bet is to make sure you are not inadvertently feeding wildlife with your kitchen scraps.

Strain your wash water to remove leftovers. Bag and carry out these scraps with your other garbage.

Where Do You Wash the Dishes?

You don't want to contaminate your water sources, so always wash your dishes 200 feet from streams, lakes, and rivers unless the local bear camping regulations say otherwise. (In some parts of Alaska, for instance, regulations call for you to wash your dishes in the rivers.)

Once your dishwater is free of floaties, you have a choice. In most parts of the country, the best practice is to fling the water around you so it is scattered over a wide area. The only time this technique is not recommended is in grizzly bear country or heavily

To broadcast means to toss the water widely, dispersing it over as large an area as possible. DAVE ANDERSON

TRICKS FOR GETTING THE POTS CLEAN

Some people like to bring along biodegradable soap for cleaning their dishes; others do not. If you do bring soap, make sure you've rinsed the pot clean to remove any soapy residue. Soapy pots can give your food an unwanted flavor or, worse, make you sick.

The best technique is to heat up a quarter of a pot of water to help soften the cooked-on residue from your meal. You can then use your fingers to pick and scrape away at the food. This usually works on all but the most stubborn burnt-on gunk (one good reason not to burn your food!). You can also use a spoon or spatula to scrape away at the pot. To ensure that your pots are germ free, rinse them with boiling water and dry in the sun or with a clean cloth.

In some situations, it helps to use a handful of dirt or sand to scrub at your dishes. The problem with this technique is that you end up with sand impregnated with fatty food residue—it's hard to dispose of that without leaving a smelly mound of dirt behind. Some people like to bring a scrubby or sponge along to help clean pots, but if you are out more than a few days, most sponges or scrubbies turn into festering, germ-laden blobs pretty quickly. You can boil them, but that seems like a waste of fuel and time when fingers and warm water really work quite well.

used areas like desert river corridors. With bears you want to concentrate and minimize odors, so your best option is to go at least 100 yards from camp, dig a cathole (a hole approximately 6 inches deep) and pour the wastewater in. If you are camped by a large, silty river, such as the Colorado, you may opt to pour your gray water directly into the main flow of the river.

Check with the land management agency that is responsible for the area you are camping in to find out what method they recommend for disposing of wash water.

THE LIGHT AND FAST COOK

The aforementioned 4 a.m. breakfast of ramen met all the criteria of a light and fast cook: It weighed very little, cooked up in a few minutes, and, with the lump of cheese floating around on top, was packed with calories to sustain somebody over the course of a long hard day of climbing. But cheesy ramen is not very creative, and your meals don't have to be that uninspiring. Light and fast does not always mean simply adding water and heat to some prepackaged concoction (although that works). You can get pretty creative—especially with some prep work at home—and still end up not having to carry much weight.

The Lightweight Kitchen

Before we get too far into the light and fast kitchen, we should say that you don't have to cook to eat well in the backcountry. You can carry food that requires no preparation—energy bars, cheese, packaged meats, crackers, bread, and so forth—and leave your kitchen behind. Your pack will be lighter (on short trips); but that said, there's nothing like a hot meal to boost morale and energy after a hard day. So let's assume you plan at least to boil water on your trip.

There is a large array of backpacking cook gear on the market, and some people like to pack a complete kitchen to make their cooking easier. However, you don't have to have all that stuff, even if you are planning to cook an elaborate meal. See "The Minimalist Kitchen" (page 144) for a list of necessities that won't weigh you down too much.

You do not have to treat water used for cooking, but you want to avoid accidentally drinking untreated water. To avoid confusion, have a system in place. A good system is: Water

Many freeze-dried meals can be rehydrated in their pouch, so you don't need to carry a bowl and there's no messy pot to clean up. DAVE ANDERSON

If you pack a collapsible water container, you won't have to hike back and forth to your water source while cooking. DAVE ANDERSON

The simplicity
of living,
eating, and
playing in the
outdoors is part
of camping's
appeal.
DAVE ANDERSON

THE MINIMALIST KITCHEN (FOR A GROUP OF 2 TO 4)

- 1–2 lightweight pots large enough to hold water to make drinks for the team (2–3 quarts)

Consider titanium or aluminum to save weight.

- Small channel-lock pliers

Acts as pot grips and useful for repairs

- Water bottle, heavy-duty plastic spoon, and cup or bowl per person

Water bottle can serve as a cup for hot drinks. Titanium cups are lightweight and can be used to heat water. If you are solo camping, leave the cup or bowl behind and eat out of your cook pot.

- Serving spoon or spatula

If someone in your group has a big metal spoon that can serve as a serving spoon, great. Otherwise it's helpful to have one large spoon for mixing, serving, and so on. Also, it's more hygienic if you don't share your eating utensils. If you opt for a spatula, leave the spoon at home.

- Water container

You can save weight by eating right out of the pot.
DAVE ANDERSON

in your personal bottle is always treated; water in the kitchen container never is.

To really minimize your kitchen setup, choose items that can be used for a variety of purposes. A large titanium cup can also be used for cooking a meal for one person. Likewise, your eating spoon can serve as a mixing spoon and even a spatula for most purposes. (Okay, it doesn't do a very good job of flipping pancakes, but if pancakes aren't on the menu, you are probably fine.) Use your water bottle for hot drinks, and leave the insulated mug at home. Bring a lightweight knife rather than a heavy multitool, unless the tool also serves as your all-purpose repair kit.

Stoves and Fuel

Today you have a wide range of backpacking stoves available, ranging from homemade alcohol-burning contraptions that weigh as little as 10 grams to expensive multifuel-burning stoves. Your choice will be dictated by several factors:

- Price
- Fuel availability
- Menu demands
- Number of people

If your goal is simply the lightest, cheapest option out there, build yourself an alcohol-burning stove out of aluminum cans (directions can be found on the Internet). The downside to this type of stove is that boiling water takes longer than it does with a blended-fuel cartridge or white gas–burning stove, and you have less control over the heat output. But they are cheap and light, so it's worth experimenting with them to see if they will work for you.

Tests show that a top-mounted blended-fuel cartridge stove is the lightest, most efficient model in terms of its heat-to-weight ratio. These stoves do not require priming, so they are simple to light. The downside is the fuel cartridges can be bulky and expensive, and they cannot be refilled. As a result, many of us end up with a box of half-full cartridges waiting to be used. Nonetheless, if your goal is to go light and fast, your best bet may be to opt for a top-mount blended-fuel cartridge or canister stove.

A top-mount cartridge stove will boil approximately 33 pints of water from a single 8-ounce canister. If you boil on average 5 pints of water per day, an 8-ounce canister will last you six or seven days.

Blended fuel canister stoves are often the model of choice for climbers and mountaineers looking for a light, reliable stove.
DAVE ANDERSON

Mixed-fuel stoves that can burn kerosene may be required if you plan to travel overseas, where fuels such as white gas are not available. Alcohol burns with the least intensity of all fuels, but the stoves are light and can be made at home. Fuel cartridges—most often containing a blend of butane and propane—are packed under pressure, so they ignite easily without pumping or priming. DAVE ANDERSON

Mixed-fuel stove

alcohol stove

butane canister stove

The MSR WhisperLite stove is a reliable backpacking stove. DAVE ANDERSON

White gas is usually cheaper than blended-fuel canisters, and you can refill your bottles before each trip. You do have to prime white gas, so lighting the stove is a little trickier than simply holding a flame to the fuel jet, but it just takes practice. For an all-around stove, you can't go wrong with a classic white gas stove like the MSR WhisperLite. It's simple, easy to repair, and relatively light.

Typically, the WhisperLite will go through approximately one-third of a liter per day for a three-person group in the summer. You'll need more if you anticipate having to melt snow for water.

There are some other stove options available that are worth mentioning. For example, you can use a solid fuel–burning stove. These stoves are tiny and light, and they burn solid-fuel tabs that fit in the palm of your hand. They are not incredibly hot, however, and fuel tabs are the most expensive fuel option out there, so these stoves aren't all that popular. But if you wish to be superlight, you may want to check one out.

The opposite extreme in terms of the cost of its fuel is a wood-burning stove. These stoves act as a chimney, inside which you build a fire from small sticks and twigs to heat your food. Such stoves work well in places where wood is plentiful and dry. They become more persnickety when the weather turns foul.

If you plan to travel outside the United States, you need to consider what fuel will be available. In many parts of the world, you cannot buy white gas or blended-fuel cartridges. For international travel, therefore, you may need a multifuel stove so you can burn whatever is available at your destination.

Fill your white gas fuel bottles away from the area where you will be cooking. Spilled fuel lights easily and can lead to an uncontrolled fire. DAVE ANDERSON

TIPS FOR CONSERVING FUEL

Organize all your ingredients, fill your pots with water, and be ready to start cooking before you light your stove. No use wasting fuel warming the atmosphere because you forgot to fill the pot.

Use a lid. A lid will keep the heat inside your pot and cause food to cook faster.

Use a windscreen. The wind sucks heat away from your stove, and cooking takes a lot longer than it should. You can also conserve fuel by choosing a protected place for your kitchen.

Don't let your pot bubble along merrily after it has reached a boil. The minute the water gets hot enough or your food is cooked, turn off the stove.

Prepping your ingredients and using a windscreen can help conserve fuel. DAVE ANDERSON

Stove Maintenance

Whatever type of stove you choose to carry, make sure you bring along—and know how to use—a simple repair kit. Stoves get clogged, brass fittings are stripped, and pumps may break, but most of these problems are easy to fix in the field if you have the right equipment. For more information on maintaining and repairing a wide variety of backpacking stoves, pick up a copy of *Backpacker Magazine's Complete Guide to Gear Maintenance and Repair* by gear editor Kristin Hostetter.

Meal Planning for the Light and Fast Cook

Food often ends up being some of the bulkiest and heaviest items in your pack. You can minimize this weight by planning your meals carefully to ensure you have enough but not too much.

With a simple repair kit, the MSR WhisperLite stove is easy to fix in the field. Make sure you know how to clean and repair the stove you choose to carry.
DAVE ANDERSON

The simplest way to plan the food for a backpacking trip is to plan the menu for each meal. This method works well for shorter trips but can become cumbersome if your trip extends over a number of weeks. For longer trips you may find that it's easier and more fun to buy food in bulk—pasta, rice, beans, sauces, cheese, and so on—and come up with a menu when you sit down to prepare each meal. We'll talk about bulk-ration planning in the next section; for the light and fast cook, let's stick to menu planning.

How you plan your meals is up to you, but one option is to divvy up the days among your team and have each team member plan meals for his or her designated days. So if there are four of you out for eight days, each of you will have two days' worth of meals for which you will be responsible. Make sure you talk to one another before you go to ensure you aren't all planning to cook the same thing.

What Kinds of Food?

If you really want the cooking to require a limited number of brain cells, you can buy dehydrated meals in a pouch and call it good. Today's dehydrated food has improved a lot over what used to be available, but it still tends to be relatively expensive per serving, and some people think the meals all start to taste the same after a while. Furthermore, the serving sizes are notoriously small, so you probably want to double the amount recommended. That said, there's not much that can beat dehydrated meals for convenience: Boil water and, voilà; moments later you are enjoying a steaming bowl of pasta primavera or beef teriyaki.

If you want to avoid the cost but like the ease of dehydrated food, you can buy sauce packets in most supermarkets for a lot less money. Add a pound of pasta, and you and your tent mates can be eating pesto penne, spaghetti Alfredo, or any number of options with little more effort than some boiling water.

Coming Up with a Menu

Talk to your teammates about the types of foods they like to eat. Use a questionnaire. Then, with this information to guide you, map out the number of breakfasts, lunches, and dinners you'll need to plan for the duration of your trip. Let's say, for example, you'll be out for four nights with two friends (making your group a total of three). You'll need a total of four dinners, four breakfasts, and four lunches.

Food-Packaging Tips for the Light and Fast Cook

All the meals listed on the sample menu can be made in one pot. For organizational ease, pack each meal together. You reduce your waste if you repackage food before you leave home. Pack everything into two-ply plastic bags. You can have your dried sauce mixes or beans in a separate plastic bag inside the larger bag of pasta or rice, so all you have to do when you sit down to cook is pull out the Monday dinner bag and you are on your way. This also precludes the need for a separate spice kit. Your meals come spiced if you've got the sauce already made at home or have mixed dried spices together in a special meal packet. You'll probably still want to bring salt and pepper and maybe some kind of hot sauce for people who like spicy food.

Boxes are bulkier and heavier than bags. They are also more difficult to pack.
DAVE ANDERSON

How Much Do You Need?

A group of three can usually consume 1 pound of pasta plus sauce and cheese or 1.5 cups of rice with 0.5 pound of dried beans in a meal with ease in the backcountry. For steel-cut oats 1 cup will give you 3 cups of cooked oatmeal. You may want to round up portion sizes a bit if you have big eaters along, and remember that there's nothing like exercise and the great outdoors to cause your appetite to kick in.

When figuring amounts, consider these factors:

- Group size
- Duration of trip
- Exertion level expected on trip
- Weather
- Altitude
- Individual appetites (age of group weighs into this)
- Food preferences
- Weight of food

Most backpackers going out on a short summer trip need to consume approximately 2,500 to 3,000 calories a day. As your trip gets more challenging or the weather becomes colder, you will probably want closer to 3,500 calories per day. If you are going to be out in winter, you should allocate as much as 4,000 to 5,000 calories per person per day! That's a lot of food, but it takes a lot of calories to keep your engine going when

Hot cereal is warm, tasty, simple, and a great way to start the day. To add extra calories and fat for long days, add a spoonful of butter or peanut butter.
DAVE ANDERSON

SAMPLE MENU

Monday:

Breakfast and lunch: On the road en route to trailhead

Dinner: Macaroni and cheese (macaroni noodles, dried milk, sliced cheese—cheddar, Monterey Jack, your choice—garlic powder, salt and pepper)

Tuesday:

Breakfast: Hot cereal (oatmeal, Cream of Wheat, and so on) with brown sugar, dried fruit, and nuts

Lunch (intended to be snacked on all day): Summer sausage, cheese, crackers, bag of gorp, granola bars

Dinner: Beans and rice (quick-cooking rice; dehydrated refried beans with such spices as salt, pepper, cumin, and red pepper flakes already added; cheddar cheese; hot sauce; dried veggies [optional])

Wednesday:

Breakfast: Bagels with cheese or peanut butter

Lunch: Tuna in vacuum-sealed packages, cheese, crackers, gorp, energy bar

Dinner: Spaghetti (spaghetti noodles, tomato sauce, Parmesan cheese, dried veggies [optional])

Thursday:

Breakfast: Rice pudding (rice, sugar, raisins, margarine, cinnamon, and nutmeg [mix up spices in small bag and pack with rice at home])

Lunch: Sardines, crackers, cheese, cookies, dried fruit, candy

Dinner: Pasta with spicy peanut sauce (penne or other type pasta; dried peanut sauce spiced with garlic, ginger, vinegar, red pepper flakes, sugar, soy sauce)

Friday:

Breakfast: Hot cereal with brown sugar, dried fruit, and nuts

Lunch and dinner on the road home

Miscellaneous:

Drinks: Hot chocolate, coffee, tea, lemonade, sports drink mix (depending on your group preferences)

Condiments: Margarine or butter, cooking oil, extra spices, hot sauce

the temperatures are below freezing and you are working hard. Compare these amounts to a typical office worker or homemaker, who needs between 1,400 and 2,500 calories per day.

Nutritional Concerns

For a short trip you don't have to spend a lot of time worrying about how your menu compares with the US Recommended Daily Nutritional Allowances. Use your judgment, include variety in your food, and you should be fine. Just keep a few basics in mind:

Carbohydrates. Provide quick energy and should make up at least 50 percent of your daily caloric intake. Examples of carbs are breads, cereal, pasta, rice, and dehydrated fruits.

Fats. Fats contain more than twice as many calories per pound as carbohydrates and are the body's major source of stored energy. Generally speaking, fats should provide about 20 percent of your daily intake of calories, but on hard wilderness trips this proportion should be higher. Fats aren't converted to energy as quickly as carbs, so they allow us to go without eating for long periods of time and are therefore a great source of energy on long, hard days. Fats are found in cheese, butter, nuts, peanut butter, cooking oil, and margarine.

Proteins. Proteins serve a number of different functions in our bodies. They act as enzymes, antibodies, hormones, and building materials. They play a role in blood clotting; transporting fats, minerals, and oxygen; and helping us balance our fluid and electrolyte levels. So it's pretty important to have enough protein in your diet. You get complete proteins from animal foods—meat, poultry, fish, eggs, milk, and cheese—and soybeans. Plant foods contain partial proteins, so they need to be combined to make a complete protein (examples of combos that result in a complete protein include rice and beans, bread and peanut butter, and hot cereal with reconstituted dry milk). You can also buy protein bars to provide you with complete proteins.

Special Treats

Okay, you want to have a balanced diet when you are camping, but being outdoors and exercising from dawn to dusk is also a time to relax a little. Treats can add some enjoyment to your trip, especially at the end of a long, hard, hot day of hiking or when it's been raining nonstop for hours. Some groups have each person bring something a little special to pull out when the going gets rough. It may be a candy bar for everyone or some hard candy. It may be a dessert such as instant cheesecake or a bag of homemade cookies. Some people opt for savory snacks such as vacuum-sealed smoked salmon. You don't have to be extravagant in your extras, but the element of surprise and a little bit of novelty can brighten your day in a matter of seconds.

Cooking Techniques

For the light and fast cook, the main thing you need to know how to do is boil water. One-pot meals are pretty self-explanatory: Bring your water to a boil, add pasta (or with rice add rice and water and then bring to a boil), simmer until soft, drain.

To reconstitute your sauces, pour the excess pasta water into someone's cup and mix the sauce up before adding it to the cooked pasta.

Staying Organized

An organized kitchen makes cooking enjoyable whether you are in the woods or back at home. Many groups fall into a pattern when they get to camp at the end of the day. First someone goes and fills up the water bladder. Then, if the temperature is cool or the weather wet, somebody else will usually pull out the stove and start water for hot drinks while people set up their tents. This helps tide people over until dinner is ready.

Cooking is more enjoyable if you are organized. Keep your ingredients handy, and divvy up tasks to make life easier when you get into camp. DAVE ANDERSON

COOKING TRICKS TO AVOID CATASTROPHE

- With pasta, always make sure you have plenty of water, at least three parts water to one part pasta. This keeps you from ending up with one big, partially cooked, stuck-together pasta blob.
- To drain your pasta, place a lid over the pot and with wool gloves on your hands to protect them from the heat, tilt the pot just enough to let the water flow. Remember, the pasta is likely to fall onto the lid in a sudden plop, so be ready for that to avoid dumping your dinner onto the ground.
- If your stove is cooking too quickly, depressurize it and the roaring flame will dim to a flicker. On a white gas stove, the best way to depressurize is to turn the stove off, blow out the flame, unscrew the fuel pump, and let some pressure escape; then re-screw the pump and relight the stove.
- If you smell burning, don't stir! Remove the pot from the heat immediately. Stirring spreads the burn taste. If your food needs more cooking, transfer the uncooked portions into people's bowls, clean the pot, and resume cooking. Make sure your pots are clean before you cook. Food sticks more readily to dirty surfaces.
- Don't over-spice! People have a wide range of taste preferences from bland to scorching hot; your best bet is to be gentle with your spices, then let people add if necessary.
- If conditions are cold and wet and people need extra calories, add a lump of margarine, butter, cheese, or peanut butter to your meal. The extra dose of fat will help restore depleted calories.
- You do not have to use disinfected water when cooking. If the water simmers or the bread bakes, you've killed off any dangerous germs.
- One of the main reasons people get sick in the backcountry is not untreated water—those bugs usually get you after you return home—but fecal contamination and shared germs. Yuck. Don't share the nasties. Wash your hands thoroughly before you begin cooking, and don't use your personal spoon for a taste test. Put a sample of whatever you are cooking in your bowl and take a bite. You'll all be happier if you stay healthy.

Once camp is set and you've changed out of your hiking boots, look for a comfortable, low-impact spot to site your kitchen. Pull out all the ingredients you will need for the meal, including hot drinks and spices, and gather your pots, water, and utensils so they are within easy reach. Make sure your stove is full (but don't fill up fuel bottles in the kitchen— spilled gas can ignite and cause a fire if you aren't careful). Now you are ready to go.

Safety in the Kitchen

Whenever you start combining fire and gas, you introduce danger. Not only do you risk setting the forest on fire if you mishandle your stove and fuel, it's also easy to get burned. Make sure you set your kitchen up in an area where there's not much to catch fire, such as on a rock or in a campsite where there is no vegetation. Keep a supply of water on hand to douse any flames that escape.

Be careful around pots full of boiling water. Make sure your stove is stable so the pot cannot fall off and dump boiling water in your lap. Keep your face averted from the stove when you light it to avoid singeing your eyebrows and hair if the stove flares up. Make sure you use either pot grips or thick wool gloves to move hot pans.

If you do end up burning yourself, immediately douse the area with cold water. Keep running cold water over the burn for 20 minutes or more (depending on the size of the injury). Once you've removed the heat from the site, use your first-aid training to treat the wound.

ADVANCED COOKING

If the goal for your trip is a bit more food oriented, or you plan to be out long enough that you think one-pot glop could get old, it doesn't take much effort to step up a bit and move into advanced outdoor cooking. The main difference really is that you bring along a frying pan and start baking quick breads, making casseroles or layered dishes, and frying things like hash brown potatoes and freshly caught trout. Some backpackers love having a frying pan because of the variety it adds to the menu, in terms of both substance and texture. Too many days in the mountains eating food that has no crunch begins to get to some people after a while. You may not be adding the texture of fresh produce, but you do get the substance of bread and the crispy flavor of fried cheese when you use a frying pan.

Another thing many advanced cooks do to add variety to their outdoor cooking is to ditch the meal plan and pack bulk food instead. This technique involves bringing a balance of different food types—pasta, rice, sauces, flour, beans, and, most important, a spice kit—that you can mix and match to create any number of meal options. So on a cold, rainy night when everyone wants instant gratification, you may choose to whip up a quick pot of mac and cheese. But when you have a rest day and the sun is out, you have the option of making something more elaborate: corn bread with cheesy beans or fresh-baked pizza.

Bulk rationing is not for everyone. Ideally suited for long trips with big groups, this method can save money as well as add an element of creativity to your diet, but some people still prefer to stick to menu planning because of its inherent simplicity. Cooking with the bulk method always

Wow your friends with piping-hot pizza. It's easy, tasty, and a nice change from one-pot glop.
DAVE ANDERSON

requires more effort and thought; some people find this inspiring, while others are intimidated by a bagful of ingredients with no directions. You decide. It's worth experimenting to see what method you prefer.

The Advanced Kitchen

You really don't need that much more equipment to advance your cooking techniques. As mentioned above, the key addition is a frying pan. Finding a good frying pan can be tricky. You want a lightweight option,

EXTRAS FOR ADVANCED COOKING

- Frying pan
- Wool gloves
- Spatula
- Spice kit

The addition of a frying pan and spatula brings versatility to your meal options. DAVE ANDERSON

you want a flat lid that you can build a fire on (more on that later), and finally you don't want the pan or lid to have any plastic parts. On many frying pans you can simply remove plastic handles and knobs to transform it into a backcountry utensil. A popular option is the Banks Fry/Bake pan. The National Outdoor Leadership School has been using these pans since 1979, and the reason is that they work. They are relatively lightweight (although no dyed-in-the-wool light-and-fast backpacker would be caught carrying one), and the lids are designed to hold a fire. They are pricey, but with a little care, they will last for years.

Otherwise the only real addition you need to your cook gear is a pair of 100 percent wool gloves. Wool gloves make baking much easier. They serve as potholders, allowing you to rotate your pan, thereby ensuring the heat is distributed evenly. They are also great for staying warm on a cold day.

Bulk Ration Planning

With a bulk-ration, you head out on your camping trip without any real plan for what you'll eat, when, and how. On the surface this sounds risky, and there is a chance that on your last night out you may end up with an odd assortment of ingredients to make a dinner from, but who knows, that creative combination may turn out to be your best meal of the entire trip.

Outdoor professionals often use bulk rationing because it is less expensive than buying prepared foods, and because it gives participants room to experiment. The systems that have been developed over the years are designed to provide enough guidelines to ensure you have balance in your ingredients.

Preplanning Considerations

Your first step in determining how much food you need for your trip requires that you consider the same factors you considered when planning a more rigid menu. You need to know your group size and age, trip length, exertion level, potential weather, altitude, and individual food preferences. Other concerns are perishability and diet restrictions. Once you've answered these questions, you can begin to get a sense of how much food you can expect to consume on a daily basis.

This amount will vary. On a short summer backpacking trip, you can usually get by on 1.5 pounds per person per day. As the weather worsens or the difficulty of the trip increases, this amount will have to increase.

Once you have calculated the amount of food per person you expect you'll need, multiply that number by the number of participants and the number of days for the total poundage you will need.

For example, you are traveling with your spouse and two teenage children on a four-day summer backpacking trip. Teenagers can be big eaters, but the trip's goals are modest, so you are probably safe planning on 1.5 pounds per person. That means your calculation is 4 days × 4 people × 1.5 lbs per person = 24 lbs total

So you need 24 pounds, but 24 pounds of what? Your next step is to divide this number into various categories to ensure you have adequate variety and balance.

For your four-day trip, figure the amount of dinner food you'll need as follows: 24 pounds × .22 = 5.28, or approximately 5 pounds of dinner foods.

Guidelines for Food Amounts		
1.5 lbs per person per day	• Warm days and nights • Group includes children, older adults • Low-intensity activities • High altitude	• 2,500–3,000 calories per person per day
1.75–2 lbs per person per day	• Warm days, cool nights • Hiking with full packs for > 7 days or more intense activity • Younger participants	• 3,000–3,500 calories per person per day
2–2.5 lbs per person per day	• Cool days and nights, chance of rain or snow • High level of physical activity (hiking, climbing, skiing, and so on)	• 3,500–4,000 calories per person per day
> 2.5 lbs per person per day	• Cold days and cold nights (e.g., winter camping) • Strenuous activity (mountaineering, skiing)	• 4,000–5,000 calories per person per day

These guidelines are based on the figures developed at the National Outdoor Leadership School after years of experimentation.

Typically, dinner foods will be pasta, beans, rice, couscous, and other staples. Breakfast foods include freeze-dried shredded potatoes, hot cereals, pancake mix, and granola. You can buy all these items in a grocery store; better yet, buy the staples in the bulk section of a natural food store.

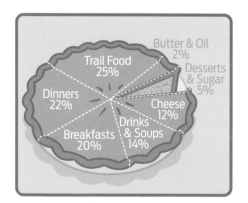

Food-Packaging Tips for the Advanced Kitchen

Before you head into the mountains, take time to repackage your food in heavyweight plastic bags. It helps to bag your food in uniform weights, just so you have a sense of how much is in each bag. Packaging in 1-pound increments is a good standard. The bags aren't too bulky to pack, and

1 pound of pasta or rice is usually a good base amount for most meals.

Spices can be packed in small plastic bags or Nalgene bottles with screw-top caps. The bottle option is heavier, but they are pretty convenient when you are cooking. Liquid spices—oil, soy sauce, vinegar, and so on—are best packed in Nalgene because the bottles are less likely to be punctured than thin-walled plastic. You may want to pack your oil bottle in a plastic bag so it won't make a mess if you spring a leak. Likewise, it is a good idea to double-bag your margarine or butter to prevent leakage in your pack.

When you load up your food, pack breakable items such as crackers or tortillas in pots or frying pans to prolong their shape. You also want to make sure that you pack your food above your fuel, just in case. Spilled fuel will destroy your food and cut short your trip.

SPICE KITS

Spice kits can be as elaborate or bare bones as you like. Here are just some ideas for spices that are can help add variety to your meals.

Salt and pepper

Garlic powder: flavoring for soups, main dishes, sauces

Cumin: flavoring for beans, rice, potatoes; good for both Indian- and Mexican-inspired dishes

Italian seasonings (or basil and oregano): flavoring for tomato sauce, pasta dishes, potatoes

Curry: flavoring for Asian dishes, rice, and so on

Cinnamon: good for sweet breads, hot cereal, and hot drinks

Baking powder: leavening agent for quick breads

Dill: good for soups, potatoes, fish, breads

Cayenne: good for a little heat with beans, curries, and other spicy dishes

Oil: for sautéing or frying

Soy sauce: flavoring for Asian-inspired dishes or as an all-around additive to rice, pasta, popcorn

Vanilla: adds flavor to sweet breads, hot drinks, hot cereal

Vinegar: adds tang to sauces

Hot sauce: great condiment for adding (or covering up) flavor and heat in main dishes

A few spices can liven up even the simplest meals. DAVE ANDERSON

Cooking Tips

As mentioned before, a frying pan is the door to your new world of out-door cooking. With a frying pan and a lid, you can create crispy hash browns and breaded pan-fried trout; you can sauté spices and brown nuts for curries; or, if you are more ambitious, you can bake pizza, cin-namon rolls, calzones, or coffee cake.

Frying

Frying doesn't require much skill, but there are a few rules of thumb to ensure your success:

- **Don't be afraid to use a lot of oil or butter.** Remember, you're burning lots of calories out there! If you skimp on the oil, you aren't going to get nice crispy hash browns or toasted bagels.
- **Don't stir.** If you stir too much, you'll never get your food to brown, and you may end up with mush. Let your food sizzle, and then flip it over without stirring. You'll be much happier with the results.
- **Don't be afraid to burn.** Obviously, it is not your goal to burn your food, but you want to give it time to cook to obtain a nice crispy crust. So let the food sit for a while, longer than you may think, before flipping it over to brown the other side.

Baking

The easiest form of baking is the flip method. The name says it all: You bake your dough on one side then flip it over to bake the other. The flip method works best for stiff dough: biscuits, flat breads, calzones—things that hold their shape.

To flip-bake, grease your frying pan, place your bread in the center of the pan, and cover. Lower the stove to its lowest possible setting. You may need to depressurize white gas stoves to get a low enough flame. Some people like to make a platform with the aluminum windscreen and place the frying pan on the platform so it is somewhat removed from the heat.

You can also take a rock that is the height of your stove and set one side of the frying pan on the rock, the other over the flame.

Balance your pan between a rock and your stove to make sure things bake evenly.
DAVE ANDERSON

One way to slow down your cooking or baking is to distance the pan from the flame by balancing it on top of your windscreen.
DAVE ANDERSON

With this method you'll want to rotate the pan "around the clock" to ensure that all sides are cooked evenly. Set a small rock on the frying pan lid to indicate your starting point; let's call it 12 o'clock. After 4 or 5 minutes at 12, rotate the pan so that 3 o'clock is over the heat, and wait another 4 or 5 minutes. Repeat the process for 6 and 9 o'clock.

Once you've gone around the clock once, remove your pan from the heat and uncover. Gently lift a corner of your bread to see if it is stiff and

BASIC DOUGH RECIPE FOR PIZZA, CALZONES, AND BREAD

Yeast breads sound intimidating, but they can be pretty straightforward and are a great way to impress your tent mates. Use this basic dough recipe for pizza, as well as for calzones and bread.

1 tablespoon yeast
1 part warm water
3 parts flour (A mixture of white and whole wheat works well. For lighter breads use more white flour. For denser, chewier breads, go heavy on the whole wheat.)
1 teaspoon salt

For one pizza, use 1 cup water to 3 cups flour. To make more dough, increase the amount while maintaining the 3:1:1 ratio (flour:water:yeast).

Mix warm water with yeast, and let sit for 5 minutes. Mixture should get frothy. Add one-third of your flour and salt to the yeast mixture, and stir thoroughly. Mix remaining flour into yeast mixture slowly, stirring well after each addition. Once the dough is relatively dry and mixed, begin kneading (make sure your hands are clean!). You can knead right in the pot without any problem. Flour your hands to help keep the dough from sticking, and add more flour if the dough is too wet. Knead for 5 or 10 minutes. The dough should feel smooth and elastic. Brush the dough lightly with oil, and place in a warm spot to rise. You can put the dough in a plastic bag to rise; if it's cold out, you can even wear your dough under your shirt to keep it warm while rising.

Meanwhile, make your tomato sauce.

Tomato Sauce:
2 tablespoons dried veggies (combination of onions and peppers works well)
1 cup water
¼ to ½ cup powdered tomato base
Spices: garlic, oregano, basil, salt and pepper to taste

Rehydrate dried vegetables in hot water for 10 minutes. Stir in remaining ingredients and heat, stirring occasionally. You can vary your thickness by adding or subtracting water.

Putting it all together:

Let dough rise for about 1 hour or until it has doubled in size. Press two fingers into the dough; if an indentation remains, the dough is ready. Punch down dough, and shape into pizza form. Bake over low heat using the round-the-clock method until bottom is cooked. Flip dough, cover with tomato sauce and cheese, and bake slowly until cheese is melted. (You can place a few drops of water into the fry pan and cover quickly to make steam and speed up the cheese melting.)

Calzone variation: For calzones, follow basic dough recipe to the final shaping steps. Punch dough out into pizza form, then cover half the top surface with tomato sauce and cheese. Fold the uncovered side over on top of the sauce, and pinch closed along the edge. Bake until dough is firm; flip and bake other side.

Use this basic dough recipe for other things, like cinnamon rolls. To make cinnamon rolls, spread butter, sugar, cinnamon, and raisins evenly across the top of your dough instead of tomato sauce. Roll the mixture up into a log, and slice into 1-inch-thick discs. Bake as normal. DAVE ANDERSON

Think of your pan as a clock and rotate through the hours systematically.
DAVE ANDERSON

For stiff breads, flip baking is a simple way to cook both the top and bottom evenly.
DAVE ANDERSON

brown. If so, you are ready to flip. If not, give it a few more minutes. To flip effectively, slide a spatula under the bread. Make sure the bread is completely detached from the pan. Once the bread is totally free, flip it. For larger bread products you can slide the bread onto a pot lid and then flip the pot lid over so that the bread falls into the frying pan with the uncooked side down.

Casseroles

Layering sauces, noodles, and cheese in the frying pan and baking into a yummy casserole is a great way to add some variety and texture to your meals. Basically you'll be modeling your meal after a classic lasagna dish, alternating cheese, sauce, noodles, cheese, sauce, noodles. But don't limit yourself to tomato sauce and noodles. You can make casseroles out of just about anything. For example, make a tortilla pie by alternating cheese, tortillas, and refried beans. Or make scalloped potatoes with freeze-dried potato slices layered with cheese and a creamy white sauce.

Here are a few helpful tips for creating a successful casserole: First, start with cheese on the bottom of your pan so you end up with a nice crispy bottom layer. Second, make sure there is enough liquid in your sauce to keep things moist and bubbly. At the same time, you don't want so much water in the pan that everything is floating around. Think of your casserole as a solid, not a liquid. You can always add a bit of water at the end to create some steam for melting the cheese on top. Finally, make sure your uppermost layer is cheese or sauce to keep noodles or tortillas from drying out.

Casseroles work best if the ingredients are precooked. So cook your noodles or rehydrate your potatoes and beans before combining everything in the frying pan. Then when you bake the final concoction, you'll only need to heat it enough to make sure it is warm and the cheese is melted, rather than having to cook everything through. Use the same round-the-clock baking technique we've already discussed to ensure even heating. (For a selection of easy and tasty backcountry recipes, see the section at the end of this chapter.)

THE BACKCOUNTRY GOURMET

Don't be intimidated by the title; any of us can be a backcountry gourmet if we're willing to experiment with our ingredients. For the purposes of this chapter, the main difference between the advanced cook and the backcountry gourmet is that now we'll be adding a top source of heat when baking to create more of an oven effect. Applying heat both above and below allows you to cook your food slowly and evenly, enabling you to bake cakes or work with batters of moister consistency that cannot be flipped readily.

Gourmet Baking

It doesn't take much to impress your tent mates. Think how happy they'll be if you whip up a chocolate birthday cake, miles from the nearest oven. The truth is, baking a cake can be pretty simple. The key is providing a steady source of low heat from both below and above your pan. Some

Lasagna Hint
You can make a kind of pseudo ricotta cheese for your lasagna by mixing dried milk with water and a teaspoon or so of vinegar. Mix the milk to a gruel-like consistency, and then add the vinegar. Pour the mixture in between a layer of noodles and cheese.

people carry along an aluminum "pot parka." Basically, a pot parka is a kind of tent made from nonflammable material that you can lower over your frying pan to create an oven-like space for holding in heat.

If you do not have a pot parka, the other tried-and-true method for creating heat above your frying pan is to build a fire on top of the lid to create an oven. Start by gathering up a pile of small (finger-size) twigs. Then grease and flour your frying pan, pour in your batter, and cover the pan with a lid. Don't overfill the pan. If your batter touches the top, it will

The Outback Oven set includes a commercial pot parka that creates a convection dome over your backpacking stove to make baking easy.
DAVE ANDERSON

burn. Give yourself at least an inch of clearance so the batter can rise without reaching the top or overflowing.

Set up the stove as you do for the flip method—either with a rock to counterbalance your pan or with the windscreen set up as an elevated platform—but before you put your frying pan on the stove, place three thumb-size twigs over the flames until they catch fire. Once the twigs are burning cheerfully, transfer them to the lid of your frying pan and add more twigs to get a small fire going. Now place the frying pan on the stove and begin your baking. If you happen to have a campfire going, rather than building a twiggy fire, simply scoop up some coals from the fire with a pot lid or shovel, place the coals on the frying pan lid, and let them serve as the source of top heat.

For twiggy fires, your sticks should be no thicker than your thumb. DAVE ANDERSON

DIFFERENT BATTER AND DOUGH CONSISTENCIES

- If you can pour the batter, it's best for pancakes or cake batter.
- If your batter is thicker and falls off your spoon in glops, it's perfect for biscuits.
- If your dough is thick and dry enough to form a ball that you can handle without getting your fingers covered with tacky dough, then it's perfect for bread.
- You can mix and match white and wheat flour in most recipes. The more wheat flour you use, the denser and heavier the bread. White flour makes lighter, fluffier breads.

You can light your twigs by holding them in the stove flame. DAVE ANDERSON

This baking method is not for children, as you are definitely playing with fire. Twiggy fires need constant attention, not only to ensure burning sticks don't roll off the lid and start a larger blaze but also because the small sticks burn out quickly so you need to constantly feed the flame. Be patient. Let your pan complete its clock rotation—which should take about 20 minutes—before you check to see if your bread is cooked. When the time comes to check, remove the frying pan lid carefully—remember you are moving a fire. Use your pot grips and plan out your route before you start. Make sure no one is in the way and that you aren't carrying coals or burning sticks over something flammable, such as your nylon clothing or a bunch

You can create your own backpacking oven by building a small fire on top of your frying pan lid. DAVE ANDERSON

of dry grass. If possible, place the lid on a large rock where there is nothing to catch fire if a coal happens to escape. If the food is cooked, just leave the twiggy fire to burn itself out in the safe place.

LUNCH

For most backpackers lunch starts the minute breakfast is over and ends when dinner begins. That's because, like with any endurance activity, you need to maintain a constant supply of calories to keep yourself from bonking. So most of us tend to snack all day on the trail.

Good Snacking

Lunch foods are one of the areas you may struggle with because of different preferences in your group. Some people may love garlic-flavored snack mix; others hate it yet love cheese-covered sesame sticks. It helps, therefore, to pack a wide variety of snacks.

Your primary goals are:
- Palatability
- Packability
- Perishability
- Variety

Snack Mixes

Most bulk-food sections of natural food stores have bins filled with all sorts of different snack mixes. There are cracker mixes, fruit mixes, spicy mixes, sweet mixes, mixes with chocolate, and mixes with pretzels. It's nice to have a selection to choose from when you are out in the mountains, so buy a few pounds of different options.

Dried Fruit

Dried fruit provides concentrated calories and a naturally sweet alternative to candy for snacking along the trail. You can also chop up

Pouring snack foods into your hands rather than digging through the bag helps minimize the spread of germs. DAVE ANDERSON

You can make your own trail mix. Gorp (good old-fashioned raisins and peanuts) is an easy favorite, especially if you add chocolate chips or M&M's to the mix.

Add some fun to your homemade mixes by experimenting with ingredients. Use dried cherries, cranberries, or strawberries instead of the normal raisin option. Try tamari-covered almonds or rice crackers. You can find lots of nuts and fruits to try in your trail mix in the bulk-food section.

Making your own mix can be cheaper, but not always; if cost is a concern, it is worth taking a moment to calculate whether you'll spend more by buying a pound of a premade mix or by buying peanuts, raisins, or whatever else separately and mixing your own concoction.

dried fruit to use in sweet breads and hot cereals. Be careful not to eat too much dried fruit in one sitting, however, as the fruit does reabsorb water in your system and can leave you feeling bloated or with a stomachache if you overindulge. If you're feeling adventurous, try drying your own fruit at home either in a dehydrator or in the sun. Bananas, mangos, apricots, apples, grapes, and papaya can all be dried (or purchased dried) and make a great trailside snack.

Crackers and Breads

It's nice to have something to accompany cheese and meats on the trail, and bread and crackers are the logical option. Look for hard breads that can withstand the rigors of being stuffed into a backpack: Bagels or pita work well. Crackers need to be packed carefully to ensure you end up with something besides a bag of crumbs. Neither crackers nor bread lasts very long in the backcountry, so plan on using these items up during the first couple of days of your trip.

Cheese and Meat

Cheese, summer sausage or salami, tuna in vacuum-sealed packages, smoked salmon, and sardines all make great trail food and are a good source of protein. The trick with these items is that once you break the seal on their packaging they tend to spoil quickly, especially in hot weather. So you should plan on consuming most of the item in one sitting.

Energy Bars, Gels, and So On

There are countless energy foods on the market, from shots of glucose-rich syrups to gummy bear–like cubes. You can buy "real food" bars or space-age energy bars that bear little resemblance to any food you have ever placed on your table. Energy foods are a great concentrated source of calories and sometimes nutrients and protein (read the label!). They can be a good pick-me-up on a long, hard day or can serve as a meal replacement in a pinch. They do tend to be rather expensive, so carry them to supplement your lunch food rather than having them serve as one of the mainstays.

Candy, Cookies, and Other Sweets

It's nice to have some sweet treats on long trips, so bring along some candy bars, cookies, or hard candy. Don't forego more nutritious options for these treats; remember, they are there for special occasions but should not replace food that is better for you.

Packing Your Lunch

Lunch food can be a bit challenging to share if you hike at different paces than your partners or if you happen to be heading out in different directions for the day. You can also run into trouble if Suzy Q always seems to end up with your favorite trail mix or Little Johnny makes a habit of mining through the bag to find every last bit of chocolate. Sometimes it helps to discuss this issue to make sure there are no hard feelings about who is eating what. You may opt to make individual bags of gorp so people can eat without worrying too much about eating more than their share. The main point is to make sure you all have talked about how to share the lunch food equitably before you hit the trail.

Mix and match your lunchtime snacks for variety and nutritional balance.
DAVE ANDERSON

Seneca Rocks, West Virginia
THINKSTOCK.COM

TASTY AND EASY BACKCOUNTRY RECIPES

We've put together some of our all-time favorite recipes and are sharing them here. We've grouped the recipes under the categories breakfast, lunch, dinner, desserts, and beverages. Each recipe includes a list of ingredients, followed by at-home tips to make meal preparation easier in camp. Then we give you detailed cooking instructions, hints for tasty variations, and occasionally reader suggestions that enhance the recipe.

Take a moment to flip through these pages, pick out some enticing recipes, gather up your ingredients, and head to the mountains armed with everything you need to change your backcountry menu from bland and boring to gourmet.

FRESH FOODS THAT LAST LONGER

Worried about foods spoiling on your camping trip? Here are a few tips to help you choose items that will stay fresh even in summer.

Chocolate. Semisweet chocolate (it lacks meltable milk solids) and carob resist melting. Store in the center of your pack.

Cheese. Waxed or hard cheeses, such as cheddar, Colby, and swiss, can last a week (several days longer than soft ones). Cheese may get oily in warm temperatures and not be all that palatable for lunchtime snacking, but it is still fine for cooking.

Eggs. Raw whole eggs, Egg Beaters, and eggs cracked and carried in a plastic container will keep about a week. Make sure to store them in a shady spot during the day.

Fruit. Apples and oranges stay good for a week plus. Buy soft fruit, like pears, hard and let them ripen on the trail.

Veggies. Storing vegetables in paper bags stalls spoilage for up to a week. Carrots, potatoes, and onions keep three weeks.

Butter. Butter lasts a week, or use ghee or margarine for a three-week lifespan.

Meats. Hard salami, jerky, and smoked meats stay good for weeks.

You've heard it countless times: Breakfast is the most important meal of the day. You may argue this in town, but in the backcountry there is little room for debate. A hearty breakfast gets you going in the morning, fuels you down the trail, and helps you stay warm in inclement weather. So load up on the calories—it's one of the few times you can justify eating with abandon.

Egg Recipes

Omelet in a Bag

Mix it, bag it, and forget about it until breakfast time. Then what do you get? An instant yummy omelet.

> 2 eggs
> 2 tablespoons grated cheese
> 2 tablespoons salsa
> 2 tablespoons chopped ham
> Pinch of salt and pepper
> 1 tablespoon cooking oil

At home: Pour lightly beaten eggs into a zip-lock bag. Add the rest of the ingredients, plus anything else that sounds good. Double-bag the mixture to prevent a "sleeping bag-and-head-lamp omelet."

In camp: Either pour the eggs out of the bag into a lightly oiled pan and fry, or bring a pot of water to a boil and drop the bag directly into the pot. Cook 5 to 7 minutes, until the eggs pull away from the sides of the bag.

(Serves 1)

Packing Tip

You don't have to settle for powdered eggs in the backcountry. Try prepackaged Egg Beaters; better yet, crack fresh eggs into a plastic container with a leakproof top. You can also double-bag liquid eggs in zip-lock bags, but be careful to seal the package carefully to prevent leaking. You might want to freeze the eggs to make them easier to pack—they'll thaw as you hike, so make sure the container is leakproof. Plastic egg containers are also available at outdoor stores.

Huevos Revueltos con Papas

The real breakfast of champions? Potassium-rich potatoes, eggs, and zesty jalapeños.

    3 ounces powdered eggs (such as Backpacker's Pantry)
    1 tablespoon powdered milk
    ¾ cup plus 1½ tablespoons water
    2–3 tablespoons olive or canola oil
    2–3 medium-size potatoes
    2–3 jalapeños, diced
    1 small onion, chopped
    ½ teaspoon adobo seasoning
    ½ teaspoon chipotle seasoning
    Salt and pepper to taste
    Tortillas (optional)

At home: Combine powdered eggs and powdered milk in a zip-lock bag.

In camp: Add water to powdered eggs/milk mixture; set aside. Coat skillet with oil. Chop potatoes and cook for 5 minutes. Add jalapeños and onion to skillet; sprinkle with adobo, chipotle, salt, and pepper. Cook for 10 minutes, or until potatoes are browned. Add eggs; stir and cook until set. For extra spice, garnish with additional chipotle or adobo seasoning. Eat as is, or wrap in tortillas.

(Serves 4–5)

Backcountry 'Cakes

Jon's Favorite Trailside Pancakes

This basic pancake recipe is designed to let you mix things up according to what's in season, on sale, or in your cupboard.

    50/50 blend of buttermilk pancake mix (Krusteaz
        preferred) and buckwheat pancake mix (Aunt
        Jemima preferred)
    Eggs—critical for maximum fluffiness—or Egg Beaters
        (check pancake mix packages to determine how
        many)
    Water as specified on package instructions
    1 teaspoon vanilla
    1 tablespoon cooking oil
    Suggested additions as available:
        Nuts such as pecans, crumbled
        Dark chocolate chips, 10 or fewer per 6-inch pancake
        Seasonal fruit (blueberries, raspberries, etc.)
        Maple syrup or honey

In camp: Mix all the ingredients from mix through oil. Fold in additions one at a time—nuts, chips, then fruit—being careful not to mash the berries. Make one extra-large pancake at a time in a medium skillet, using very hot (but not smoking) oil for extra-crispy edges. Bring a real spatula, and use a heat diffuser if you have a stove with a very tightly focused flame that burns the middle of the cake while leaving the outside raw. Serve with warmed real maple syrup or honey.

(Serves 2)

Lemony Maple-Blueberry Syrup

Spice up your pancakes, oatmeal, french toast, breads, or cakes with this fun variation on classic maple syrup.

½ lemon (juice and rind)
1 tablespoon butter
½ pint fresh blueberries (substitutes: any other berry, or a soft fruit such as peach, pear, or plum)
½ cup real maple syrup
1 tablespoon brown sugar

At home: Pack syrup in a leakproof bottle; pack sugar in a zip-lock bag.

In camp: Using a sharp knife, gently peel the yellow part of the lemon rind. Avoid cutting too deeply into the white part of the skin (it's bitter). Finely chop the yellow peel and set aside. Squeeze remaining lemon over a bowl to extract juice. In a skillet, melt the butter over low heat; add the blueberries. Mash some of the blueberries with a fork; add the remaining ingredients, including the lemon rind and juice. Simmer over low heat for about 5 minutes until the mixture starts to thicken.

(Makes 1 cup)

Blueberry-Hazelnut Rice Flour Pancakes

This gluten-free variation on the traditional recipe serves up superlight cakes.

1¼ cups rice flour
2 tablespoons sugar
2 teaspoons baking powder
½ teaspoon salt
¼ cup chopped hazelnuts
¼ cup fresh or dried blueberries
1¼ cups water
1–2 tablespoons canola oil

At home: Combine flour, sugar, baking powder, salt, and hazelnuts (plus blueberries, if you're using dried) in a large zip-lock bag.

In camp: Combine dry ingredients with water and oil (plus blueberries, if you're using fresh) in a medium-size bowl. Heat a lightly greased skillet over medium flame. Spoon 3 tablespoons of batter onto skillet; cook 2 to 3 minutes per side until browned.

(Serves 3)

No-Frills Crepes

Crepes can be made with either sweet or savory batter and served with just about anything: sugar, fruit, cheese, meat. Your only limitation is your imagination.

3 large eggs
1⅓ cups whole milk
¾ cup unbleached, all-purpose flour
¾ teaspoon salt
5 tablespoons unsalted butter, melted

At home: Mix all the ingredients together and blend until smooth. Pour ¼ cup at a time into a buttered 8-inch skillet over medium heat. When the edges are noticeably crispy, flip the crepe. Lift the edge with a spatula, then flip with your hands to avoid tearing. Cook until golden brown. Let the crepes cool, then stack them, separated with pieces of wax paper, and put into a large zip-lock bag. Store flat like a stack of tortillas in the fridge. Crepes last up to three days on the trail.

(Serves 3)

Chef's Secret

Use watered-down pancake batter to make crepes in camp. Pancake mix is sweeter than crepe mix, which makes it better for dessert crepes than meal crepes.

Hearty Potato Breakfasts

Sausage and Potato Breakfast

A hearty breakfast like this one hits the spot on cold, wet mornings in the mountains.

2 tablespoons powdered scrambled egg mix
Enough powdered milk to make the milk required for potatoes
1 3.5-ounce packet instant cheesy mashed potatoes
½ cup chopped cooked Italian sausage
½ teaspoon garlic powder
1 tablespoon butter

In camp: Mix powdered eggs, powdered milk, and potato flakes. Add boiling water (use the amount specified on potato package directions). Stir in sausage, garlic powder, and butter. Eat!

(Serves 3–4)

Hunger waits for no one. THINKSTOCK.COM

Bacon and Cheese Breakfast Taters

This recipe is a little more involved than pouring hot water into oatmeal—but thanks to extra-convenient ingredients, not much.

1 2-ounce Jack Link's Jack Pack! (combo of cheese sticks, beef sticks, and pretzels)

1 3-ounce pouch bacon bits

Small green onion, chopped

1 tablespoon oil

1 3.5-ounce packet instant cheesy mashed potatoes (we recommend Hungry Jack Easy Mash'd Mashed Potatoes, Cheesy Homestyle)

1 tablespoon grated Parmesan cheese (use one of the packets from your last pizza delivery)

2 teaspoons Kraft Macaroni & Cheese Topping

In camp: Dice the Jack Pack cheese sticks and set aside. Slice beef sticks into ¼-inch-thick rings. Sauté beef with bacon bits and chopped onion in oil until barely tender. Add 2 cups water; cover and bring to a boil (now's a good time to eat those pretzels that came in the Jack Pack!). Remove from heat and stir in mashed potato mix and Parmesan cheese. Potatoes will thicken quickly—smooth out any lumps with a spoon or spatula. Sprinkle with cheese topping and diced cheese. Enjoy!

(Serves 2)

Hot Cereals

Cheesy Grits

The secret to grits lies in how well they complement any and all toppings. Whether you add sweet sundries (like bananas with brown sugar), salty and savory tidbits (ham, cheese, bacon, beans), or spicy foods (a handful of jalapeños), the ground cornmeal's mild flavor and amazing velvety texture enhance all accoutrements.

Pinch of salt

1 cup water

3 tablespoons regular grits

Your choice of toppings (see below)

In camp: Add a pinch of salt to the water, bring it to a boil, and then add the grits. Cover the pot and turn the heat to low, stir ring the grits regularly to make them soft and silky smooth. Keep cooking until the desired softness is reached. Different grits cook at different rates. Quick-cooking varieties usually take 8 to 10 minutes; regular grits take about 20 minutes. To finish off your breakfast, add your desired toppings.

(Serves 1)

Toppings and Mix-ins

- Handful of diced cheese cubes (any cheese works, but American melts easily) and some slices of summer sausages, or cheese and freeze-dried broccoli for a veggie alternative (toss the dried broccoli in with the grits to cook)
- Apple and peanut butter—fantastic!
- Powdered milk (no need to reconstitute the milk first; just add slightly more water to the pot if needed) plus garlic and onion powder
- A handful of gorp
- Plain ol' delicious butter and salt

Trail Brecky

If you think oatmeal is boring and tasteless, think again. This recipe will change your mind. Plus everybody knows oats are good for our hearts.

　　3 cups water or milk (use powdered milk)
　　1 cup rolled oats
　　Handful of dried cranberries
　　Handful of sunflower seeds
　　1 teaspoon ground cinnamon
　　2 tablespoons butter
　　2 tablespoons brown sugar or beet syrup

In camp: Place water and oats in a pot and bring to a boil. Reduce heat to a simmer and cook until soft and creamy. Add the rest of the ingredients, stir, and enjoy.

(Serves 2–3)

LUNCH

On most backcountry trips, lunch begins with the completion of breakfast and ends with the start of dinner. Typically we snack throughout the day—a handful of gorp, an energy bar or two—to keep our energy up on the trail. This section provides ideas for immediate on-the-trail gratification, plus suggestions for more elaborate fare—because sometimes it's nice to enjoy a leisurely meal that involves a little preparation. Finally, some fast, easy twists on typical sandwiches and trail food add variety and flavor to your hikes.

Packable, Portable Wraps

Tuna Salad Wraps with Sprouts

A simple tuna salad gets a nutritional punch with the addition of bean sprouts.

　　1 4.5-ounce pouch tuna
　　¼ cup mung sprouts
　　2 tablespoons mayonnaise and/or mustard
　　Garlic powder to taste
　　2 corn tortillas

In camp: In a bowl, mix tuna with mung sprouts, mayonnaise and/or mustard, and garlic powder. Wrap into a warm tortilla, roll up, and bite in.

(Serves 1)

JUSTIN BAILIE

Olympic Wrap

The lunch choice of champions . . . or at least it should be.

  1 tube tomato paste
  1 or 2 whole-wheat tortillas
  Manchego cheese (Hard cheeses are best because they
     last longer. Plus, they're delicious.)
  Turkey pepperoni

On the trail: Squeeze tomato paste onto a tortilla. Slice cheese and layer with pepperoni on the tortilla, then wrap and eat. Repeat as necessary.

(Serves 1)

Classic Sandwiches with a Twist

Supreme Crusty Bread Sandwiches

This hot sandwich is perfect for those days when you're sticking close to camp with a fire still smoldering.

  1 loaf crusty bread (French, sourdough, etc.)
  Butter or olive oil
  Swiss cheese*
  Ham*
  Mushrooms (canned is lovely)*

In camp: Lay the loaf of bread on a piece of tinfoil big enough to cover the entire loaf. Make slices in the bread without completely cutting through the loaf. Swipe a little butter or olive oil on the insides of every cut. Layer your toppings within every other cut. Run a little butter/oil across the top of the whole loaf (or don't; this is not an essential step). Wrap the tinfoil snugly around the overflowing loaf. Heat over campfire coals or in a frying pan over stove until the cheese is melted. Cut or tear into sandwich size pieces.

(Makes 6–8 sandwiches)

*Substitute anything of your choosing.

Smoked Salmon Sliders

Sliders are greasy little burgers that are supposed to slide right down your throat. These sandwiches are little and do slide right down, but not because they are greasy. They're just that good.

  6 ounces smoked salmon
  1 tablespoon chopped green onions
  1 tablespoon chopped red onions
  1 tablespoon capers
  2 tablespoons minced fresh dill
  1 tablespoon fresh lemon juice
  1 teaspoon mustard
  1 tablespoon olive oil
  10 mini bagels

In camp: Shred salmon in a bowl and mix in other ingredients, except bagels. Split and toast bagels; make sandwiches with salmon mixture. Optional: Add cream cheese or cucumber.

(Makes 10 sliders)

Sandwich Packing Tip

For some of us, it is hard to imagine a sandwich being complete without lettuce and tomato. But keep in mind those items have high water content (hence the sog factor). Instead consider vegetables such as fennel, spinach, or shredded cabbage. If you want toppings like tomato, pickles, or cucumber, pack them separately.

Cinnamon-Raisin PB Sandwiches

Add a few secret ingredients and you have gourmet PB&J suitable for all ages.

½ cup peanut butter
2 tablespoons honey
1 teaspoon ground cinnamon
6–8 slices bread
4 tablespoons raisins

At home: In a bowl, mix together peanut butter, honey, and cinnamon. Spread peanut butter mixture over a slice of bread. Sprinkle approximately 1 tablespoon raisins evenly over peanut butter mixture and place another slice of bread on top to complete the sandwich. Repeat with remaining ingredients.

(Makes 3–4 sandwiches)

Variations: Try different dried fruit and nut butters, like cranberries with cashew butter, or bananas with almond butter or even sunflower seed butter.

Middle Eastern Lunches

Falafel with Tahini Sauce

Boost your on-trail protein intake with this tasty dish.

1 cup falafel mix
Vegetable oil (enough for frying)
2 tablespoons tahini (sesame paste)
2 cloves garlic, minced
2 tablespoons lemon juice
Salt to taste
2 large pita pockets, halved

In camp: Add ¾ cup water to falafel mix and mix thoroughly; let sit for 10 minutes. Shape falafel into small patties and fry in oil, on both sides, to desired crispiness. To make the sauce, combine remaining ingredients (except pita), and thin it with warm water to the consistency you want. Put falafel patties into pita pockets, spoon on sauce, and dig in.

(Serves 2)

JUSTIN BAILIE

Crunchy Tabbouleh

Tabbouleh's minty taste provides a welcome change from your regular backcountry flavors.

    1 6-ounce box tabbouleh mix (including spice packet)
    1 small cucumber
    2 green onions
    1 carrot
    2 radishes
    ½ cup broccoli florets
    4 sprigs parsley
    2 tablespoons lemon juice (optional)
    2 tablespoons olive oil
    2 flour tortillas or pita pockets

At home: Combine bulgur from tabbouleh mix with contents of spice packet; pack in a zip-lock bag.

In camp: At breakfast, chop the veggies and parsley; combine all ingredients in a leakproof container with 1 cup cold, filtered water. By lunchtime, the bulgur will be rehydrated and the salad will be ready to devour. Serve with tortillas or pita pockets.

(Serves 2)

Apple-Raisin "No Freeze" Oatmeal Bars

An easy, year-round homemade snack.

    1½ cups rolled oats, uncooked
    1⅓ cups all-purpose flour
    ⅔ cup light brown sugar
    ¾ cup butter (softened)
    1 large apple, chopped into pieces (about 1½ cups)
    ½ cup raisins
    ½ cup shredded carrots (optional)
    ¼ teaspoon ground cinnamon
    ⅛ teaspoon salt

At home: Preheat oven to 400°F. Mix together oats, flour, and brown sugar. Cut in butter until mix is crumbly. Add apple, raisins, carrots, cinnamon, and salt, mixing well. Pat mixture into a greased 9 × 9-inch pan and bake for 40 minutes; cool in pan before cutting.

(Makes 18 chewy, all-natural energy snacks)

JUSTIN BAILIE

DEHYDRATING FOOD

Dehydrating your own food is one of simplest ways to upgrade your backcountry menu. You can pack healthier foods and reduce your pack weight significantly.

Here are a few tips for successful drying:

Buy a dehydrator. Yes, you can dry foods in a standard oven set to 150°F (leave the door open slightly), but the circulating air in a commercial device does a faster and more even job. You also get trays specifically made for drying sauces, fruits, jerkies, and more. *Backpacker* is a big fan of the American Harvest Snackmaster (nesco.com).

Slice it thin. The first thing everyone makes is dried fruit, and with good reason: Apple slices, pineapple rings, berries, and other sweet treats are a great way to carry dense calories and vitamins and spruce up bland gorp. Next up is usually jerky, which takes a few tries to master. (*Hint:* Buy the leanest meat or fish you can find.) For all of these foods, our advice is to cut your sections thinner than the books recommend. You might wind up a bit on the crunchier side with your apples (leave the skins on—yum!), but the fruits and especially the jerkies will last longer in the field. They also dry faster and more evenly if you cut ¼-inch slices rather than the typical ⅜-inch.

Spice it up. Tabasco on your salmon jerky is just a start. Next time you're in the spice aisle, check out the flavored salts and sugars. A tiny pinch of green chili sugar (yes, it exists!) sprinkled pre-drying on apples and pears will create the most popular snack in camp. Another favorite: smoked sea salt (popular in the Northwest) on dried peppers, tomatoes, and jerky. For something simple, try cayenne on pineapple chunks or brown sugar on bananas.

Burger Jerky

Say good-bye to rock-hard, overpriced, gas-station jerky with this cheap and easy recipe.

    1 pound 80 percent lean ground beef
    ½ teaspoon garlic powder
    2 tablespoons tamari or soy sauce
    1 tablespoon chili powder
    1 tablespoon Worcestershire sauce

At home: Preheat oven to 150°F (or "warm" setting). Mix beef and spices well in a large bowl. Place half the meat on a sheet of wax paper and roll it to ⅛-inch thickness with a rolling pin. Cut the beef into 1 × 6-inch strips with a knife or pizza cutter and place on ungreased cookie sheets. Repeat with the other half. Dry in oven 7 to 12 hours (until strips break when bent) on the middle rack, flipping strips and patting excess fat dry with a paper towel every 3 to 4 hours. Let cool completely before storing in a zip-lock bag. ***Note:*** Jerky can also be dried in a dehydrator set to 150°F.

(Makes 12–14 strips)

Ted's Herky Jerky

Jerky is the classic backcountry snack.

1–1½ pounds flank steak
⅔ cup Worcestershire sauce
⅔ cup soy sauce
1 clove garlic, finely minced (or 1 teaspoon garlic powder)
2–3 teaspoons freshly ground black pepper
2 teaspoons onion powder
1 teaspoon liquid smoke
1 teaspoon cayenne pepper (or red pepper flakes)

At home: Trim excess fat from the steaks and cut into strips. Place meat and remaining ingredients in a gallon-size, zip-lock freezer bag. Squish everything around for about 10 minutes, until all powder clumps are broken up and ingredients are well mixed. Place in refrigerator and marinate 3 to 6 hours. When marinating is done, evenly distribute the strips of meat across the trays of your dehydrator. (*Oven version:* Put them directly on the racks, with a sheet of aluminum foil below to aid cleanup.) Set the dehydrator (or oven) to 150°F and bake jerky for 7 to 10 hours, checking and patting dry every few hours. When jerky is fully dry, pack in a zip-lock bag.

(Makes enough for 2 jerky lovers for 2 to 3 days)

Packing Tip

Kept cool in an airtight zip-lock bag, most jerky will last a month (the fattier the meat, the shorter the shelf life). Stash it in the freezer when at home to extend freshness.

Fruit Leathers

This snack is convenient and sweet without lots of added sugar.

1-pound bag of frozen berries, thawed and pureed in a food processor (try raspberries, strawberries, blueberries, cranberries, or a mixture)

Alternative: Applesauce in a jar (comes in a variety of flavors such as watermelon, berry, and peach-mango)

At home: Spread the fruit puree thinly on a plastic dehydrator tray lined with wax or parchment paper. Place in the dehydrator for 8 to 16 hours, or until the fruit peels off in a thin sheet. Roll in wax paper and store in a zip-lock bag.

Variations: Experiment with a dash of nutmeg or cinnamon. Or, for an exotic twist, add some kick to your fruit leather with a bit of cayenne pepper.

DINNER

By the time most of us roll into camp after a day on the trail, we're hungry. Very hungry. Most people's appetites go into overdrive when they are backpacking. Under these conditions, almost anything tastes good—the first night. But after several evenings eating the same thing, that bland dish may have you gagging. You also want to make sure your meals contain enough calories and nutrients to refill the tanks. So don't just settle for anything. It can be fun to make creative, flavorful—and easy—meals to savor in the evening. Consider it a reward to yourself for a job well done.

South of the Border Fare

Anaheim Skillet Quesadillas

Meet the comfort food of the Southwest.

- 1 small red onion
- 1 small red bell pepper
- 1 Anaheim chili pepper
- 2 tablespoons chopped flat-leaf parsley
- 2–3 tablespoons olive oil
- 4 flour tortillas
- ¾ cup each shredded sharp cheddar and pepper jack cheese
- ½ teaspoon ground cumin
- ½ teaspoon chili powder
- Chopped jalapeños
- Orange Chili Salsa (see below) for garnish (optional)

JUSTIN BAILIE

At home: Put shredded cheese in a zip-lock bag.

In camp: Cut onion and peppers into thin 2-inch strips. Sauté them with parsley in olive oil until slightly tender (about 10 minutes); set aside. Place one tortilla in a skillet, adding slightly more olive oil if needed. Sprinkle with cheese, pepper mixture, cumin, and chili powder. When crispy, fold tortilla over and remove to a plate. Cut into wedges and top with jalapeños and salsa. Repeat for each quesadilla.

(Serves 4)

Orange Chili Salsa

This light, fruity garnish is so good, you'll make it to eat at home.

- 1 red jalapeño
- 1 green jalapeño
- 1 tablespoon olive oil
- ¼ cup slivered raw almonds
- 1 tablespoon chopped fresh cilantro or parsley
- 2 large navel oranges

In camp: Dice jalapeños and sauté in olive oil for about 8 minutes. Add almonds and chopped cilantro or parsley and sauté for 6 to 7 minutes more, or until almonds are lightly browned. Peel oranges and slice out segments, holding each orange over a bowl to catch the juice; cut segments into bite-size chunks. Squeeze juice from leftover orange membranes into bowl. Add chili mixture and toss.

(Serves 4–5)

Chef's Tip

Tone down the heat by removing seeds and membranes from jalapeños.

Backcountry Pizza Party

Pepperoni Pizza in a Pan

Now you don't have to wait until you get back to town to enjoy a slice of pizza.

- 5-ounce block Asiago cheese (or another hard/semi-hard cheese, such as Gouda, Monterey Jack, or Parmigiana Reggiano)
- 1 6.5-ounce pouch baking mix (such as Bisquick or Betty Crocker Pizza Crust Mix)
- 1 tablespoon olive oil
- ½ cup tomato sauce (use Contadina's pack-friendly Pizza Squeeze bottle)
- 1 4-ounce pouch pepperoni slices
- 1 tablespoon Italian seasoning

At home: Transfer Italian seasoning to zip-lock bag. Pack oil in a leakproof container.

In camp: Finely dice cheese. In a bowl, combine baking mix and ½ cup water; stir until dough forms. Pour oil into a 10-inch skillet. Roll dough thin on a plate with a rigid plastic water bottle and transfer to skillet (or spread dough evenly across skillet with a spoon). Top with tomato sauce, cheese, and pepperoni. Cover the pizza with a pot lid and cook over medium heat for 5 minutes, or until cheese melts. Top with Italian seasoning.

(Serves 2)

Variations: Try these variations to make more great pizza!

- Greek: feta cheese + chopped olives + chopped peperoncinis
- Spicy Southwest: pepper jack cheese + black beans + chili powder
- Vegan: soy mozzarella + chopped portobello mushrooms + broccoli
- Purely Potent: Gorgonzola cheese + chopped garlic + anchovies
- Dessert Pizza: Nutella + dried strawberries + walnuts

Fast Dough

Take whole-wheat pitas and make pizzas on them—that way, you don't end up with sticky hands or doughy centers! They are super yummy and make pizzas super fast.

Chef's Secret

Make sure your pizza doesn't burn by spreading the dough thinly and removing it from the heat as soon as the cheese is melted. You might be wondering why we don't suggest using pre-shredded mozzarella (or another soft variety). That's because the harder a cheese is, the longer it'll last in the backcountry. And if you leave it in block form and dice right before baking (rather than shredding ahead of time), it'll stay fresh even longer.

If your cheese is slow to melt and the dough is cooked through, add a few drops of water to the hot skillet and cover quickly with your lid. The steam will help melt your cheese.

Perfect Pasta Dishes

Kickin' Mac and Cheese

Fast, filling, and yummy macaroni and cheese is comfort food wherever you pitch your tent.

1 pound pasta
4 tablespoons powdered milk
Red pepper flakes to taste
Garlic powder to taste
1 cup or more (depending on preference) diced sharp
    cheddar cheese
3–4 tablespoons butter or margarine
Salt and pepper to taste

At home: Put butter in a hard container. Place powdered milk, red pepper flakes, garlic powder, salt, and pepper in separate zip-lock bags.

In camp: Boil water and add pasta; cook until done (about 8 to 12 minutes). Stir occasionally to keep the noodles from sticking. Meanwhile, rehydrate powdered milk following package directions (add enough water to give it the consistency of milk). Once the pasta is done, remove it from heat. Drain water. Add milk, red pepper flakes, and garlic powder; stir to coat pasta. (*Note:* For a creamier mac, use more milk.) Mix in cheese and butter. Return pot to stove and heat slowly, stirring constantly, until cheese melts. Add salt and pepper to taste.

(Serves 3)

EIGHT TIPS FOR MAKING PASTA

Easy to cook and packed with carbohydrates, noodles are ideal for helping you refuel after a long day on the trail.

1. Use at least 1 quart (4 cups) of water for every 4 ounces of dry pasta. Using plenty of water will help prevent the pasta from clumping and sticking together.
2. Cover the pot with a lid to help bring the water to a boil faster. This doesn't mean that the water won't boil over, so be sure to watch it.
3. Salt the water to boost the pasta's flavor. Use a maximum 2 tablespoons of salt per pound of pasta. Do not add salt until the water comes to a boil. If you add the salt to cold water, it will take a little longer for the water to boil and the salt could also pit the bottom of your pot.
4. Stir the pasta after you add it to the boiling water and occasionally throughout the cooking process. This will prevent noodles from clumping and sticking to the bottom of the pot.
5. Don't add oil to the water. Oil will coat the pasta and prevent your sauce from sticking.
6. Pasta can overcook quickly. Test for doneness about 4 minutes before the time given on the package instructions. Most pastas cook in approximately 8 to 12 minutes. Noodles should be tender but still firm, or al dente. Remember that pasta will continue to cook and soften even after you drain it. For fresh pasta, you know it is done when it rises to the surface.
7. Don't rinse the pasta (except when making a cold pasta salad or lasagna). Rinsing the pasta will remove the starch that helps your sauce adhere to the noodles.
8. Try whole-wheat or whole-grain pasta. It has more fiber, which will keep you fuller longer.

Cheesy Sausage Pasta

Vary ingredient amounts to taste.

Handful of sun-dried tomatoes
Handful of dried mushrooms of choice
1 4-ounce pouch Knorr-Lipton Four Cheese Bow Tie
   Italian Sides
1 chunk gruyère cheese
1 chunk summer sausage

At home: Pack the tomatoes and mushrooms in a zip-lock bag.

In camp: Rehydrate the dried ingredients in hot water for 20 to 30 minutes, or until soft. Drain. Cook pasta according to package directions. While pasta cooks, dice cheese and chop sausage into bite-size chunks. Add cheese, sausage, tomatoes, and mushrooms to pasta. Stir until cheese melts.

(Serves 1)

Fancy Fish Feasts

Cold-water trout contains healthy doses of omega-3 fatty acids and protein. This means that while the catching is fun and the eating is great, the fish is good for you!

Mediterranean Stuffed Trout

Lemons and olives deliver a flavorful punch.

1 lemon
⅓ cup oil-cured olives
2 cleaned whole trout
1 cup flour
½ teaspoon salt
1 teaspoon lemon pepper
1 teaspoon dried thyme
1 tablespoon cooking oil

At home: Combine flour, salt, and lemon pepper in a gallon-size zip-lock bag.

In camp: Slice lemon into ½-inch sections and set aside. Slice olives. Place trout in the zip-lock bag containing flour, salt, and lemon pepper; toss gently to coat. Sprinkle the inside of the fish with thyme; cover with lemon and olive slices. Heat oil in pan to sizzling and cook trout until flesh is flaky. To keep your trout from curling when frying, score the skin.

(Serves 2)

THREE WAYS TO COOK TROUT WITHOUT A PAN

If you forgot your fish kit (see page 190) but caught the fish, you can still enjoy a yummy trout dinner without a pan.

Baked: Make a campfire and get a good bed of coals going. Place a thin, flat rock on the coals, pizza oven–style. Bank coals around the rock. Clean the trout, brush it with olive oil, and cook, flipping a few times until done.

Grilled: Weave together green branches to make an improvised grill. Set the grill on rocks over your fire and cook—just be sure to remove the fish if the branches start to burn.

Ceviche: Clean trout and chop into 1-inch pieces. Place in a zip-lock bag filled with fresh lemon or lime juice (use 6 fruits per pound of fish). Chill in a snowbank or cold pond for 4 to 6 hours, stirring after the first hour.

Whole Trout with Cranberry-Almond Sauce

Crunchy and flavorful, this gourmet dish is the trail mix of fish recipes.

¼ cup dried cranberries
2 cleaned whole trout
1 cup flour
½ teaspoon salt
¼ teaspoon ground black pepper
Pinch of cayenne pepper
Pinch of ground cinnamon
1 tablespoon cooking oil
¼ cup minced onion
⅓ cup chopped toasted almonds
1 tablespoon butter (optional)

At home: Combine flour, salt, black pepper, cayenne, and cinnamon in a gallon-size zip-lock bag. Store cranberries, almonds, and onions in separate bags.

In camp: Soak cranberries in 1 cup water for 5 minutes to soften. Place trout in bag with flour and spices; toss to coat. Heat oil in pan to sizzling and fry trout until flesh is flaky (3 to 6 minutes per side, depending on size of fish). In the meantime, make sauce: Add onions to pan and sauté 30 seconds. Add almonds, cranberries, and their water (and butter, if using); stir to combine. Pour sauce over cooked trout.

(Serves 2)

Spicy Southwest Trout

Give your fish a kick with green chilies and cornmeal.

2 cleaned whole trout
1 cup cornmeal
1 teaspoon mild chili powder
½ teaspoon salt
¼ teaspoon pepper
2 tablespoons cooking oil
¼ cup minced onion
1 4-ounce can chopped green chilies

At home: Combine cornmeal, chili powder, salt, and pepper in a gallon-size zip-lock bag.

In camp: Place trout in the bag with flour and spices; toss to coat. Heat oil in pan to sizzling and fry trout until flesh is flaky. Remove trout and keep warm. Add onion to pan and sauté 30 seconds. Stir in chilies and serve over trout.

(Serves 2)

PACK-A-FISH KIT

For most fish dinners you'll need a few basic supplies for cleaning and cooking:

- 10-inch frying pan (nonstick coatings speed cleanup)
- Plastic spatula
- Pocketknife or multitool with knife for filleting fish. (If you anticipate catching big fish [12 inches or more], pack a 6-inch fillet knife.)
- Olive oil packed in leakproof container
- To accompany your trout, plan on a side dish such as flavored rice. We like Lipton's Creamy Garlic Parmesan, and Herb and Butter.

Hearty One-Pot Stews

Mushroom Soup with Gremolata

An Italian-style relish adds the robust taste of garlic, parsley, and lemon to your basic mushroom soup.

1 small garlic clove, minced
1 tablespoon finely chopped fresh parsley (or 1 teaspoon dried)
1 teaspoon lemon zest
3 cups dried mushrooms (cremini, shiitake, oyster, or white)
2 tablespoons olive oil
3 tablespoons flour
4 cups water
4 chicken bouillon cubes
Salt and pepper to taste
3 green onions

At home: Put lemon zest in a zip-lock bag.

In camp: To make the gremolata, combine minced garlic, parsley, and lemon zest; set aside. For the soup, slice mushrooms and add to a pot with the olive oil. Sauté for 5 minutes. Add flour, stirring for 2 to 3 minutes, or until flour browns slightly. Gradually add water and stir until smooth. Add bouillon cubes; heat to a boil and simmer 5 minutes. Season with salt and pepper. Slice green onions and add to the pot. Spoon soup into bowls and garnish with gremolata.

(Serves 2–3)

Chef's Secret

You don't have to rehydrate the mushrooms before sautéing them; they'll rehydrate in the broth as you cook the soup. However, if you prefer, you can let the mushrooms soak for 15 minutes in cool water before you begin cooking.

Double Onion and Potato Stew

A crispy, cheesy garnish tops this winter comfort dish.

　　4 cups water
　　2 tablespoons cornstarch
　　1 cup dried potatoes
　　4 beef bouillon cubes
　　¼ teaspoon dried thyme
　　1 medium onion
　　1 tablespoon chopped fresh parsley (or 1 teaspoon dried)
　　Salt and pepper to taste
　　¾ cup shredded Parmesan cheese
　　½ cup french-fried onions (such as French's)

At home: Place potatoes, bouillon cubes, and thyme in a zip-lock bag.

In camp: Put water in a pot and stir in cornstarch until smooth. Place over high heat. Add potato mixture; heat to boiling and simmer for 6 to 7 minutes. Thinly slice onion and add to the pot. Simmer 5 more minutes. Season with parsley, salt, and pepper. Spoon stew into bowls and garnish with Parmesan cheese and french-fried onions.

(Serves 2)

Chicken and Dumplings

This simple one-pot meal can be made from leftovers you bring from home.

　　1 tablespoon chicken bouillon
　　1 tablespoon dried veggie flakes
　　1 tablespoon dried onion flakes
　　½ teaspoon celery salt
　　¼ teaspoon black pepper
　　¼ teaspoon dried thyme
　　7 ounces leftover chicken
　　2¼ cups Bisquick
　　1 teaspoon dried parsley

At home: Put the first six ingredients in a zip-lock bag. Freeze the chicken in a second bag. Put the Bisquick and parsley in a third bag.

In camp: Boil 3 cups water; add contents of first bag and simmer. Slice and add chicken. Make dumplings by adding ⅔ cup water to Bisquick bag. Seal and squish to mix. Snip off corner of bag and squeeze dough into soup. Cover until dumplings float to top.

(Serves 2)

Portable Pub Grub

Mushroom-Asiago Veggie Burgers

Okay, it's not beef, but there's still something very satisfying about a burger, veggie or not.

1 cup (6 ounces) veggie burger mix
1 cup boiling water
2 large cremini mushrooms
½ cup grated Asiago cheese
Olive oil (optional)
4 large burger buns
Condiments such as mayo, ketchup, mustard, lettuce, onion, and tomato

At home: Pack buns in your cook pot or a smash-proof plastic container. Do not dice or wash mushrooms, which can accelerate spoilage.

In camp: Place burger mix in a heat safe bowl. Add boiling water, stir, and let stand for 10 to 15 minutes, or until mixture is cooled and set. Dice mushrooms and work into mix along with cheese. Form into 4 patties. Pan-fry in a nonstick skillet (with olive oil, if using). Fry each side until browned and burger is cooked through. Place on bun and add fixings.

(Serves 4)

JUSTIN BAILIE

JUSTIN BAILIE

Spicy Sweet Potato Fries

Backcountry fare tends toward one-pot glop meals. So if you are looking for something crispy, try these fries.

2–3 medium sweet potatoes
Olive or canola oil
1–2 teaspoon sea salt
Seasonings such as onion powder, Italian seasoning, and/
    or seasoning salt

At home: Place potatoes in paper bag.

In camp: Wash or peel sweet potatoes; cut into 2-inch strips. Coat a large skillet with oil. In batches, add sweet potatoes and sprinkle with sea salt and seasonings. Fry until browned on both sides, about 10 to 15 minutes. Remove to a plate and top with additional seasonings, if desired.

(Serves 4–6)

Chef's Secret
To bake fries, wrap them in foil along with the seasonings and place the packet directly on hot coals; omit the oil.

Hot Spinach and Artichoke Dip

If your meal takes more than 5 minutes to cook and you have a lot of hungry campers eager to chow, try serving this tantalizing appetizer to tide people over.

 1 5-ounce can evaporated milk
 1 tablespoon cornstarch
 ¼ teaspoon salt
 1 12-ounce jar quartered and marinated artichoke hearts, chopped (we like Cento's)
 2 cups fresh baby spinach, lightly chopped
 2–3 tablespoons chopped fresh basil
 ¾ cup grated Parmesan and Romano cheese blend

At home: Place spinach, basil, and cheese in a large zip-lock bag.

In camp: Whisk evaporated milk, cornstarch, and salt in a medium saucepan until smooth. Place over medium heat, stirring frequently until thick and bubbly. Remove from heat; add artichoke hearts, spinach, basil, and cheese. Stir and return to heat for 6 to 7 minutes, or until spinach is wilted and cheese is melted. For dipping, pack a bag of pita chips (they're less fragile than other chips) or a loaf of crusty bread; or make tortilla chips in camp (see recipe below).

(Serves 4–6)

Toasted Tortilla Chips

Chips turn into dust in your backpack, so your best bet is to make your own on the spot.

 4 10-inch tortillas (try Mission's Garden Spinach Herb or Jalapeño and Cheddar)
 2 tablespoons olive or canola oil (optional)
 Pinch of sea salt

At home: Cut tortillas into wedges and place in a zip-lock bag.

In camp: Fry tortilla wedges in a skillet with oil until crisp and browned, or use a dry nonstick skillet. Remove from heat and sprinkle lightly with sea salt.

(Serves 4–6)

Hearty Potato Recipes

Sesame White-Bean Potato Cakes

These potato cakes are heavy on the carbs and taste.

    1 15-ounce can great northern beans
    1½ cups instant potato flakes
    2 teaspoons powdered milk
    2 tablespoons onion soup mix
    1 cup cold water
    4 tablespoons sesame seeds
    4 tablespoons olive oil

At home: Drain and rinse beans; double-bag in zip-lock bags.

In camp: Smash beans into a paste with a spoon. Combine potato flakes, powdered milk, and soup mix. Mix with bean paste and water. Shape dough into 8 balls and flatten each into a 1-inch-thick patty. Pour sesame seeds in a shallow plate; press each patty firmly into the seeds to coat both sides. Heat oil in a skillet and cook patties about 3 minutes per side, until golden brown.

(Serves 4)

Wasabi Potatoes with Salmon

The wasabi adds a kick to instant potatoes, while the salmon is a perfect protein source.

    1½ cups water
    1½ cups instant potato flakes
    2 teaspoons wasabi powder (check the Asian section of
        your grocery store)
    1 6-ounce pouch salmon

At home: Pack potato flakes and wasabi powder together in a zip-lock bag.

In camp: Bring water to a simmer. Add the potato-wasabi mix and stir until smooth. Remove from heat, add salmon, and serve.

(Serves 2)

Chef's Secret

Skip the salt—it brings out the wasabi's bitterness and dampens its spice.

Lost Coast, California.

Curry Variations

Masaman Curry
Lemongrass and peanuts accent this creamy Thai dish.

- 1 4-ounce pouch instant mashed potatoes
- 1 tablespoon Masaman curry paste (contains lemongrass, garlic, cumin; available at tastepadthai.com)
- 1 1.75-ounce pouch coconut cream powder (available at Asian or Indian groceries) and 1 cup water (or 1 cup canned coconut milk)
- ½ medium onion, peeled and thinly sliced
- ½ cup matchstick-cut carrots
- 1 tablespoon brown sugar
- ⅓ cup crushed peanuts
- 1 7-ounce pouch precooked chicken breast (vegetarian option: 1 14-ounce can chickpeas)

At home: Combine brown sugar and crushed peanuts in a zip-lock bag. (If using chickpeas, place in a separate zip-lock bag.) Place precut onions and carrots in two more zip-lock bags.

In camp: Prepare potatoes according to package directions; set aside. In a separate pot, combine curry with coconut powder and water (or canned coconut milk). Bring to a boil. Add onions and carrots and cook, stirring, for 3 minutes. Add sugar, nuts, and chicken (or chickpeas), and cook until sugar is dissolved and everything is hot. Spread over potatoes.

(Serves 2)

Spicy—and Ultralight—Curried Noodles

Lighten your load and still eat like a king or queen with this ultralight meal, courtesy of *Backpacker* magazine's discriminating gear editor, Kristin Hostetter. As she puts it: "It requires a bit of upfront prep work at home, but pretty much zero work in camp. It's superlight (just 6 ounces per serving!) and, man, does it taste good! Way better than anything prepackaged." The secret: dehydrated ingredients + a freezer bag.

1 serving of Asian cellophane noodles (They typically come in large bricks. Break off a chunk about 3 by 6 inches.)

¼ cup dehydrated meat of your choice (burger or chicken)

¼ cup dehydrated mixed veggies

1 tablespoon curry

1 tablespoon cumin

1 tablespoon coriander

1 tablespoon garam masala

½ teaspoon ground ginger

2 tablespoons coconut cream powder

2 tablespoons powdered milk

Dash of cayenne

Salt and pepper to taste

Handful of cashews

At home: Combine all ingredients except the cashews in a quart-size freezer bag.

In camp: Add about 1½ cups boiling water to the ingredients in the freezer bag. Squish it around and wrap it in a coat or sleeping bag for about 10 minutes, or until everything is tender. Top with cashews.

(Serves 1)

Thai Green Curry

This sweet-tasting dish is more fragrant than spicy.

6 ounces rice noodles or linguine

2 teaspoons green curry paste

1 tablespoon brown sugar

1 1.75-ounce pouch coconut cream powder (available at Asian and Indian groceries) and 1 cup water (or 1 cup canned coconut milk)

½ small onion, peeled and thinly sliced

½ cup matchstick-cut carrots

2 3.5-ounce pouches precooked shrimp (vegetarian option: 1 12-ounce package firm tofu, cut into 1-inch cubes)

½ lime (optional)

¼ cup chopped cilantro (optional)

In camp: Cook noodles according to package directions; drain and set aside. In a separate pot, combine curry and brown sugar with coconut powder and water (or canned coconut milk) and bring to a boil. Add onions and carrots and cook, stirring, for 3 minutes. Stir in shrimp (or tofu) and cook till heated through. Serve over noodles; add lime or cilantro if desired.

(Serves 2)

Doctoring Ramen Noodles

Easy Pad Thai

Ramen noodles have always been a go-to lightweight favorite of backpackers. You can up the ante and still enjoy the ease of instant noodles with this recipe, which transforms ramen from boring to exotic.

> 3 packages ramen noodles
> 1 7-ounce pouch precooked chicken breast
> ½ cup Asian sesame dressing (try Newman's Own Asian Sesame Natural Salad Mist, which comes in a pack-friendly 7-ounce plastic bottle)
> 1 cup shelled peanuts

At home: Crush peanuts into pieces with the bottom of a bowl or mug. Pack in a zip-lock bag.

In camp: Cook ramen noodles according to package directions and drain (save the seasoning packet and add it to soup or rice later). Stir the chicken and dressing into the pot and cook for 1 minute. Sprinkle crushed peanuts over the noodles and serve.

(Serves 3)

JUSTIN BAILIE

Okay, most of us don't get much beyond s'mores when we think about backcountry desserts, but there are lots of easy treats you can whip up to satisfy your sweet tooth that don't require a campfire or a lot of effort.

UPDATING THE CLASSIC S'MORE

You know the basics: Toast a marshmallow over the fire, place on a graham cracker with a square of chocolate, top with second graham cracker, and enjoy. It's hard to imagine an improvement on this, but try one of these variations—you may be surprised.

The Johnny Appleseed
Apple-cinnamon graham crackers + marshmallow + apple slices

The Minty Fresh
Chocolate grahams + marshmallow + Andes mints

The Kindergarten Classic
Honey grahams + peanut butter + marshmallow + chocolate

The Tropical
Grahams + dried mango + marshmallow + coconut shavings

The Mexican S'more
Grahams + chili powder + cinnamon + marshmallow + chocolate

The Inside-Out
Roast a marshmallow; while it's still on the stick, roll it in a shallow plate full of chocolate syrup and crushed graham crackers.

Chocolate-Dipped Ginger and Mango
A sweet and savory dried-fruit dessert.

1 7-ounce package semisweet baking chocolate
2 tablespoons peanut oil
10 pieces crystallized ginger
10 slices dried mango

At home: Pour peanut oil into a small plastic bottle. Place mango and ginger in a zip-lock bag.

In camp: Fill a pan three-quarters full of water and place on stove over medium heat. Put chocolate in a metal cup or small pot and place in the pan of water (this prevents the chocolate from burning). Pour in peanut oil and stir until chocolate melts. Dip ginger and mango slices into chocolate, eating as a fondue.

(Serves 2)

JUSTIN BAILIE

Campfire Baked Apples
Another variation on baked apples.

4 tart apples
½ cup raisins
½ cup unsweetened shredded coconut
½ cup brown sugar
1 teaspoon ground cinnamon
½ teaspoon ground nutmeg
Pinch of salt
4 teaspoons maple syrup

At home: Mix all the ingredients except the syrup and apples in a zip-lock bag.

In camp: Core the apples. Fill each apple halfway with spoonfuls of the raisin-coconut-sugar-spice mixture. Add 1 teaspoon syrup to each apple; top off with more mixture. Wrap apples individually in foil and bury in warm, ashy campfire coals for about 20 minutes, or until apples are soft.

(Serves 4)

Coconut-Mango Rice Pudding
Try this with one of your curry dinners for an all-Asian meal.

2 teaspoons potato starch
8 tablespoons powdered milk
2 tablespoons coconut cream powder or powdered coconut
2 teaspoons sugar
4 tablespoons chopped dried mango (or dried fruit of your choice)
2 cups instant rice

At home: Combine all the ingredients in a zip-lock bag. Shake.

In camp: Divide dry mixture equally into four insulated mugs. Add boiling water to each mug. Stir well; cover and wait 5 minutes before eating. *Bonus:* Makes a fine breakfast too; serve as is, or add 4 tablespoons oatmeal to the dry ingredients for more texture and flavor.

(Serves 4)

Black Canyon Chocolate Cake

Molasses works best in this delectable dessert if you don't mind carrying a tiny Nalgene bottle.

1½ tablespoons powdered milk
¼ cup sweetener (molasses recommended)
½ cup chocolate chips
1½ tablespoons oil
½ cup all-purpose flour
1 tablespoon cornstarch
¼ teaspoon baking soda
⅛ cup powdered sugar

At home: If using a dry sweetener, combine with chocolate chips in a zip-lock bag. Also pack flour, cornstarch, and baking soda together. Leave other ingredients separate.

In camp: Mix powdered milk with ¼ cup cold water in a nonstick saucepan. Add sweetener and chocolate chips, and melt over medium heat. Remove from heat and stir in oil; then stir in flour mixture. Pour into a nonstick skillet lined with parchment paper and bake. We recommend the Outback Oven; baking time is about 40 minutes after the thermometer reaches "Bake." Or you can bake the cake above coals or a fire. Just make sure to rotate the pan periodically so that all parts get heated evenly. (You can also ensure even heating by placing the cake pan inside another pan that's lined 1 inch deep with pebbles, which distribute heat. Both pans then go atop a fire or stove.) If not using a backcountry oven, it also helps to cover the pan and put coals on top, to apply heat from above. Bake until a fork comes out almost dry. Sprinkle with powdered sugar.

(Serves 3)

Alpine Lake, Wallowa Mountains, Oregon.
THINKSTOCK.COM

Chocolate Cheesecake

No-bake cheesecake mix makes this dessert easy and fast.

2 1.25-ounce packages Mini Oreo Bite Size! Chocolate
  Sandwich Cookies
Jell-O No-Bake Real Cheesecake Dessert Mix
⅓ cup plus 3 tablespoons powdered milk

At home: Open cheesecake box and pack only the filling mix. Place powdered milk in a zip-lock bag.

In camp: To make the crust, crush the cookies inside their bags into a chunky powder. Open bags and pour powder equally into the bottom of four bowls. Mix 1⅓ cups water (the colder, the better) and powdered milk in a rigid plastic water bottle; shake well. Pour milk into a bowl and add cheesecake mix. Whisk with a fork for 3 minutes or until thick. Spoon over Oreo crust in each of the bowls and enjoy.

(Serves 4)

Variations: Use shortbread cookies, Girl Scout Thin Mints, or Golden Oreos for the crust.

For Super Chocolate Cheesecake replace ¼ cup of the basic cheesecake mix with ¼ cup instant chocolate pudding mix.

For Lemon Cheesecake replace ¼ cup of the basic cheesecake mix with ¼ cup instant lemon pudding mix.

Chef's Secret

Best toppings for cheesecake include these favorites:
  Chocolate syrup
  M&M's
  Caramel syrup
  Crushed Heath bar pieces
  Pecans
  Dried fruit
  Jelly beans

Use granola, nuts, and fruit for toppings and snacks.
THINKSTOCK.COM

Hmm, what do you bring to drink when you go backpacking—a flask of whiskey maybe? Or perhaps you forego cocktail hour to save weight. But for many there's nothing quite like a sip of something around the campfire at the end of a long day to round out a great trip. Here are a few fun recipes for everything from a warming hot toddy to a snowy mint julep, plus a new twist on hot apple cider.

BUILD A BACKCOUNTRY BAR KIT

Can't decide on just one cocktail for your adventure? Then put together a mobile backcountry bar kit. This kit is geared toward whiskey drinkers, but you can be creative and come up with your own cocktail makings for any liquor type.

The first step in this endeavor is finding a toiletry kit or other closable container in which to store all the necessary ingredients. REI's Stasher Kit is the perfect size, plus it has separate compartments to keep everything organized, zips completely shut, and has a handle on the outside for easy carrying. To properly prepare this mini mobile bar for stocking, you'll also need the following gear (available at rei.com):

- REI Stasher Kit or similar nylon zip toiletry kit
- 1 8-ounce flat oval bottle
- 3 2-ounce flat oval bottles
- 1 3 × 5-inch zip-lock bag

The Ingredients

Once you have all the necessary equipment, the bar will need to be stocked. This will make 5 drinks.

8 ounces whiskey (we like Stranahan's Colorado Whiskey)
½ ounce vermouth
3 dashes Angostura bitters
¾ ounce simple syrup (equal parts sugar and hot water)
5–8 mint leaves
¾ ounce maple syrup
Small piece of ginger, sliced
1 cinnamon stick
2 cloves
2 slices lemon
1 individual packet of honey
1 packet black tea
1 straw (optional)

At home: Pour 8 ounces whiskey into the 8-ounce bottle. In the three smaller bottles, combine vermouth and bitters in the first; simple syrup and mint in the second; maple syrup, ginger, cinnamon, and cloves in the third. Plan ahead so these ingredients have at least a day to infuse. Lastly, place 2 lemon slices in the small zip-lock bag and pack everything into the Stasher Kit.

Cocktails

Hot Toddy

Heat 4 ounces water. Add honey, squeeze of lemon, and 1½ ounces whiskey. Stir to dissolve honey.

Manhattan

Add 1½ ounces whiskey to the smaller bottle (vermouth and bitters). Give a gentle shake to mix, and allow to chill slightly before enjoying (pack in snow or secure in a cold stream).

Upper Peninsula Black Maple Spice

Heat 4 to 6 ounces water and brew black tea per instructions. In a glass, combine tea, 1½ ounces whiskey, squeeze of lemon, and contents of the maple syrup bottle. Stir until dissolved.

Mint Julep

If it's winter or you are up around permanent snow, find a nice clean patch of snow and pack a snowball to fit in your glass. Add 1½ ounces whiskey to the small bottle containing the simple syrup, and shake to mix ingredients. Pour over the top of the snowball and enjoy. *Tip:* A straw comes in handy here.

Whiskey Neat

Enjoy the remaining 2 ounces of whiskey straight out of the bottle or in a glass with a dash of water.

Pumpkin Spice Toddy

This tempest of flavor is nothing less than fall in a flask. Enjoy in moderation, as alcohol will chill and dehydrate you.

    2 ounces cream
    4 tablespoons canned pumpkin pie mix (not pumpkin
        puree)
    ¼ ounce unsweetened hazelnut syrup (found in a gro-
        cery's coffee section)
    1½ ounces añejo tequila (we like Milagro Añejo)

In camp: Mix equal parts (by volume) of cream and pumpkin pie mix. Add cream, pie mix, and hazelnut syrup to a pot; bring to a light boil. Add tequila, stir, and pour into a cup. Garnish with shaved chocolate if desired.

(Serves 1)

Wintermint

Leave the Altoids at home. Minty refreshment never tasted so good.

    1 peppermint tea bag
    1½ ounces Baileys Irish Cream

In camp: Steep tea for 4 to 7 minutes; add Baileys and enjoy.

(Serves 1)

Ginger-Spiced Apple Cider

Warm up with this recipe for apple cider with a kick.

3–6 ounces unfiltered apple juice (unfiltered apple cider made from fresh apples is even better)
1 individual packet mulling spices
1 ounce Domaine de Canton ginger liqueur
1 ounce Absolut vanilla vodka
¼ ounce agave nectar

In camp: Heat apple juice with mulling spices and brew according to package directions. Once juice comes to a boil, remove from heat. Add ginger liqueur, vodka, and agave nectar; stir until agave is dissolved.

(Serves 1)

Variation: For a Halloween theme in the fall, modify this drink for little ones by leaving out the booze. Miniature Day of the Dead–type candy skulls add a fun twist if you can find them at a Mexican grocery store. They also sweeten the cider as they dissolve. If you can't find candy skulls, check out this idea for a garnish by Martha Stewart: Peel a small apple and carve a face into one side; throw it onto a skewer and lightly toast over a fire before floating in cider.

South-of-the-Border Coffee

A jolt of caffeine tempered by a shot of tequila.

2 cups brewed coffee
2 tablespoons powdered milk
1 tablespoon brown sugar
1 ounce tequila

At home: If you grind your own beans, grind them shortly before you leave home for maximum freshness. Pack the ground beans in a zip-lock bag.

In camp: Make the coffee; the rich flavor of a French-pressed cup works well with this recipe. Add the powdered milk, brown sugar, and tequila, stirring gently.

(Serves 1)

Variation: Substitute bourbon for tequila for a fine Kentucky coffee.

Warming up on a cold winter day. THINKSTOCK.COM

Nonalcoholic Hot Drinks

Tangy Hot Apple Cider

Sometimes hot chocolate just doesn't hit the spot.

¼ cup raisins

3 whole cloves

3 cups water

4 packets instant apple cider mix

3 tablespoons Tang

2 cinnamon sticks

At home: Combine the cider mix and Tang in a zip lock bag.

In camp: In a pot, combine raisins, cloves, and water; heat slowly over a low flame until the water is aromatic and amber-colored (about 10 minutes). Remove from heat and stir in the cider mix and Tang. Pour into two large mugs, add a cinnamon stick, and nibble on the raisins (skip the cloves—they're not very tasty). Or pour the cider through a strainer to remove the chewy bits. This recipe contains lots of vitamin C, which makes this drink a perfect on-the-trail substitute for morning OJ.

(Serves 2)

Fruit and Spice Tea

A spicy, refreshing, and warming after-dinner drink.

4 cups water

4½ tablespoons Tang

1 tablespoon instant tea powder

1 tablespoon instant lemonade (presweetened)

About 2 teaspoons cherry Jell-O powder (or experiment with flavors to find your favorite)

¼ teaspoon ground cinnamon

⅛ teaspoon ground cloves

Sugar to taste (optional)

At home: Mix all the dry ingredients in a zip-lock bag.

In camp: Boil water. Combine 2 tablespoons (2½ if you prefer stronger tea) of dry mixture and 2 cups hot water. Add a spoonful of sugar if you like. Sip this tea in the morning for a hit of nutrients: Tang is a good source of vitamin A and riboflavin and an excellent source of vitamin C.

(Serves 2)

CHAPTER 8

HAZARDS AND WEATHER

Waiting for the next strike, the three hikers crouched on a steep incline just below the wide open tablelands of the Alpine Gardens on Mount Washington in the White Mountains of New Hampshire. Rain and hail lashed against their faces and the wind cut through their T-shirts, causing them to shake with cold. The lightning storm had them pinned down with no shelter. The group had an overwhelming urge to run across the exposed terrain above to the descent trail. Instead they stayed in the gully below, spread a few dozen feet apart, squatted on their packs and waited. It was the best decision they had made all day. Another flash of light lit up the darkened mountainside, followed in a few seconds by a loud boom of thunder. The storm was moving away and the threat of being struck by lightning was diminishing.

These hikers had survived the lightning storm, which many people would consider the main outdoor hazard that day. In reality, hypothermia, caused by the cold, wet conditions, was probably a greater threat to their lives. However, being caught in the storm and becoming hypothermic were both caused by a series of small mistakes that, when added up, could have proved disastrous.

None of the three had visited the White Mountains before, and the group was unprepared for the hike. To start with, they had failed to check the weather forecast, which called for afternoon thunderstorms. While they knew the length of the hike in miles, they had not taken into consideration how rugged the terrain would be and how the dramatic change in elevation would slow their progress. As a result, the three started their adventure much later in the day than they should have. The intended route was on a trail, so the group did not feel the need to bring a map. Later, when the main trail diverged into several unmarked trails, the three spent considerable time arguing over the correct path to take. When they left the car at the trailhead, the August temperatures and the morning sun had them sweating in T-shirts and shorts, and they decided against bringing extra warm layers and rain gear. The steep terrain took

Educate yourself about potential hazards before you go into the backcountry.
DAVE ANDERSON

longer than anticipated, and the hikers quickly consumed all their water and food. All these factors left them cold, wet, hungry, dehydrated, and scared while crouching on the ground during an electrical storm.

Luckily, the summer storm passed quickly, and after a few jumping jacks to warm up, the group continued across the Alpine Gardens down the Lions Head Trail back to their car.

SUBJECTIVE HAZARDS

While objective hazards—such as lightning, blizzards, and swiftly moving rivers—can exist independently of anything you might do, subjective hazards can be controlled, at least in part, by the decisions you make as a backcountry traveler.

Lack of Preparation

For any type of outdoor activity there should be a planning session about what to bring and what skills you need before you head out in the wilds. Lack of such preparation is one of the primary hazards backcountry hikers and backpackers face.

Water and Food

Humans have a few basic needs: water, food, and shelter. Inexperienced backcountry travelers often underestimate the amount of water needed to maintain healthy body functions. The common recommendation of

Staying hydrated boosts energy, attitude, and acclimatization.
DAVE ANDERSON

consuming at least eight glasses of water per day might be appropriate if you are working in an environmentally controlled office, but it's woefully inadequate if you are hiking through Death Valley in July. During periods of intense exertion in hot conditions, your body can process 1 to 1.5 liters of water per hour. Signs such as thirst, decreased and darkened urine, a headache, and general fatigue are indicators that you are not ingesting enough liquids. However, you also need to ingest food to maintain adequate electrolyte balance within the cells of your body and proper glucose (sugar) levels in your blood. Carbohydrate-rich, fluid replacement drinks and gels are quickly absorbed by the body and contain important electrolytes such as calcium, potassium, and sodium. Carrying a backpack up a steep trail will burn a lot of calories. Consuming 135–270 calories of carbohydrates per hour will help maintain an adequate level of glucose in the blood. Complex carbohydrates (sugars) found in energy bars and dried fruit will provide continuous energy without the sugar crash caused by candy bars. Adding fats and protein-rich foods that digest slowly (like cheese) to evening meals will help you sleep warm throughout the night and revitalize your muscles.

Shelter, Clothing, and Footwear
Prior research into the type of terrain you will encounter, possible weather conditions, and estimated length of your adventure will determine what type of clothing, equipment, and shelter you bring. Before venturing into

Improperly fitted boots can produce painful blisters.
DAVE ANDERSON

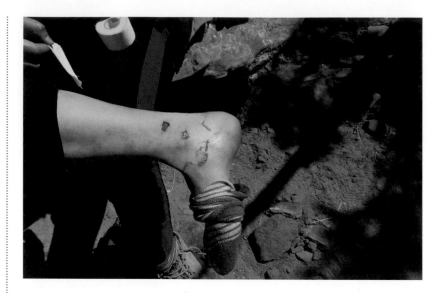

the backcountry on an extended trip, it is always a good idea to test out your gear beforehand to make sure things like the tent zippers are working and hiking boots are broken in. Clothing systems should include items that can be comfortably layered on top of each other, allowing hikers to easily adapt to changing weather conditions. Shelter systems (tents) should be strong enough to withstand the worst possible conditions you might face. The challenge in deciding what to bring boils down to the need to have enough gear to be safe and relatively comfortable. However, bringing too much increases your pack weight, which could lead to athletic injuries, blisters, and a generally unhappy experience.

Getting In over Your Head

One of the most common hazards people encounter in the backcountry is exceeding their own technical skills or abilities. Most people would agree that learning to drive a car in Manhattan in the middle of rush hour would be a bad idea. Likewise, learning how to place climbing protection when you're halfway up El Capitan in Yosemite seems equally foolish. The difference between the two examples is you can always park the car and take a taxi in New York; on El Capitan your life depends on your skill. Whether you are hiking through a boulder field, crossing a river, or kicking steps up a steep snow slope, all of these activities require competent movement skills and the knowledge of the risks associated with each type of terrain.

Outdoor travelers generally fall into one of five categories: novice, beginner, proficient, expert, or master. Novices are often unaware of what they don't know, while beginners at least realize what skills they are lacking. Proficiency is the next tier of outdoor skills, where the person has the skills and awareness but needs always to be making a conscious effort to focus on safety. The expert's skills are so well developed that they come automatically without much conscious thought. Finally, the master maintains his automatic competence by reflecting back on his skills to make improvements. Knowing which category you fall into is a primary component of not getting in over your head on a backcountry trip. The best way to avoid this hazard is to research what challenges you will face during your adventure, bring the appropriate equipment, know how to use it, and make sure your backcountry skills are sufficient for the journey.

Learn How to Use Equipment Properly

There is a plethora of outdoor gear available that can make your backcountry experiences safer and more enjoyable. You need to avoid taking too much equipment, and you need to know how to use the equipment you do bring. Some people see an ice ax as a glorified walking stick for traveling on snow and ice. In well-trained hands, however, an ice ax can be used to chop steps, ascend vertical ice, and quickly self-arrest falls on steep snow. In the hands of a novice it is often dropped or, worse, accidentally impales its owner during a poorly attempted self-arrest maneuver. No matter how much money you spend on the latest state-of-the art piece of gear, it does not buy automatic competence. It's up to you to seek proper instruction.

Proper ice ax technique reduces risk and effort.
DAVE ANDERSON

Learn Proper Navigation Skills

Each year, search and rescue organizations across the country are called to look for lost hikers. The main reason people get lost is that they fail to bring or do not know how to use navigation tools such as a map or GPS receiver. While new technology such as GPS is a great tool to aid your navigation, being able to interpret topographical features on a map is a basic skill all wilderness users should have. Trails get rerouted, new buildings appear, others burn down, a new dam might change a river flow, but the

Basic navigation skills are
a must in the backcountry.
DAVE ANDERSON

contours of the land do not change. Looking at the three-dimensional
terrain of a landscape in front of you and then trying to extrapolate that
information to a two-dimensional map takes practice. However, once you
hone your map-reading skills, they can be used anywhere in the world.
And unlike a GPS, map-reading skills won't break or run out of batteries.

Poor Physical Conditioning

Backcountry adventures can require a repertoire of technical outdoor
skills. However, the core skill that many novice hikers often underestimate is how physically challenging carrying a backpack can be, especially
a pack loaded with gear for several nights in the backcountry. Throw in a
surprise snowstorm while crossing a large boulder field and even a sea-
soned backpacking veteran will have her hands full. A loss in balance, as
the result of poor general fitness, can quickly turn into a sprained ankle
or worse in rugged trail conditions.

While running and lifting weights will increase your aerobic capacity and muscle strength, there is no better training for carrying a heavy
pack than actually carrying a heavy pack. Some people try to simulate
the rigors of backpacking by filling a pack with some weight and regularly climbing up sets of stairs or walking around the block several times
a week. Although such routines will help get you used to carrying a pack,
the main thing they lack is duration. A typical backpacking day usually
consists of carrying a pack for at least 6 to 8 hours, and the wear and

Running is a good way to get yourself in better shape for your next outdoor adventure. DAVE ANDERSON

The best way to train for a backpacking trip is to go on a short backpacking trip! DAVE ANDERSON

tear on muscles and joints is cumulative over time. Before venturing out on a two-week section of the Appalachian Trail, a long weekend excursion with a fully loaded pack is a great shakedown trip. You can see what muscles and joints are the most impacted and then train specifically to strengthen that area of your body.

Preexisting Medical Conditions

Preexisting medical conditions should be carefully evaluated before attempting any outdoor adventure. Obviously, people with heart conditions, diabetes, or other serious health concerns should seek advice from their physicians. Also, people's backs, knees, ankles, and other joints can be weakened by age, previous injuries, or genetics, and these impairments need to be taken into account during the planning stages of a backcountry trip. Fortunately, there are several resources available to ease the wear and tear on the body. Today there is a tremendous amount of high-quality, extremely lightweight gear available for consumers that can drastically reduce pack weight. Trekking poles are great for incorporating the arms when ascending steep trail, helping cushion the knees and ankles during steep descents, and maintaining balance in rough terrain. For longer excursions into the wilds, horses, llamas, goats, and even human porters can be hired to carry camping gear, leaving you with just a daypack on your back.

Phobias and Fears

For every kind of outdoor activity or environment, there is a named phobia associated with it, from hydrophobia, the fear of water, to xerophobia, the fear of dry places. Fear of potentially dangerous activities or environmental conditions is a normal, healthy, human reaction. However, the definition of a phobia is an irrational fear that affects a person's daily actions. Knowing what aspects of the outdoor environment make you uncomfortable will help you choose appropriate objectives and is key to having a pleasant experience. You do not want to hike up the exposed Angels Landing trail in Zion National Park only to discover you have acrophobia (fear of heights) and be frozen in place with fear halfway up the trail.

While some people enjoy traveling in the backcountry to escape the stresses of the modern world, outdoor adventures often have their own challenges. Trying to wrap up personal issues and work deadlines before

When planning an adventure, make sure you are comfortable with the terrain you will encounter.
DAVE ANDERSON

you head into the wilderness will allow you to be more present on your outdoor trip. Having a clear mind will allow you to enjoy the environment around you and the people in your group, and to focus on safely traveling in the backcountry.

Problems in Communication and Decision Making

During a weekend backpacking trip with one close friend, communicating and making decisions occur naturally, as you already have a relationship established and know each other's strengths and weakness. As the size of a group increases, not only do the logistics increase but so do the complexities of communicating and making decisions. Having a designated "leader" can aid in a number of ways during a backcountry trip, such as securing the necessary permits, organizing what to bring, and planning the daily activities. The leader's role will be dependent on his skills and those of the rest of the group. If the leader is much more experienced than the rest of the group, a directive leadership style could be the most effective, whereas in a group of similarly skilled participants, a consensus style might be best for decision making. Establishing open communication within a group of backcountry travelers is important so that everyone feels like his or her thoughts and concerns have a chance to be heard. A group of outdoor enthusiasts usually has considerable knowledge and experiences that can make a trip in the wilderness a safe

The larger the group, the more you have to work together to accomplish your goals. DAVE ANDERSON

and fun experience. The challenge is utilizing all of the group's attributes so everyone feels appreciated and invested in the experience.

WEATHER

Exposure is one of the leading causes of death among backcountry travelers. It has a single cause: being outside in weather for which you are unprepared. Even if conditions are not life-threatening, they can still be miserable. In town, getting a weather forecast is often easier than finding a glass of water, but the farther you get from civilization, the less likely it is that you'll be able to pick up the forecast on a radio, a cell phone, or any other electronic device. What's more, the forecast in town is likely much milder than the weather in the woods.

Weather can change quickly too. There's an old saying in the Presidential Range: "If you don't like the weather, wait a moment." Funny how that saying also crops up in the southern Appalachians, the Rockies, the Sierra Nevada, and most any other mountain range! The key is determining what threat a change in the weather might pose so you can respond appropriately. Every mountain range is susceptible to lightning strikes, which are particularly dangerous if you are above tree line. Or a snowstorm might pass through the area even in the middle of summer.

Then there's desert backcountry, where it's hot, hotter, and hottest during the day, contrasted with cold at night. But how hot or cold? The

difference between hiking on an 85°F day and a 105°F day can mean the difference between serious perspiration and serious heatstroke.

Weather forecasting in the backcountry provides more than comfort and campfire talk—it can be a matter of life and death. This section will help you understand how weather works and how to guard against it; more important, it will give you key weather-predicting skills to help make your trips into the backcountry more enjoyable and safer.

Precipitation

The term *precipitation* is used to describe rain, snow, sleet, hail, and grau-pel. Each of these forms of precipitation has its own associated hazards. A blizzard can cause limited visibility, which can make navigation chal-lenging; becoming soaked by a cold rainstorm can lead to hypothermia;

Mount Washington in New Hampshire looks benign on a clear day but is home to some of the wildest weather in the world. LISA DENSMORE

TECHNIQUES FOR COPING WITH PRECIPITATION IN THE BACKCOUNTRY

- **Keep your gear dry.** Some experienced hikers swear by lining the inside of their backpack with a heavy duty trash compactor bag to waterproof their pack and stuffing everything inside. Other people have good luck using a commercially made pack cover. Still other backcountry users line their sleeping bag stuff sack and other stuff sacks they want to keep dry with plastic bags and let other items like cookware, food, and the shelter get wet. Whatever technique you decide to use, your sleeping bag and extra clothes should be dry when you arrive at camp.

- **Choose the right clothing system.** There are two main schools of thought for dealing with hiking in cold, wet conditions on overnight trips. The first is not to worry about getting wet and to rely on heat generated by the act of hiking to keep you warm. Then when you arrive in camp, you quickly change into dry clothes and full rain gear. This technique works as long as the temperature is not too cold. The second technique involves wearing appropriate layers to try to stay dry during the hike. The challenge with this technique is not overheating and soaking your clothes in sweat. Modern outerwear has a wide continuum of waterproof/breathable levels, and it is now possible to find clothing that matches almost any condition. Finally, bring adequate gloves and mittens to keep your hands warm and dry. Wet, cold, nonfunctioning fingers will limit your ability to change layers, set up a shelter, light your stove, and perform other essential cold-weather travel skills.

- **Dry out your wet clothing.** Regardless of the hiking clothing system you choose, chances are you will end up with some wet clothes during extended rainy periods. Some hikers just pile up their wet clothes in the vestibule of the tent and change back into them before starting to hike the next morning. Another technique is to dry out some of your wet clothing while you sleep. Your body continually pumps out heat, and by placing damp clothing inside your sleeping bag you can dry it out during the course of the night. A synthetic sleeping bag is essential for this technique. Trying to dry too many wet clothes will leave both you and your clothes soggy and cold in the morning, so some experimentation is required to figure out your own human clothes drier capacity.

- **Compare down versus synthetic insulating gear.** The benefit of down is that it is extremely lightweight and compresses well for packing when compared to synthetic insulation. However, when untreated down gets wet it clumps up, losing almost all of its insulation value, while synthetics retain their insulating capacity even when wet. Your decision on what type of sleeping bag or puffy jacket you will use should be based on the weather conditions, where you are going, and how careful you are about keeping things dry.

- **Compare tents versus snow shelters when winter camping.** Some backcountry travelers use snow shelters instead of tents when winter camping. Snow shelters can be very warm compared to the outside temperatures, but they require considerable work to build, which can cause clothing to get soaked from snow and sweat. If you plan to build a snow shelter, practice in a benign environment (like the backyard) before trusting your life to one in the backcountry.

High-quality rain gear, including rain hats and pack covers, will help hikers deal with rainy conditions. A good attitude doesn't hurt either. DAVE ANDERSON

and heavy hail can damage your tent. Choosing the right equipment and appropriate hiking and camping techniques is essential for improving your comfort and safety in wet conditions.

For backcountry users, the two most important types of precipitation are rain and snow. The impact of a rainstorm or snow event on a wilderness experience varies depending on the temperature. For example, a three-day hike on the island of Kauai in steady rain with the temperature never dipping below 90°F is much different than three days of rain in Denali National Park in 40°F conditions, which is also different than a long weekend spent winter camping in 5°F temperatures during a snowstorm in Rocky Mountain National Park. In Kauai, even if all your gear gets soaked, there is no danger of any cold-related injury. However, during a cold rainstorm in Denali, there is a real threat of both hypothermia and trench foot, and in the Rocky Mountains during winter, you have the added threat of frostbite.

Obviously, the gear needed for each trip will be drastically different; so will hiking and packing techniques. Prior research into what average temperatures and precipitation you can expect will go a long way toward helping you plan for your outdoor adventure.

Wind

Hurricanes, tornadoes, and dust storms are major meteorological events that have associated high winds. Hurricanes are formed by warm air rising off the surface of the ocean and the action of other wind events such as thunderstorms. As the warm air rises into the atmosphere, it creates a vacuum, which in turn sucks more air and energy into the tropical storm, creating high winds. When the wind speeds reach over 74 miles per hour, the storm is classified as a hurricane. Tornadoes are often part of hurricanes, but they can also form independently on land as well as over the ocean. Dust storms occur when high winds pass over arid land and pick up small sand particles, carrying them suspended in the atmosphere.

Lenticular clouds are striking but indicate high winds and incoming weather. DAVE ANDERSON

The highest documented surface wind speed, 231 miles per hour, was recorded at the weather station on the summit of Mount Washington in 1934. However, even mild wind events can affect hikers in several ways. First, hiking in windy conditions takes more energy, and strong wind gusts can cause you to lose your balance; add a large pack that can catch the wind like a sail, and the difficulty of walking is increased dramatically. Second, in cold climates wind speed can cause a variety of cold injuries. If the wind is blowing at 15 miles per hour and the outside temperature is 0°F, the windchill factor makes it feel like it is 20°F. Exposed skin can freeze within 30 minutes under these conditions. Third, visibility is often decreased due to blowing snow or sand, making navigation challenging and increasing the likelihood of getting lost.

In exposed campsites, use extra guylines and rocks to secure your tent.
DAVE ANDERSON

Steps for Dealing with Windy Conditions

- **Do your research.** Check weather data to see the likelihood of wind events as well as the current conditions in the backcountry area you will be visiting.

- **Plan your travel day accordingly.** In many locations, wind speed tends to increase during the day, so plan on doing the bulk of your hiking when wind speeds are the lowest.
- **Cover up.** Wear windproof clothing to reduce heat loss and prevent frostbite. In blizzard conditions, goggles, hoods, scarfs, and neck gaiters will prevent snow from getting in your eyes, ears, nose, and mouth. Finally, in sandy conditions, wear prescription glasses instead of contacts to reduce eye irritation.
- **Choose your campsite wisely.** Avoid camping in exposed windy locations. Look for shelter created by trees, boulders, and other natural wind blocks, but watch out for dead branches or trees that could blow down on your tent. Orient your tent with the door facing toward the prevailing wind direction. Learn how to secure your tent to the ground using cord, tent stakes, rocks, and other anchors. If you are camping in snow, build wind walls to protect your tent or excavate a snow shelter.

Snow-block walls make great wind walls to shelter your tent from high winds.
DAVE ANDERSON

- **Keep your equipment organized.** At camp make sure to secure all of your gear either inside your tent or in your pack so that it does not blow away or get buried by snow and become lost while you sleep.

Follow these special precautions for dealing with hurricanes, tornadoes, and dust storms: Move away from dangers such as dead limbs or dead trees in a forest. Take shelter in caves, rock overhangs, in between large boulders. If you are caught in the open, look for a low point such as a trench or ditch and lie as flat as possible in these features. Goggles and bandannas will prevent sand and other debris from getting in your eyes, ears, nose, and mouth. Be aware of other hazards associated with wind events. Hurricanes can also produce torrential rains, ocean storm surges, and flash flooding, so be aware of these dangers and how they relate to your location.

Lightning

Lightning is a powerful natural phenomenon that has evoked curiosity and fear for thousands of years. Lightning is a gigantic discharge of electrostatic energy. This is the same kind of electricity that can shock you

Lightning often strikes the high locations that backpackers and climbers frequent. DAVE ANDERSON

when you touch a doorknob after walking across a carpet. Lightning can occur between clouds and the ground, between clouds, or within a cloud.

Scientists still do not fully understand how lightning forms, but they do know the conditions needed for lightning to occur. Wind, humidity, change in atmospheric pressure, and the friction between ice particles within a cloud combine to produce a separation of positive and negative charges creating lightning. Lightning can travel at speeds over 140,000 miles per hour and reach temperatures of over 50,000°F. The associated thunder we hear is the result of rapidly expanding gases caused by the lightning bolt. Despite the incredible forces generated by lightning and its frequent occurrence, fewer than seventy-five people are killed by lightning each year in the United States.

Tips for Avoiding Lightning Strikes

- **Plan activities to avoid being in high-risk areas.** If you are climbing a peak or crossing a high pass or plateau, time your travel so that you are not in a high, exposed area during prime lightning time (typically noon or later).
- **Use the sound of thunder to help predict lightning strikes.** You can hear thunder up to 10 miles away and should modify your travel plans as soon as you hear it. To further estimate how close lightning is to your location, count the seconds from when you see a lightning strike to the time you hear the associated thunder and divide by 5. This gives you a rough estimation of how many miles away the storm is.
- **Avoid dangerous locations.** While seeking shelter inside a building or a vehicle provides shelter from lightning strikes in the frontcountry, in the backcountry we are more vulnerable and try to avoid being in high and exposed places. Avoid mountaintops, exposed ridges, and wide-open flat ground. In addition, stay clear of individual long or tall objects such as lone trees or fence rows that can attract lightning. Also, do not stand in the mouth of a cave or rock overhang where your body can act like a spark plug, bridging the gap and allowing electrical current to travel in the most direct path—through you.
- **Get into a safe lightning position.** Sometimes it is impossible to move to a safe location and you must wait out a storm. To avoid the effects of ground current and direct lightning strikes, crouch

on a sleeping pad with your feet together and simply wait out the storm. Get away from long objects such as tent poles and ice axes that attract lightning.

Extreme Temperatures

As humans, our normal core body temperature averages 98.6°F. A temperature of even a few degrees above or below that normal level causes extreme stress on our bodies. As a result, we have many physiological reactions to deal with changes in the temperature. Traveling in the backcountry often places us in challenging climatic conditions and increases the risk of injuries related to cold (hypothermia) and heat (hyperthermia).

Hot Environments

Three factors affect hikers in hot environments: temperature, humidity, and direct solar radiation. In response, your body uses several mechanisms to stay comfortable in hot conditions. When your muscles contract while you are hiking, they generate heat. To get rid of excess heat, blood flow to the vessels in the skin increases, causing a red or flushed look when exercising hard. As the outside temperature increases, getting closer to our body's core temperature of 98°F, this method of getting rid of extra heat is less effective. Another physiological response is sweating. In dry environments our sweat evaporates, cooling the surface of the skin. In climates with high humidity, sweat does not evaporate, leaving you feeling hot and damp. This factor helps explain why you feel hotter and more

Two young women overlooking rural landscape.
THINKSTOCK.COM

DESERT ENVIRONMENTS

The fantastic geological features, as well as the unique plant and animal species, found in many deserts make them appealing destinations for hikers. Deserts are defined as areas of land that receive less than 10 inches of precipitation a year. In the United States there are over 350,000 square miles of desert habitat. The low rainfall and high temperatures of this harsh climate require visitors to plan ahead and use caution when traveling in the desert backcountry.

The desert can be a dangerous place for the unprepared. DAVE ANDERSON

uncomfortable hiking in the Florida Everglades than in the Grand Canyon, even if the ambient air temperature is the same in both locations.

Along with losing water through sweat, we also lose water through breathing and urinating, so staying hydrated is very important in hot environments. The body can process up to 1 quart of water per hour during intense exercise or hot conditions, so drink up during your backcountry adventures.

In addition, the ambient air temperature of any environment can be further increased by the sun's solar radiation. Reducing your level of exertion, the amount of time you spend in the direct sunlight, and covering exposed skin when you travel will make you feel cooler.

Steps to Avoid Heat Injuries

- **Choose an appropriate time of year.** Visit the desert during cooler seasons, when temperatures are lower and water sources may be more available. During hot seasons plan to do most of your travel in the early morning, when the temperatures are lowest.

- **Cover up.** The ambient air temperature of any environment can be further increased by the sun's solar radiation. Wearing loose-fitting, lightweight, breathable clothing, a wide brimmed hat, and even gloves to cover exposed skin will actually make you feel cooler and reduce the risk of sunburn. Also, less water evaporates from covered skin than from exposed skin, reducing dehydration. Apply waterproof sunblock to exposed skin.

- **Protect your eyes.** Sunglasses will reduce the chance of your corneas getting burned by the sun's ultraviolet rays and developing "snow blindness."

- **Create your own shade.** Hike with a lightweight umbrella.

- **Stay hydrated.** Carry enough water with you to safely navigate between known water sources. Do not rely on unknown springs or tanks listed on a map, as they may only contain water during wet periods of the year. Using a hydration system such as a water bladder and attached drinking tube allows for constant intake of fluids while on the move.

- **Remember to eat.** Ingest enough calories to have energy for the day's activities and to maintain adequate electrolyte balance within your body. Hyponatremia is a condition in which there is not enough salt (sodium) in the body; this can quickly affect muscle, nerve, and even brain function, causing cramps, nausea, and a reduced level of consciousness. Eating a small amount of salty snacks will keep your electrolytes at proper levels.

- **Take care of your feet.** Hikers' feet often swell in hot temperatures, and choosing well-fitting footwear that is both breathable and protective is important. In addition, low-cut gaiters can prevent sand and small pebbles from getting into your shoes and causing hot spots or blisters.

- **Watch out for other desert dwellers.** The harsh climatic conditions and relatively open terrain of the desert have caused the plants and animals that live there to develop unique defenses to survive. Many desert plants have thorns and spines, and a number of arachnids (spiders and scorpions) and reptiles are venomous.

Cold Environments

When most novice backcountry users think about dealing with the cold, they often think about weather conditions typically encountered during the winter season. However, experienced hikers realize cold, "winter-like" conditions can be encountered during any season. Wilderness travel in mountainous regions can have an extreme range of temperatures dependent on the elevation. For every 1,000 feet gained in elevation, the temperature decreases by 3.5°F. The elevation gain of the popular Keyhole Trail to the top of Longs Peak in Colorado is close to 5,000 feet, and that 60°F temperature encountered in the parking lot will plummet to the low 40s by the time you reach the summit—and that does not take into account the potential windchill effect.

People have a wide range of metabolisms and varying tolerances for cold conditions, but understanding how we lose heat to the environment is crucial in terms of outfitting ourselves in cold backcountry conditions. As we mentioned in the previous section, we generate heat by moving our muscles and other basic metabolic processes. This means that while hiking, especially carrying a heavy backpack, it is relatively easy to stay warm as long as you have been ingesting sufficient food and water.

Dealing with cold challenges every group. DAVE ANDERSON

Cold hazards often manifest themselves when you run out of energy or after you have stopped for the day. Two heat transfer mechanisms, conduction and convection, can quickly channel away body heat. We lose heat by conduction from direct contact with a cold surface through the soles of our boots while standing on a cold surface or in snow or when sitting or sleeping on the ground. Convection is the loss of heat when the warm air next to your skin is displaced by cold air, often by wind, in the outdoor environment.

Steps to Avoid Cold Injuries

- **Layer up.** Having several lightweight layers that can be worn together will allow you to fine-tune your clothing system to match the outside temperature conditions. The old saying "If you are cold put on a hat" makes sense; but in reality, any exposed skin will lose heat at the same rate, so cover up.
- **Don't sweat it.** Try and anticipate how your metabolism will respond to a specific outdoor activity and wear just enough clothing to keep yourself warm without sweating. In the desert environment, sweating was our friend, but in cold conditions evaporative cooling can quickly lower your core temperature. In addition, having sweat-soaked clothes against your skin will conduct additional heat away from your body. Choose fast-drying synthetic or wool blends instead of cotton base layers.

- **Sleep warm.** A 40-below-zero bag will do little to keep you warm during a frigid night unless you have an adequate sleeping pad to insulate you from the cold ground. Bringing an extra pair of dry socks that are worn only when you are sleeping will keep your toes toasty at night. For those people who sleep cold, putting a hot water bottle and having a snack in your sleeping bag are two ways to stay warm through the night.
- **Remember that calories equal warmth.** The caloric demands during a winter camping trip are huge—it is not the time to start a diet! During the day choose foods high in complex carbohydrates that digest at a medium rate, keeping your energy at a constant, well-fueled level. For the evening meal, add fats or proteins that digest slower and will help keep you warm throughout the night.
- **Avoid dehydration.** Unlike hot environments, where you will often be thirsty, the urge to drink liquids can be reduced in a cold environment. Bringing a lightweight thermos to carry hot drinks during the day can increase your fluid intake.

Predicting Weather

Weather surrounds you. It is simply the condition of the air and how it's flowing. But it's always changing. Sometimes that change is very, very slow; sometimes it comes with blinding speed and drenching, staggering force. Various aspects of our world—some local to where you might be backpacking, such as a massive peak, and others distant, such as an ocean—affect the weather and the rate at which weather changes. Basic forces of nature, such as gravity and sunlight, also affect air movement, both cyclically and in relation to a specific weather event.

The evaporation-precipitation cycle

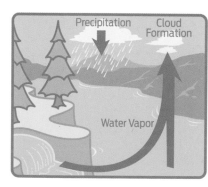

The atmosphere moves constantly and in more than one direction. Air near the ground warms up during the day, pulling moisture in the form of water vapor into the atmosphere as it rises. As moisture gains elevation, it cools, condensing around dust particles and forming clouds. When it cools to its dew point, it falls back to the earth as precipitation.

How simple weather forecasting would be if it were just based on hot air rising, but in addition to moving up and down, air also moves across the land as wind. In the backcountry, we are acutely aware of wind. We feel it as a refreshing breeze, a gusty gust, or a numbing chill. And then there are those nasty

overbearing winds that cause your tent to shake and rattle, keeping you up all night.

As if things aren't complicated enough with air moving both vertically and horizontally at the same time, the temperature of the air, the speed of the air, and the atmospheric pressure also contribute to the weather around you and, more important, to what's coming. Weather forecasting is complex. The National Oceanic and Atmospheric Administration (NOAA) recently completed the installation of a $180 million computer system, which can make 69.7 trillion calculations per second, to more accurately predict weather. Even with this state-of-the-art computer, weather forecasting, at least long-range forecasting, remains inexact. You can accurately predict the weather over the next 24 to 48 hours, and you don't need a computer to do it. You only need to observe and interpret the air around you.

When the weather feels calm, air molecules still move but slowly and in unison, therefore making the weather more predictable. On the other hand, when a mass of cold air collides with a mass of warm air and the amount of moisture in each air mass is different (which is usually the case), the air molecules move in different directions and speeds depending on how high they are above the ground. The faster the air mass travels, the more violent the collision and thus the weather. The slower the air mass, the more gradual the change, and if that change is toward bad weather, the longer the unpleasant conditions will linger.

Backpackers approaching Mount Wood in Montana's Absaroka-Beartooth Wilderness on a clear day.
LISA DENSMORE

Four Ingredients of Weather

The recipe for weather contains only four ingredients:

1. Air temperature
2. Wind speed
3. Humidity
4. Barometric pressure

When you mix these ingredients together, not only do you get the atmospheric conditions at a particular moment but you can also predict what's coming in the next 24 to 48 hours with a high degree of accuracy.

Air Temperature. Air temperature affects you in the backcountry in two ways. First, the temperature of the air around you near the ground determines how many layers you need to wear in order to stay comfortable. Second, the temperature of the air high above you determines whether you wear or carry your rain gear. As warm air rises and cools off, it gets closer and closer to its dew point, which is the temperature at which water vapor in the air turns to water droplets. If the droplets become heavy enough, they fall back to earth as precipitation.

Low scud clouds under cirrus clouds mean the sun may shine for a moment, but the rain will return soon.
LISA DENSMORE

Wind Speed. Like air temperature, wind speed affects you in the back-country in two ways. First, the perceived temperature on exposed skin is lower than the actual air temperature due to the wind. The stronger the wind, the colder the air feels. Second, wind is a symptom of changing weather. A strong wind can mean a cold front is approaching, with the possibility of severe thunderstorms on its leading edge.

Humidity. Humidity is the amount of water vapor in the air, though "relative humidity" is more important when it comes to predicting weather because it is related to the dew point. When the air reaches its dew point, it cannot hold any more water vapor and must release it. As air rises, it cools off, getting closer and closer to its dew point. In addition, as air rises, relative humidity increases. A relative humidity of 100 percent means the air temperature equals the dew point, thus the air is saturated with water. Be prepared for a wet day outdoors if the relative humidity is high.

Barometric Pressure. Barometers measure air pressure. The air in a warm air mass is always lighter (less dense) than the air in a cold air mass; thus warm air exerts less pressure on the earth than cold air. If the barometric pressure is falling, that means a warm front is coming in. If the barometric pressure is rising, a cold front is arriving. If the barometric pressure is steady, the weather is unlikely to change until the air pressure begins to move up or down.

Reading the Sky

Want to know what the weather will be when you crawl out of your tent tomorrow? Look at the clouds today! The types of clouds in the sky, along with the speed and direction they are moving, are helpful forecasters.

There are four families of clouds: cirrus, cumulus, stratus, and lenticular, though lenticular clouds are often lumped in with stratus clouds. Within these major cloud families, there are several subfamilies based on altitude, size, and color. In addition, there are combinations of clouds. Here's how to identify what's in the sky above you and what weather to expect:

Cirrus

Cirrus clouds form high in the sky, at elevations over 20,000 feet. Sometimes called mare's tails, they look like wisps and swirls. Though cirrus clouds do not release precipitation, they typically signal an incoming warm front, which means worsening weather, though it might take 12 to

Cirrus clouds form high in the sky. LISA DENSMORE

Cumulus clouds look like piles of cotton in the sky. LISA DENSMORE

24 hours to arrive. **Note:** Cirrus clouds that result from the condensation trails from jet airplanes do not signal an incoming storm.

Cumulus

Cumulus clouds, sometimes called "heap clouds," look like piles of cotton that build upward in the sky. The bottom elevation of the cloud depends on the amount of moisture in the air. In humid climates the base can be as low as 6,500 feet. In arid climates and in the mountains, it might be as high as 20,000 feet. If the top of a cumulus cloud becomes cold enough, it reaches its dew point and precipitation falls from it. If the ground temperature is above freezing, expect rain. If the ground temperature is below freezing, expect snow. While snow sometimes falls when ground temperatures are slightly above freezing, ground temperature is a good gauge for determining what form precipitation will take. First, it's available; you can carry a thermometer. Second, it's almost always below freezing aloft, especially at the top of tall cumulus clouds, which can grow to elevations above 40,000 feet. But the snowflakes that form high in the sky usually turn to raindrops by the time they reach you on the trail if the thermometer on your pack reads above 32°F.

Stratus

Stratus means "layered," although stratus clouds have no discernable form. They can form at zero feet as fog or at 20,000-plus feet. Stratus clouds turn the sky a featureless sheet of white or gray, often blocking out the sun. It's a gloomy day under stratus clouds, though you might escape precipitation. If rain does come, it will likely fall in the form of drizzle.

Stratus clouds have no real discernable form.
LISA DENSMORE

Lenticular

Lenticular clouds are elongated clouds caused by wind as it passes over the top of a mountain. Air is forced upward as it hits the side of the mountain, then curls over the peak. A lenticular cloud forms on the leeward side of a summit at the "wave break." These clouds look stationary, but they signal very strong wind.

Lenticular clouds are elongated. They look stationary but signal a very strong wind. LISA DENSMORE

Common Combination Clouds

Cirrostratus: Cirrus clouds forming a sheet across the sky at a very high elevation.

Forecast: Approaching warm front. Precipitation in 12 to 24 hours.

Cirrostratus clouds.
THINKSTOCK.COM

Cirrostratus with halo: An intensifying sheet of very high clouds, barely discernable at first except for a halo around the sun or moon.

Forecast: Cloud ceiling is lowering. Possibility of precipitation within 48 hours.

Cirrostratus clouds with halo. LISA DENSMORE

Cirrocumulus: Very high clouds that look like a mass of puffballs or fish scales rather than wisps.

Forecast: Fair but cold weather now. Precipitation may be on its way due to an unstable air mass. In tropical regions cirrocumulus clouds may indicate an impending hurricane, thus the expression "Mackerel sky, storm is nigh."

Cirrocumulus clouds.
LISA DENSMORE

Altocumulus: Similar to cirrocumulus clouds but lower (about 8,000 feet).

Forecast: Precipitation or thunderstorm within 24 hours. If you see altocumulus clouds in the morning, keep your rain gear handy. You'll likely need it after lunch.

Altocumulus clouds.
LISA DENSMORE

Cumulonimbus: Massive cumulus clouds, often with anvil-shaped tops.

Forecast: Take cover! An intense downpour and possibly hail are imminent, probably accompanied by a violent thunderstorm, but it should be over in 20 minutes.

Cumulonimbus clouds.
LISA DENSMORE

Cumulus congestus: The precursor to cumulonimbus clouds but still forming. The top is uneven and growing higher and higher.

Forecast: Unstable air mass. A thunderstorm is coming, but you've got a little more time than with cumulonimbus clouds.

Cumulus congestus clouds.
LISA DENSMORE

Fair-weather cumulus: Puffy white clouds that form later in the day. They may form in lines across the sky, indicating the direction of the breeze. Birds may circle in the thermals under them.

Forecast: Slather on more sunscreen. The air mass is stable. Enjoy the rest of a beautiful day.

Fair-weather cumulus clouds. LISA DENSMORE

Altostratus: Medium-high clouds (8,000 feet) that turn the sky medium gray. You can see a bright spot where the sun is.

Forecast: Light precipitation may fall now. Expect rain within 48 hours if the sky gets darker.

Altostratus clouds.
LISA DENSMORE

Nimbostratus: Low, dark, thick clouds with ragged edges and undefined shapes. Also called "scud clouds."

Forecast: Tent cribbage, anyone? It's going to rain steadily all day.

Nimbostratus clouds.
LISA DENSMORE

More Clues from the Clouds

A savvy weather watcher can make fairly accurate predictions based on what the clouds are doing. Here are a few more clues to help you decide whether to wear your poncho or your sunglasses:

It's going to be wet today if . . .
- the clouds build in size and quantity;
- the speed of the clouds increases;
- the higher clouds move in a different direction than that of the lower clouds;
- low dark clouds scurry under high dark clouds.

It's going to be dry today if . . .
- the sky is blue and there's no wind;
- the sky is white with very high clouds and there's no wind;
- the sky is dotted with rows of white, puffy clouds.

Figuring Out Fronts

Colliding air masses are known as fronts. In the Northern Hemisphere, the prevailing winds move from west to east. As a result, general weather patterns move from west to east. Like one car rear-ending another, the incoming front from the west rams into the outgoing front, pushing it eastward. Also as in a car collision, the faster and more aggressive the new front is, the more violent the collision and thus the stormier the weather it causes. That's why some changes in weather are merely fender benders and others cause irreparable wreckage.

There are three types of weather fronts: cold fronts, warm fronts, and occluded fronts. Each brings bad weather; it's just a matter of how bad and what comes after the front passes through.

Warm front

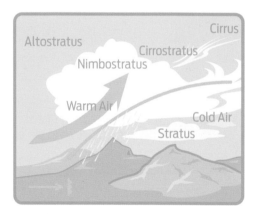

Cold front

Warm fronts

Symptoms: Low barometric pressure, high humidity, low cloud ceiling, poor visibility.

What's Really Happening: A warm air mass rises slowly above the cold air in front of it. As the warm air rises, it eventually cools to its dew point.

Resulting Weather: Relatively calm with maximum winds of 20 miles per hour at the leading edge of the front. Steady rain for several days.

Cloud Sequence: Cirrus, followed in succession by cirrostratus, altostratus, and finally nimbostratus rain clouds.

Cold Fronts

Symptoms: High barometric pressure, high cloud ceiling, good visibility unless precipitation is present.

What's Really Happening: Unstable, fast-moving cold air pushes under the warm air in front of it. The warm air mass is forced upward, which cools it. If it reaches its dew point, the resulting precipitation may be heavy and violent.

Resulting Weather: Fair weather, although it may change with little warning. Strong winds up to 35 miles per hour, generally from the north or west in the Northern Hemisphere. Severe but short-lived thunderstorms or heavy snow squalls.

Cloud Sequence: Altostratus, then nimbostratus or cumulonimbus rain clouds.

Warm Occluded Fronts

Symptoms: Change of wind direction, usually from south-southeast to north-northwest; falling, then rising barometric pressure; poor visibility during precipitation, then improving.

What's Really Happening: A cold front overtakes a warm front, lifting (occluding) the warm air mass off the earth's surface. This allows the incoming cold front to collide with the cold front that's departing ahead of the lifted warm air mass. The incoming cold front is warmer than the departing cold front, climbing over it while keeping the warm front in the middle above both cold fronts.

Resulting Weather: Thunderstorms possible. Light to heavy rain followed by dry weather after the front moves out. Cold temperatures followed by slightly milder temperatures.

Cloud Sequence: Cirrus, cumulostratus, altostratus, nimbostratus, scattered cumulus.

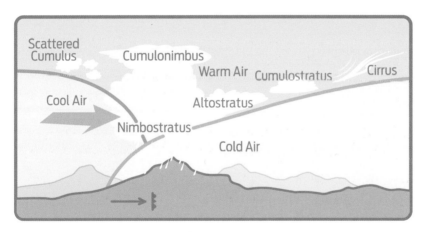

Warm occluded front

Cold Occluded Fronts

Symptoms: Change of wind direction, usually from south-southeast to north-northwest; falling, then rising barometric pressure; poor visibility during precipitation, then improving.

What's Really Happening: A cold front overtakes a warm front, lifting (occluding) the warm air mass off the earth's surface. This allows the incoming cold front to collide with the cold front that's departing ahead of the lifted warm air mass. The incoming cold front is colder than the departing cold front and wedges under it.

Resulting Weather: Thunderstorms possible; light to heavy rain, followed by drying weather. Funnel cloud in severe cases. Cold temperatures get even colder.

Cloud Sequence: Cirrus, cumulostratus, altostratus, nimbostratus, then scattered cumulus.

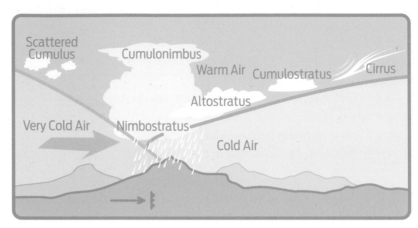

Cold occluded front

Dealing with Dew

Here are several ways to avoid having dew ruin your morning, especially if you have to break camp:

- Pick a campsite that is as high as possible. A small plateau or high rocky shelf above water will be slightly drier than a spot by water's edge. Put on the tent fly if the humidity is above 50 percent. Though it's lovely to lie in your tent and gaze at the Milky Way through the netting, you will wake up wet without the fly.
- If your pack doesn't fit inside your tent or in the tent vestibule, put a rain cover over it or cover it with a large plastic garbage bag before you go to sleep.
- Put your cooking gear inside a garbage bag, or lay a tarp over it to keep it dry overnight. In the morning use a dry garbage bag or small tarp under your cooking gear to keep it off the wet ground while you prepare breakfast. ***Note:*** Never use your cook stove on the tarp!
- If you put a tarp under your tent, make sure the tarp does not extend past the edges of the tent; otherwise dew drops will collect under your tent floor, and you might wake up in a puddle.

Use the tent fly to keep dew off you while you sleep.
LISA DENSMORE

Put cooking items on plastic to keep them dry.
LISA DENSMORE

- Allow your tent to dry before packing it up. You might have to wait an extra hour before departing, but it's a lot more pleasant to set up a dry tent at your next campsite.

Predicting Weather by Dew

Heavy dew early in the morning or late in the evening typically means fair weather for at least the next 12 hours, though all bets are off if it rained the night before—rain increases the amount of moisture at ground level.

Dealing with Frost

As with dew, keep everything covered or inside plastic, and put the fly on your tent. Here are a few more suggestions to make breaking camp more comfortable on a frosty morning:

- It's difficult to pack up a stiff, frost-covered tent, so relax with another cup of coffee and wait for the day to warm up a little before trying to break down your campsite.
- Like black ice on the road, if frozen dew formed overnight, the rocks on the trail may be slick. Let the day warm up before hiking for friendlier footing.
- Wear gloves. If there's frost, temperatures remain chilly even when they rise above freezing. A pair of waterproof gloves or quick-drying fleece gloves will keep your hands warmer while handling metal tent rods and camping pots.

Predicting Weather by Frost

As with dew, a heavy frost in the morning or late evening usually means fair weather for at least 12 hours. Frozen dew in the morning is a sign that a cold front came through during the night. The high temperature for the day may not be high at all, but the sun will shine.

Dealing with Fog

- If you are in the mountains, stay in the trees, or at least on the edge of them, to add contrast in low-visibility conditions.
- Above tree line, follow the rock cairns (stacks of rocks) to remain on the trail.
- Unless you are competent at navigating with a compass and a GPS, if the fog is so thick that you can't see the trail markers, stay put until it lifts.
- Stay ashore.
- Wear rain gear and put a rain cover over your pack to keep yourself and your gear dry.
- If you are hiking or paddling after dark, use a flashlight instead of a headlamp and hold the beam low to the ground or water for better visibility. A yellow or colored light penetrates fog more effectively than a white light.

Depositional frost on tent.
LISA DENSMORE

Predicting Weather by Fog

If the dawn is gray and there is fog in the valley, the weather will likely become nicer as the day goes on. A foggy morning that burns off by noon will usually stay clear for the remainder of the day.

STREAM CROSSINGS AND FLASH FLOODS

Many established hiking trails have bridges that allow hikers to easily cross over streams and rivers. However, bridges can get washed away in floods and many wilderness trails do not have bridges. The backcountry traveler is left to her own devices in terms of figuring out the best way to cross a stream or river. As a result, crossing moving water is a major outdoor hazard that all backcountry travelers encounter at some point. Moving water by its nature is constantly changing and no two crossings are the same, requiring you to be proficient in a number of different crossing techniques.

Safely Crossing Rivers and Streams

Stream and river crossings can be divided into two main types: wet and dry crossings. Dry crossing involves using rocks, tree trunks, logjams, and Tyroleans (see below) to get across rivers, hopefully keeping your feet dry in the process. Consider scouting a dry river crossing without packs to determine its difficulty and what the repercussions would be if you did fall into the water. Rock hopping across flat, closely spaced, featured rocks can be a fast and effective way to cross a river. However, if the rocks are covered with algae and far apart, it might be safer to simply wade rather than risk injury leaping between slippery rocks. Throwing sand on the surface of slick rocks or logs and using trekking poles to maintain balance are a couple ways to make dry crossing easier. Logjams can be very unstable, and great care should be used in determining the overall solidity of the mass of debris. A Tyrolean traverse is a section of rope or cable tensioned between two trees or boulders on opposite banks of a river, and onto which people attach themselves to cross above the water. Tyrolean traverses take time to set up, require a fair amount of technical equipment and rope skills, and require at least one person to initially cross the river to set the rope up on the opposite side. However, they are a useful crossing technique with a large group or if you have to cross the river several times.

Wet crossings involve getting in the water and wading or swimming from one bank to the other. When determining what type of crossing technique is best, outdoor travelers should look at the volume, speed, and depth of the water, as well as the type of substrate on the river bottom.

There are different opinions on the best way to safely cross moving water. Some people believe crossing one at a time using trekking poles, with the other group members stationed downstream acting as spotters, is the safest. The spotters need to be very careful not to make the mistake of getting swept into the water trying to make a rescue. If you have a rope, the spotters can use it as a throw line. Never tie the rope around the waist of either the crosser or the spotter.

Others subscribe to group-crossing methods. It is best not to attempt these crossings without some training, but you may have to.

Two basic types of wet crossings are often used with a group of people. The first is the chain method, in which people face upstream, hold hands or lock arms, and step together across the river. The second method, the "eddy" technique, is used in deep, faster-moving water, where one person positions himself facing upstream, the rest of group stands behind the lead person in either a train or pyramid formation, and everyone walks in unison across the waterway.

Once you determine the type of river crossing you will use, check out the entrance and exit points on the banks of the river. Determine what the hazards are downstream if you swim, where spotters should stand, and determine if you should cross now or wait until the water flow is less. To get ready for the crossing, remove long jackets or other clothing that

Forming a human chain can increase your stability when crossing rivers and streams.
DAVE ANDERSON

will catch the water and act like sails. In addition, unless the riverbed is soft sand, you should wear some type of footwear to reduce injuries and give you more support during the crossing.

Safety Tips for River Crossings

- Spend time to look at the potential hazards of each river crossing, and remember you always have the option of not crossing the river.
- Waterproof important items in your pack.
- Don't look down into the water; swirling current might cause you to lose your balance.
- Have spotters downstream in case things go bad.
- Loosen your pack straps and consider undoing your hip buckle in case you fall in and need to quickly jettison your pack and swim to shore.
- If you do fall into the water, do not try to stand back up in the middle of the river, as your feet can become trapped between rocks. Instead, swim or float on your back toward shore, using your legs to push away dangers in front of you.

Flash Floods

Flash floods can occur in any environment. They are caused by heavy rainfall, thunderstorms, and hurricanes, sometimes in conjunction with melting snow. In such conditions the soil and vegetation become completely saturated and the excess water pours into the surrounding drainages. The arid regions of the desert Southwest are especially susceptible

SAFELY HIKING IN TIDAL AREAS

Coastal hiking and backpacking is a popular activity along the shoreline of many areas of the United States. Some trails and regions can only be accessed during low tide. Careful planning using a tide chart for reference is required to make sure you do not get stranded when the tide comes in. Ocean tides are affected by the gravitational pull of the moon, sun, and Earth. The highest high tides occur near the spring and fall equinox, when the Earth, moon, and sun are all in alignment. When choosing a campsite for the night, you should position yourself well above the high-tide mark, which can easily be identified by sticks, detached seaweed, and other buoyant debris piled up on the far edge of the shoreline or beach.

Watch out for high tide during coastal hikes, as your trail might be underwater.
DAVE ANDERSON

While high tides caused by the orientation of the moon, sun, and Earth can be planned for, there are other ocean conditions, such as storm surges and tsunamis, that are more random. The worst natural disaster in the United States occurred in 1900, when between 6,000 and 12,000 people were killed in Galveston, Texas, by a storm surge during a hurricane. A storm surge is caused when the high winds of a hurricane push down on the ocean's surface, displacing water. This event, in combination with the low pressure created by the hurricane and an abnormally high tide, creates monster waves.

Tsunamis are huge waves of water created by a buckling or other disturbance in the sea floor, often the result of an earthquake. This buckling displaces large volumes of water and forms giant waves that travel for thousands of miles across the ocean, retaining enough lethal energy to destroy buildings, trees, wildlife, and people. Since the waves travel such far distances before striking land, they are difficult to anticipate because the area devastated by the tsunami might not even feel the initial earthquake. However, if you see the ocean receding at an unusually fast rate, it is a good indication that a big wave is on its way and you should immediately seek high ground.

Tight desert canyons like this can fill quickly with water during flash floods.
DAVE ANDERSON

to flash flooding in the summer season. Powerful thunderstorms can produce several inches of rain in a short period of time. The desert soil cannot absorb much of the rainfall, and the vast majority of the water runs immediately into creeks and other tributaries, tearing through canyons and ripping up vegetation and other debris at the bottom of the watershed.

Flash floods are a serious danger for desert canyon hikers because there is often little warning before the flood. The thunderstorms that produce the flooding can be many miles away, and hikers might not even see clouds or feel rain before the water levels begin to rise.

Steps to Avoid Getting Caught in a Flash Flood

- When planning a canyon trip, study topographic maps of the region and identify sections of your route that are subject to flash floods. At the same time, identify potential escape routes.
- Monitor the weather before you begin your backcountry adventure. Check the long-range forecast for the area you will be traveling through, as well as areas upstream of your location in the same watershed.
- Never camp in a wash at the bottom of a canyon, even though the often level open ground makes a comfortable, low-impact campsite.

- If you have to camp in a narrow canyon, look for the highest signs of flooding and camp well above that line.
- If you are caught in a canyon during a flash flood, do not try to outrun a wall of water. Instead, climb up above the water and wait for the storm to abate.

STEEP AND CHALLENGING TERRAIN

Hikers face challenges not only due to the angle of a route but also due to the "trail" medium. Even established hiking trails can present obstacles such as loose gravel, rocks, boulders, roots, and downed trees to navigate through. Leaves, rain, snow, and ice produced by changing seasons and inclement weather can further complicate your foot travel. Off-trail hiking can add bushwhacking, boulder fields, rock slabs, snow slopes, and even glaciers into the mix.

Scree, Talus, Boulders, and Small Cliffs

The terms *scree*, *talus*, and *boulders* all refer to rocks and are sometimes used interchangeably, but they can be differentiated by their size and how they are formed. Scree and talus slopes are formed when chunks of rock cleave off a cliff due to some types of physical weathering processes—often freeze-thaw—and fall onto a slope below a cliff. The small rocks, roughly smaller than a football, are often called scree and the larger rocks are called talus. Scree and talus pile up at the steepest possible angle until gravity or an additional accumulation of eroding rocks pushes the scree farther down the slope. As a result, scree fields are often very unstable and challenging to walk through. Established trails through this type of terrain tend to be traverses or low-angle diagonals up a slope. Attempting to hike straight up a scree slope is often an exercise in futility, as you will find yourself sliding one step back for nearly every step upward. On certain scree slopes that are composed of small golf ball-to-baseball-size rocks, hikers can "scree ski" by doing a controlled

Scree slopes are often loose and unstable. DAVE ANDERSON

Navigating through boulder fields can be time-consuming, but rushing can make them even more hazardous. DAVE ANDERSON

slide on their feet down the slope. Before you start "skiing," make sure no one is below you to get hit by tumbling rocks and that you do not go too fast and lose control—a fall into a rock slope is much more painful than on a snow slope.

Tips for Avoiding Rockfall

Whenever you travel through steep terrain, observe the base of a cliff or slope and look for recent signs of rockfall. If there are other people above you, consider choosing a different route or waiting in a safe zone until they have moved through the terrain. When traveling as a group through loose scree or talus, stick close together so that if a rock is dislodged, it will not have time to generate a lot of force as it rolls toward someone else in your party.

Tips for Safe Navigation of Rocky Terrain

- Travel through tough terrain at the beginning of the day when you are fresh, and take frequent rest breaks.
- Choose a route based on the ability of the weakest member of your group.
- If the terrain looks challenging, consider scouting it without packs to make sure your route will work.
- Stay mentally focused and save the sightseeing for the rest breaks. One misstep can result in a sprained ankle, broken leg, or worse.
- Trekking poles can reduce trauma to your joints and aid in balance, especially on descents, but they can also get in the way when you need to use both hands.
- Choose footwear that gives you support but is flexible enough to allow you to "feel" the rocks and boulders.
- When climbing up or down large boulders or short vertical steps, consider passing the packs through the difficult section and/or "spotting" people as they climb so you are in a ready position to stop a fall and prevent injury.
- Rain can make boulders—and especially lichen growing on the boulders—very slippery. Careful foot placement helps.
- If you do dislodge a rock, yell "ROCK!" so that other hikers know of the hazard potentially coming at them.

The "butt scooch" is a good technique for getting down large boulders.
DAVE ANDERSON

Steep Snow and Ice

While steep snow and ice are usually considered the domain of mountaineers, general hikers and backcountry users can find themselves in this environment and should be aware of the common hazards associated with these types of terrain. Avalanches are a serious danger on steep snow slopes and will be covered in the next section.

The biggest hazard in both steep snow and ice travel is falling on the slope. More specifically, it is the inability to stop or arrest your fall once it occurs. While there are technical rope systems you can learn to protect against a fall, they are beyond the scope of this book. Instead we will examine techniques and precautions you can use to safely move through steep snow and ice.

Snow is an incredibly variable medium. Unlike a steep gravel trail, where the conditions remain the same throughout the day and night, a snow slope can change dramatically in a 24-hour period. You might use snowshoes, crampons, or light hiking boots to climb the same steep snow slope, depending on the conditions. Knowing the appropriate ascension technique to be safe and efficient is a big part of climbing snow and ice slopes. There are certainly dangers while climbing up a slope, but most accidents occur on the way down. Most novices recognize the dire consequences of a fall on a steep cliff without a rope, but a slip on a 35-degree snow slope seems much less serious. However, snow and ice have very little friction, and a person can quickly rocket out of control. Beginner backcountry travelers should stick to terrain they will not be likely to fall on. If you do slip, you should have the skills to be able to stop (arrest) the fall before it gets out of control.

Equipment for Negotiating Steep Snow and Ice

The ice ax is the iconic image of mountaineering, and many people believe that simply purchasing an ice ax and carrying it in their hands will keep them safe in the mountains. However, without the necessary skill and training, an ice ax is at best something that gets dropped in a fall on a steep slope; at worst it might impale its owner. Ice ax techniques, like the self-arrest, should be mastered in a safe environment with proper instruction before being used in the backcountry. A better option for novices is to stick to moderately angled slopes with less exposure and use trekking poles, which are a more intuitive way to help with balance and short slips.

Crampons are another climbing tool that is often misused. The two points sticking out of the front of the crampons are used for climbing steep ice, and putting your weight on these "front points" stresses your calf muscles. The points on the bottom of the crampons are better used for climbing moderately steep snow and ice. This flat-footed crampon technique uses the larger quadriceps muscle of the leg and conserves energy. The main reason beginners fall when using crampons has nothing to do with the frozen terrain they are climbing; instead it is often the result of mistakenly catching their pants leg or gaiter with their crampon points. Another reason people fall while wearing crampons is because

wet snow "balls up" on the bottom of the crampons and makes footing difficult. Use your ice ax or trekking poles to periodically tap the sides of your crampons to dislodge the snow; alternatively, consider removing your crampons if the snow is soft enough that you don't need them.

Ascending Techniques for Steep Snow and Ice

- **Kicking steps:** While maintaining a diagonal direction up a moderately soft snow slope, slice your boots (without crampons) into the snow, creating a level platform for each foot. The next person up the track will walk directly in your tracks and try to improve the steps.
- **Front pointing:** On steep snow or ice, kick the toes of your boots (with or without crampons) into the snow and travel directly up the slope. Try to lower your heels to relax your calves.

Descending Techniques for Steep Snow and Ice

- **The plunge step:** In moderately soft snow, face away from the slope, aggressively kick your heels into the snow, and walk directly down the slope. If the snow is harder, you can face the slope and "front point" down, being careful not to catch a point and flip over backward.

- **Glissading:** This is a great technique for quickly descending a snow slope. It can be done from a standing, crouching, or seated position. First check to make sure there is not a sheer cliff or other hazard at the bottom of the slope. Second, take your crampons off, as the points can catch in the snow and break your ankle or lower leg. Start off by slowly sliding down the slope. You can check your speed by digging your heels into the snow while in the

"Plunge stepping" down a steep slope on soft snow can make for a quick descent. DAVE ANDERSON

Glissading offers a fast, fun way down, but don't let the slide get out of control. Learn self-arrest techniques with the ice ax. DAVE ANDERSON

STEPS FOR STAYING SAFE IN AVALANCHE TERRAIN

Fresh snow on a glacier or snowfield can create avalanche conditions in a hurry. Avalanche training is beyond the scope of this book, but here are a few tips for staying safe in avalanche terrain:

- Remember that learning how to interpret the snowpack and accurately predict how safe or dangerous a particular slope is takes time and experience under the tutelage of experts.
- Stay on slopes less than 25 degrees.
- Look for signs of previous avalanche activity.
- Ridges or buttresses are safer choices for travel than convex slopes or gullies, where the tension fractures can cause avalanches.
- Stay near snowpack anchors, such as dense stands of trees and rock outcroppings.
- Know the weather history of the snowpack.
- Wear an avalanche transceiver and know how to search for a buried victim with it.
- In questionable terrain, travel one at a time across a suspect slope. If you are caught in an avalanche, try to get rid of skis, snowshoes, and other items that might drag you down, and swim or roll to the side of the slide path. Those not caught should watch and take note of where the victim was last seen. Begin searching from that point down and look for other signs of the victim, such as ski poles, gloves, packs, etc.

seated position. If you feel you cannot slow down, use your ice ax to self-arrest by quickly flipping onto your stomach and digging into the snow with your ax while simultaneously kicking the toes of both boots into the snow to stop.

BEYOND BEARS: OTHER WILD ANIMALS

Hiking and camping in bear country is covered in chapters 4 and 6, respectively. But bears aren't the only animals to be aware of when backpacking. While encounters with these wild animals are extremely rare, it's helpful to be armed with information when hiking.

Mountain Lions

Mountain lions, also called panthers and cougars, are a large wild cat species living in North America. Adult males can weigh over 200 pounds. Mountain lions are found in a variety of habitats, from deserts in Arizona to the coniferous forest of British Columbia. While their primary prey is deer, they are opportunists and will hunt and eat a variety of game. Mountain lions usually take down their prey by pouncing on the back of the intended victim. Cougar attacks are rare and, when they do occur, usually happen as the result of human development encroaching on mountain lion habitat. Small women and children traveling alone in the backcountry are most at risk for mountain lion attacks.

Mountain Lion Safety Tips

- As with bears, if you see a mountain lion in the wild, especially a female with young or a lion defending its prey, move away from the area.
- Do not run or crouch down when you see a cougar.
- Pick up small children and, if you are in a group, bunch together and try and make yourself look bigger; then slowly back away from the mountain lion.
- Never stare into the eyes of a mountain lion.
- If a cougar comes toward you, act aggressive, yell, wave your arms, and throw rocks and branches at it.

Wolves and Coyotes

Like grizzly bears, wolves were once found in many states, but hunting brought them to near extinction in the continental United States. Gray wolves have been reintroduced to parts of Montana, Wyoming, Idaho, Minnesota, Wisconsin, and Michigan. An adult wolf can weigh up to 80 pounds and range in color from white to black. Wolves are pack animals and hunt large game such as deer, elk, and moose but will also kill small mammals and birds. Wolves usually tend to avoid people. There have been only a handful of documented aggressive encounters, and these have often been the result of people hiking with their dogs.

RABIES

Rabies is a viral infection that affects the brain and nervous system of mammals. Once the neurological symptoms present themselves, the disease is almost always fatal. All mammals can contract rabies, and the virus is spread through bites from an infected animal. Rabies deaths in the United States are almost nonexistent, but worldwide the disease kills more than 50,000 people annually. In the United States raccoons are the most common carriers of the virus, but bites from bats are the most likely reason for infections in humans. Anytime you are bitten by a wild animal, you should see a physician. The treatment for a suspected rabies infection is a series of three to five injections given in the arm. People who are working in or traveling to areas where rabies is common can get a series of pre-exposure vaccines.

Coyotes are found in every state except Hawaii, which attests to their ability to thrive in a variety of ecosystems. Their size depends on the environment. In the desert coyotes rarely weigh more than 25 pounds, but in the Northeast, where they often hunt deer, they can weigh as much as 70 pounds. They have adapted well to suburban environments by eating garbage, small dogs, and cats. Coyotes rarely attack humans; however, infants and small children should not be left unattended when in coyote habitat.

Coyotes are found throughout North America. They rarely bother humans, but small children should not be left unattended when coyotes are around.
DAVE ANDERSON

Hooved Mammals (Ungulates)

There have been a few documented cases of people being attacked by moose, elk, mountain goats, and bison. Moose can be particularly aggressive during the fall, when bulls go into the rut. As with most other animals, mothers with their calves can also be antagonistic. Almost all of these incidents occur when people try to approach too closely, often while trying to photograph the animals. If a moose is blocking the trail, don't try to scare it off. Instead, take the long way around, steering far clear of the animal so as not to disturb it.

Bull moose can be aggressive in the fall during mating season.
DAVE ANDERSON

Venomous Snakes

Currently there is at least one type of venomous snake found in every state in the United States, the exceptions being Maine, Alaska, and Hawaii. These snakes include the copperhead, cottonmouth (water moccasin), rattlesnake, and coral snake. Copperheads and cottonmouths are found in the East, coral snakes in the Southwest, and rattlesnakes throughout the continental United States. Coral snakes are black with alternating yellow and red bands. Copperheads, cottonmouths, and rattlesnakes have a variety of color patterns.

Despite the hype surrounding the dangers of snakes, fewer than a dozen people are killed each year by venomous snakes. When confronted by some type of danger, all snakes, even venomous ones, will try to slither away instead of striking out at people. Rattlesnakes have rattles on the end of their tails, which they vibrate to warn people and other animals of their presence. The typical person to get bitten by a venomous snake is a young male who has been trying to catch or pick it up. The toxins in snake venom cause severe pain, and the amount of venom depends on the species and size of the snake. Common effects of envenomation include nausea, swelling, weakness, and blurred vision. In addition, some toxins affect the central nervous system, causing paralysis and lung and heart failure. All victims of venomous snakebites should be evacuated to a hospital as soon as possible to receive antivenin.

A rattlesnake will usually warn you with its rattle if you get too close.
DAVE ANDERSON

Treatment of Venomous Snakebites

Note that some treatments that have been commonly accepted in the past are now known to be more harmful than helpful.

- Try to determine the species of snake based on visual inspection.
- Keep the person calm.
- Remove rings, bracelets, etc., as the affected area will swell.
- Keep the snakebite lower than the heart to reduce the flow of venom.
- Evacuate the victim quickly with as little movement as possible.
- Do not make an incision in the skin with a knife or other cutting device.

- Do not try and suck venom out with your mouth.
- Do not apply a tourniquet.
- Do not give any medication or alcohol.

BUGS AND MICROSCOPIC ORGANISMS

Biting bugs have always been a nuisance. But in this age of West Nile fever (mosquitoes) and Lyme disease (ticks), both seriously debilitating conditions, preventing bug bites has taken on a new urgency.

Mosquitoes

The old standby, DEET, is still the best bug repellent on the market and lasts for about 4 hours, although the 30 percent strength is all you need. So far, none of the herbal repellents have proven effective for more than an hour or two. And the electronic gizmos are a joke. When conditions are especially bad, a mosquito-proof head net worn over a wide-brim hat and long-sleeve clothing treated with permethrin are your best option.

Ticks

When ticks are bad in summer, wear a long-sleeve shirt and long pants with gaiters or the legs tucked into your socks. Lighter-colored clothing makes it easier to spot ticks and will be cooler in the sun. Hike in the center of the trail and avoid tall grass and bushes. If you hike with a dog, be sure it has protection against ticks as well.

If you discover a tick on yourself or a friend or pet, the most effective way to remove it is to use a pair of tweezers and slowly pull with increasing force until the tick lets go. Spraying exposed skin areas with a solution containing DEET will discourage ticks, but the best thing to do is to check yourself for ticks during rest breaks and more thoroughly at the end of the day.

Scorpions

Scorpions are a member of the arachnid group to watch for in the backcountry. Commonly found throughout much of the Southwest, scorpions, like black widow and brown recluse spiders, are nocturnal. Scorpions have large pinchers and a stinger on the end of their trail. While deaths from scorpion stings are rare, the sting is very painful, similar to a bee or hornet sting. Check your boots in the morning to shake out any scorpions.

Spiders

Did you know that every spider is venomous? Yes, all spiders have some type of venom that they inject into their prey. Fortunately, very few spider bites actually are harmful to humans. Two species of spiders whose venom can be harmful are the black widow and brown recluse, both of which are found throughout North America.

Both male and female black widows usually have a red hourglass shape on their abdomen. These spiders are not aggressive and bite only when provoked or protecting their eggs. The black widow bite is very painful. Other symptoms include headache, severe abdominal pain, and sweating. An antivenin is available for black widow bites and is often used in conjunction with narcotics to reduce the pain associated with the bite.

The brown recluse sometimes has a violin-shaped pattern on its abdomen, but a more reliable identifier is that the brown recluse has six eyes instead of the normal eight of most spiders. Unlike the black widow's venom, which is a neurotoxin, the brown recluse spider has hemotoxin venom that kills red blood cells and can lead to large tissue death around the wound site. The initial brown recluse bite is often not painful, and symptoms don't develop until 24 hours later. As a result, many other ailments, such as skin ulcers and staph infections, are sometimes blamed on brown recluse bites. There is no effective treatment for brown recluse bites except to treat the resulting dead cell and tissue areas of the bite.

Tarantulas are large spiders found in the southwestern United States. DAVE ANDERSON

Backpackers in areas that are known to have high populations of black widow or brown recluse spiders can reduce their chances of being bitten by sleeping in tents and carefully checking their clothing and hiking boots for critters in the morning.

Bees, Hornets, and Wasps

If bees, hornets, wasps, and honeybees did not exist, neither would humans—these insects pollinate the vast majority of the foods we eat. Most bees are not aggressive. People come into contact with bees, hornets, and wasps by either getting too close to their nests (or hives), or by leaving out food that attracts certain species of hornets. Honeybees and bumblebees have a stinger on the end of their abdomen; when they sting, the stinger and venom sack stay attached to their victim. As a result, the bee can only sting once and then dies a short time later.

Hornets and wasps have a retractable stinger and can sting many times. Honeybees, hornets, and wasps build nests in hollow trees, on the underside of branches, and on rock overhangs. The observant traveler can avoid these hazards. However, some hornets like yellow jackets make their nests underground. The hiker is only aware of a nest after she inadvertently steps on one and a horde of angry hornets swarms around. The venom in a sting is very painful and causes swelling and redness. Some individuals develop an allergic reaction to bee stings. Symptoms include hives and difficult breathing, which are signs of a severe, whole-body allergic reaction, anaphylaxis—a life-threatening condition that needs to be treated immediately.

Hornets make nests out of paper-like material.
DAVE ANDERSON

"Killer bees," or Africanized honeybees, are a nonnative species that is very similar to our native honeybee. They are less tolerant to cold conditions, so their range is restricted to the Southwest, although they have also recently been found in Florida. All bees will swarm a perceived threat to their nest or hive, but killer bees tend to be very aggressive In this behavior. Their sting is not any more potent than that of regular bees, but they will swarm and sting a perceived threat hundreds or thousands of times.

Steps to Avoid Confrontations with Stinging Insects

- Avoid known nest and hive areas.
- Seal smelly food items in plastic bags.
- If stung, remove yourself from the area quickly. Bees, wasps, and hornets have a territory they will defend.
- After vacating the area, pull the stinger out as soon as possible to reduce the amount of venom injected.
- People with known anaphylactic episodes should carry appropriate drugs such as epinephrine and antihistamines and know how to administer them.

Microscopic Organisms

Although you cannot see microscopic hazards such as bacteria, viruses, and protozoans, you can certainly feel the effects in your body once they take hold. The most common way these small creatures get inside us is through eating and drinking. Two parasitic hazards hikers are often concerned about are *Giardia* and *Cryptosporidium*. The cysts (eggs) of these protozoans get into water sources from fecal contamination by mammals infected with the disease. Any mammal can carry the cysts, including, cattle, moose, beavers, and people. These one-celled organisms are found throughout the world and in many water sources; even public drinking water may contain very low levels of the cysts. The cysts of *Giardia* and *Cryptosporidium* hatch inside the small intestines and cause diarrhea, fever, nausea, vomiting, and abdominal pain. Some people will recover in a few weeks, but most will need medication to combat the parasite.

Prevention is easy. Wash or sanitize your hands before eating or cooking, treat suspect drinking water, and cook all food thoroughly. You can treat questionable water sources several ways. Boiling, filtering, and chemical treatments are all viable options. For more information on water treatment options, see chapter 6.

PLANTS

Hiking along the Appalachian Trail in early fall while the leaves are turning provides you with an inspiring kaleidoscope of colors. However, bushwhacking through a dense stand of willow and slide alders in Boston Basin in Washington's North Cascades often leaves you sweating and cursing. All plants are not created equal in terms of backcountry enjoyment, and some can be hazardous to your health.

Bushwhacking

Off-trail travel adds problem solving and the excitement of the unknown into your backcountry experiences. However, when you are bushwhacking, you can do a number of things to make the experience safer and more enjoyable. First, get ready for your off-trail adventure by streamlining your pack. Take items that are clipped or strapped to the outside of the backpack, such as water bottles and sleeping pads, and pack them inside. Put on a long-sleeve shirt and pants to protect yourself from abrasions. Consider wearing sunglasses to protect your eyes and gloves to protect your hands. Know what types of plants you are going to encounter so that you do not grab a branch to keep your balance and end up with a hand full of thorns. While navigating through thick vegetation, try to keep enough distance between you and your hiking partners so you do not get hit by "fly back" branches.

Almost all plants in the desert have some type of thorn like this ocotillo.
DAVE ANDERSON

Poisonous Plants

While ingesting poisonous plants can be a serious backcountry hazard, it is totally preventable by simply not eating any plant you cannot exactly identity. However, other poisonous plants can still cause problems for the wilderness traveler. If you spend enough time walking around in the woods, you will most likely develop a rash on your skin as the result of contact with one of these three plants: poison sumac, poison ivy, and poison oak. All three of these plants contain urushiol, an oily substance that is a potent skin irritant in small quantities. Poison sumac is an uncommon shrub that is found in very wet areas in the Southeast. Poison oak and poison ivy can grow as ground cover, vines, or shrubs and are found throughout North America. They have leaves in groups of three and can sometimes display a shiny luster on the leaves. After just a few minutes of direct skin contact with one of these plants, the oils are bonded to your skin and a very itchy rash develops. The best treatment is to wash the affected area with soap and water to remove the oil and not scratch the rash, which can cause scarring. Once the oil has been removed, the rash cannot spread to other areas of your body or to another person; after a week or two, it will disappear on its own. To reduce the itching, dermatologists recommend oatmeal baths or putting baking soda on the rash.

Poison ivy has leaves in groups of three. Even dead poison ivy still contains the oils that irritate skin.
DAVE ANDERSON

Dead Snags and Widow Makers

When selecting a campsite for the evening, there are many things you should take into consideration to increase your comfort and reduce your environmental impact. These include camping at least 200 feet from a trail and water source and looking for a flat site that has been used before or, if not previously used, is on a durable surface. One thing most people do not do is look up into the tree canopy to see if there are any dead branches that might fall on their tent during the night. In established campsites, other users may have killed or weakened the trees by girdling the bark or by cutting off branches for firewood. Even in remote areas, trees killed by insect infestations can quickly change a nice sheltered spot into a potentially deadly campsite during high winds. Early fall snowstorms, while leaves are still on the trees, can take down living branches and even trees. The leaves allow more snow and weight to accumulate. An early snow event might be hard for you to plan for in advance, but once it is happening, you should move your camp to a safe location.

HUMANS

Other visitors recreating in the same wild region can be potential hazards. These visitors might be doing the same type of activity as you, such climbing on the same rock face, or they might be participating in a different activity, such as snowmobiling or cross-country skiing, but sharing the same terrain. Before you go into the backcountry, part of your research should be to find out what other types of users recreate in the region. Often, if the speeds of the activities in the shared terrain are very different, problems and dangers arise. Some public lands allow only certain activities and might even suggest trail etiquette for different types of user groups. In many locations horses, hikers, and mountain bikers share the same trail. The common and sometimes posted rule states that bikers should yield to hikers, and hikers and bikers should both yield to horses. This rule is based on the speed and maneuverability of the activities. If you encounter horses while hiking on a trail, step off on the downside and let the horses pass.

Dogs

Dogs are one hazard associated with other people. Some areas require dogs to be on a leash at all times; others do not, but all canine owners are expected to be able to control their dog. Dogs are naturally territorial and protective of their owners, and some get confused about how much territory they need to protect. They will aggressively defend a section of the trail by barking as you approach. Usually talking to the dog in a calm manner will diffuse the situation. However, if you feel the dog is going to attack, defend yourself with trekking poles, sticks, rocks, even pepper spray. Often, quickly taking off your pack and holding it in front of you will provide protection from a dog attack until the owner can get control of his animal.

Hunters

Hunting is a popular activity on many public lands. Almost every state requires new hunters to take a hunting safety course that helps prevent conflicts and accidents with other users. However, there are several things you can do to increase your safety when interacting with hunters. First, know what type of hunting seasons are in effect for the area you are visiting and when and where they occur. That way you can predict in what type of terrain you might encounter hunters and what time of day they will be most active. Second, make yourself visible to hunters by wearing blaze orange vests, hats, and other clothing. Make noise to alert hunters of your presence, and do not wear camouflage.

Criminal Element

There have been a few accounts of theft and even violence directed toward hikers in the backcountry. However, these incidents are extremely rare. Crime, when it does happen, usually occurs near the trailhead (so don't leave valuables in your car). Criminals aren't likely to hike a long way into the wilderness, because there are few potential victims in there. Also, criminals typically seek out victims they can easily overpower and then quickly leave the area, which is not an option deep in the wilderness.

There are self-defense options for the solo traveler, such as hiking with a dog or carrying pepper spray, even a gun. Make sure you have proper knowledge of how to safely use a firearm and what permits are necessary to carry a gun in the area you are visiting. The easiest and potentially most enjoyable way to make yourself safer when hiking is to invite a few friends along. The more people in your group, the less likely you are to be the target of criminals.

Either wear or strap to your pack some blaze orange during hunting season to make yourself more visible.
DAVE ANDERSON

Green River Overlook, Canyonlands
National Park, Utah THINKSTOCK.COM

CHAPTER 9

BACKCOUNTRY FIRST AID

If you spend a lot of time in the wilderness, you are likely to encounter some kind of first-aid situation. Proper planning helps minimize this likelihood. You can choose routes and activities appropriate for your skill level. You can train to prepare yourself physically. You can carry the appropriate equipment. But you cannot avoid everything. Sometime someone is going to take a misstep in a boulder field or get a stomachache in camp. You may need to patch a blister or tape an ankle; you may find yourself faced with a broken limb or worse. Having some basic first-aid skills is imperative in these situations.

By definition, the wilderness is a place far from civilization. You can't pick up the phone, call 911, and expect an ambulance to show up in 10 minutes. If someone in your party gets sick or injured, you may have to provide care for hours, if not days, until help arrives. While not a substitute for hands-on first-aid training from a qualified instructor, this chapter includes basic information for assessing your patient's condition, treating immediate threats to life or limb, caring for minor injuries, and gathering important information to pass on when help arrives. (For information on how to prevent and treat bug bites, stings, and snakebites, see chapter 8 on outdoor hazards.)

If you find yourself in a first-aid or rescue situation, remember that the first priority is the safety of the rescuer. Too often people compromise their own safety in an effort to save someone else. Before you approach an injured or sick person, stop and survey the scene to determine if it is safe for you to approach. Deciding not to help could be one of the most difficult situations you ever face, but creating two victims helps no one.

Accidents happen quickly and without warning, so it helps to be prepared.
DAVE ANDERSON

PATIENT ASSESSMENT

Initial Assessment

In any first-aid scenario—illness, injury, mystery—care begins with an initial assessment. You may have heard of the ABCs of first aid—this acronym addresses the immediate threats to life: **airway, breathing, circulation, cervical spine.** Your first priority is to ensure that your patient's ABCs are stable: that he or she is breathing and that his or her heart is beating. This is the time you "look, listen, and feel" for breath sounds, heartbeat, bleeding, and other signs of trauma. If any of an individual's ABCs is compromised, you need to stop and fix the problem immediately. No air means you have just minutes before your patient will die; no heartbeat, the same. To address these problems, you must have training in cardiopulmonary resuscitation (CPR) and artificial breathing. You must know how to clear an airway and how to stop bleeding. You need to know how to avoid adding further damage to a spinal cord injury.

Most bleeding can be controlled by direct pressure and elevation. Take a wad of cloth (ideally sterile gauze pads, but anything will do in an emergency) and place it directly over the wound. Press down firmly with the flats of your fingers. Raise the affected body part above the heart. You can also push on specific pressure points—the brachial artery in the upper arm or the femoral artery in the leg—to slow blood flow into the

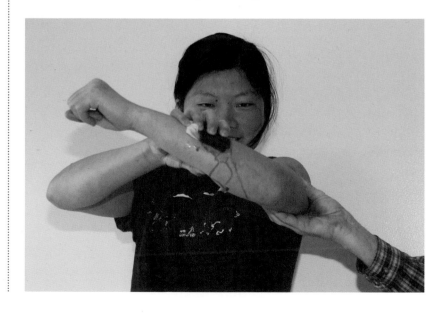

Most bleeding can be controlled by applying pressure directly to the wound, elevating the affected limb, and pressing down on the closest pressure point, in this case the brachial artery in the patient's upper arm.
DAVE ANDERSON

limb. (See the upcoming section on wound management for more detail on controlling bleeding.)

If you suspect the patient has injured her spinal cord—something possible with any fall from body height or above—do not move her. Use a jaw thrust to open her airway. A jaw thrust is done by placing your fingers under the corners of the individual's jaw and lifting it up and away from her throat.

The ABCs have been expanded to include D and E. D stands for **disability** and clues you in to look for obvious deformities resulting from trauma. E stands for both **exposure** and **environment** and serves to remind you

Get close and give yourself time to look, listen, and feel for breath sounds.
DAVE ANDERSON

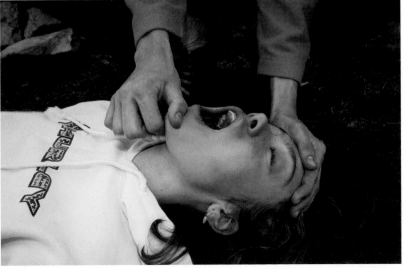

If your patient is not breathing, open her airway using the head-tilt, chin-lift technique. Place one hand on your patient's forehead, the other beneath her chin, and tilt her head back.
DAVE ANDERSON

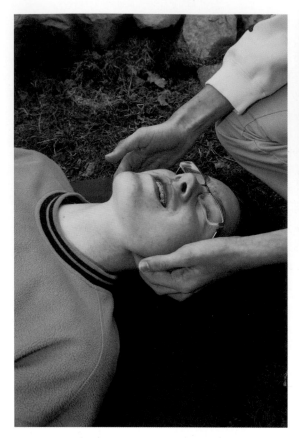

If you suspect your patient has injured his spine, open his airway by lifting up on the outer edges of his jawbone to avoid moving his head and neck. DAVE ANDERSON

If your patient is not breathing, pinch his nose closed and breathe into his mouth once every 5 seconds. DAVE ANDERSON

to look at or expose the patient's body as you conduct your assessment to ensure you do not miss anything. Environment just reminds you to be aware that the environment may be life-threatening in and of itself. Is your patient submerged in freezing cold water or lying in direct sun? Are you both exposed to rockfall or avalanche hazard? These factors may also demand immediate attention.

Stabilize Your Patient

Once you have determined that the ABCDEs are okay, you need to make your patient comfortable. The big difference between wilderness and frontcountry medicine is the time it takes to get a patient to a hospital. At the very best, you may get help in a matter of hours, but it is more likely that you will need to care for an individual for a day or two before you can get him or her out of the backcountry.

Stabilize your patient in a position of comfort. If he can talk to you, let him help you figure out the best position. If he cannot, rest him on his side in case he vomits. Put him on some kind of pad to protect him from the ground; cover him with a sleeping bag or warm clothing. If the patient is conscious and capable of feeding himself, give him food and water. Monitor the individual's vital signs, and go for help. Ideally, you have enough people in your group to allow someone to remain with your patient while others go for help. If there are just two of you, you are faced with a decision. Can you leave your patient to seek aid? Or do you need to stay put to provide care? Some form of communication device such as a personal locator beacon can help in this kind of situation.

You can find a pulse alongside your patient's jugular. DAVE ANDERSON

Secondary Survey

After your patient is stable and resting, take time to go through a more thorough history of her illness or injury. The more information you can relay to rescuers, the better. Ask questions about everything: history of the present illness or injury, what your patient ate, when she last had a bowel movement, when the illness began, what her pain is like, whether she has taken any medications or illegal drugs, if she has any chronic illnesses that may have contributed to her current condition—anything that may help doctors determine what is going on.

You should also conduct a thorough physical exam to make sure you haven't missed anything. Sometimes one injury or problem will mask others, so it's important to double check. Start at your patient's head and move down to her toes. Look, listen, and feel. Be systematic.

Finally, take your patient's pulse and count her breaths. Remember, a normal pulse ranges from sixty to eighty beats per minute, while we breathe between twelve and twenty times per minute. Check skin color and temperature. Ask questions to determine your patient's level of consciousness: name, date, time, what happened? These vital signs—heart rate, breathing rate, skin color and temperature, and level of consciousness—are good ways to monitor your patient over time. Check vital signs regularly, and record your findings. Any changes may indicate a change in your patient's condition.

Make a Plan

You now have to make a judgment call. Is this a life-threatening situation? Is your patient about to die? Hard as this may be to accept, if someone is about to die from an injury or illness that demands advanced medical care in the next hour, it is unlikely you can do much more than try to make him comfortable. You may be carrying some kind of communication device—a satellite phone or personal locator beacon—that allows you to call for immediate help. You may even be able to get a helicopter to your side quite rapidly, but it's unlikely it will arrive within an hour unless everything falls into place. You cannot beat yourself up if this is the situation. The wilderness attracts us because it is wild, not safe. You may not be able to do anything to help your patient.

That said, often you can. Now is your time to come up with a plan for what comes next. This includes immediate steps—splinting the fractured leg or cleaning the wound—as well as long-term care, such as how you intend to make your patient comfortable until the injury heals or you can get him to a hospital. Can your patient stay with you in the wilderness or does he have to see a doctor? If your patient needs medical attention, can he walk out of the wilderness or are you going to need assistance? What kind of assistance is available? These kinds of questions all need to be addressed in your plan.

The remainder of this chapter will be dedicated to conditions you can do something about in the field with little medical training.

SHOCK

Shock is insidious. Your patient can appear fine; suddenly he faints and his vital signs plummet. Shock is caused by circulatory system failure. For a number of different reasons ranging from blood loss to severe dehydration or a heart problem, your circulatory system fails to deliver adequate oxygen to your body. Untreated, shock causes death.

Shock is associated with other injuries and can be managed—or at least slowed—if recognized. Any time you have someone who has experienced trauma, either physically or emotionally, you should treat for shock.

Signs and Symptoms of Shock

- Pale, clammy skin
- Rapid, weak pulse
- Shallow, rapid respirations
- Changes in levels of consciousness
- Thirst
- Anxiety

Treatment

The most important treatment for shock is to remove the cause. This means stopping bleeding, addressing ABCDEs, stabilizing fractures, and alleviating pain as much as possible. Help keep your patient calm by maintaining your personal composure and talking in a soothing, professional manner. If your patient is conscious and capable of holding and drinking from a cup, give him fluids.

Have your patient lie down and prop up his feet with a pillow or some kind of footrest (make sure to support the knees). Ideally, the feet should be approximately 10 inches above the heart. Make sure the patient is comfortable—neither too hot nor too cold. Monitor vitals.

In any traumatic event, you should treat for shock, just in case. Help your patient lie down. Elevate his feet. Make sure he is comfortable and speak to him in a calm, reassuring voice.
DAVE ANDERSON

FRACTURES, SPRAINS, AND TENDONITIS

Athletic injuries, or injuries to the skeletal system and its connective tissues, are one of the most common injuries encountered in the backcountry. People are pushing their physical limits, they may not be in the best shape, they are carrying heavy loads, and the terrain is varied, inconsistent, and unstable. It's easy to fall or step wrong and end up with some kind of injury.

Whether your patient can remain in the wilderness after suffering an athletic injury depends on its severity, but you can definitely do a lot to help her be more comfortable while you come up with a plan.

Bone Fractures

Fractures can be open or closed, which means either the skin is broken (open) or intact (closed). Open fractures are very serious. Exposed bones can dry out and the tissue die, plus the opening allows the introduction of bacteria, which can lead to infection. Open fractures demand immediate attention. Clean the wound carefully (see the upcoming section on wound management for basic wound care) and keep bone ends moist with a damp dressing. Splint the wound (see sidebar) and evacuate your patient as soon as possible.

For closed fractures, the threat is less immediate or dire (with the exception of femur fractures).

Signs and Symptoms

- **Mechanism of injury:** What happened? Probably the most common sign of a fracture is the simple fact that you fell and heard something snap.
- **Deformity:** Fractures often result in some deformity. The bones don't line up as they should, or there's a bend where there should not be.
- **Discoloration:** You may have swelling and discoloration associated with a fracture, but this won't happen immediately, so don't sigh with relief if you don't see it right away.
- **Pain and tenderness:** Often with fractures, a patient can point out exactly where it hurts.
- **Crepitus:** You may detect the sound of bones grinding against each other when the injury moves.

Treatment

Once you've identified a fracture, your treatment involves a number of steps. First, remove all clothing surrounding the injury. You may need to cut off a sleeve of a shirt or part of a pants leg. You need to see what you are working with, and clothing gets in the way. Remove all jewelry, watches, shoes, and so forth. You are likely to have swelling associated with a fracture, so it's a good idea to get rid of any potentially restrictive items before you no longer can.

Once you have exposed the injury, look to see if the bones are aligned. Most medical professionals now believe you should apply gentle, in-line traction to realign bones if medical attention is distant. To do this, have a helper hold the injured limb above the site of the fracture (this can be the patient if you have no one else to help), while you take hold of the limb below the injury and pull gently until the bone is straight. Stop if the movement is causing more pain.

Assess the limb for any tingling or numbness to ensure adequate circulation. Make sure to continue checking as you treat.

Immobilize the injury. If you've broken a long bone, you need to also immobilize the joints on either side of the fracture, such as your elbow and wrist if you have a forearm fracture. In the case of a suspected fracture in a joint, immobilize the long bones on either side, such as the upper and lower arm in the case of an elbow injury.

For a lower arm fracture, apply in-line traction by stabilizing the upper arm with one hand and pulling the lower arm gently until it is straight. DAVE ANDERSON

SPLINTING MADE EASY

Splints need to be firm, comfortable, simple, adjustable, and allow access to fingers or toes to check circulation. Most of us don't carry splinting materials in our first-aid kits; there's no need really, as the likelihood of encountering a fracture is slim and you can improvise with materials at hand. Everything from spoons to jackets and bandannas, even backpacking seats, can be transformed into an effective splint with a little improvisation.

Firm: You can use a variety of things to provide support to your splint, including rolled foam pads, sticks, tent poles, and so forth. The idea is to have something that prevents movement without being too cumbersome.

Comfortable: Use abundant padding throughout your splint to make sure it is comfortable. Talk to your patient as you work; he will tell you if the splint feels good. If you are unsure, you can experiment on someone else before actually subjecting your patient to the splint. Padding also provides insulation.

Adjustable: Tie your splint in place with wide straps—bandannas, cravats, or strips of cloth from a shirt work well. Use loose knots or even bows that you can untie easily in case the splint needs to be loosened as the limb swells.

You can improvise a splint from almost anything. Here a shirt, sleeping pad, strip of cloth, and a trekking pole provide materials. DAVE ANDERSON

Simple: People have a tendency to get a bit carried away with splints. They are fun to build, demanding ingenuity to accomplish their purpose, but they don't have to be too elaborate. The simpler the splint, the easier it is to assess the injury. Splints should be usable. For example, you don't want to splint someone's arm straight out from his side: He could not move in that position without banging into something.

Finally, make sure you leave a window to peep in through so you can check your patient's fingers or toes. You want to make sure he has good skin color and temperature and there is no tingling from lack of blood flow.

A good splint must be rigid, provide stability, and be comfortable. DAVE ANDERSON

Once you've created your splint, secure the injured arm to your patient with a sling. DAVE ANDERSON

Treat for shock by lying your patient down, comforting him or her, and administering fluids. Fractures may be associated with internal bleeding and extreme pain that can cause shock.

Finally, elevate the limb to help reduce swelling. You can RICE the area (rest, ice, compression, elevation) as well.

Dislocations

Dislocations involve bones being pulled out of the joint sockets. Signs and symptoms of a dislocation include obvious deformity, popping sound at time of accident, extreme pain, and loss of function.

If you take a wilderness first-aid course, you will probably be taught to reduce or fix some dislocated joints in the field—typically patellas, fingers, and shoulders—as it is best to minimize the time a joint is out of alignment both for the patient's comfort and for the long-term health of the joint. If you do not have this training, splint the injury as you find it and get your patient out of the wilderness as quickly as you can.

For some fractures, such as broken arms or wrists, your patient may be able to hike out with her arm splinted and supported in a sling.
DAVE ANDERSON

Evacuation

You'll want to get someone to see a doctor after he has broken a bone, but if you are able to create an effective splint and see no signs of circulation impairment, you can have your patient walk out if he feels up for it (usually this is only possible with arm or shoulder injuries, but some people can hobble out with makeshift crutches or leaning on others for lower leg fractures).

If you are unable to maintain adequate circulation or if the patient shows signs and symptoms of shock, you need to expedite your evacuation process to ensure your patient's continued well-being.

FEMURS

Femur fractures are very serious because of the size of the muscles in your thigh, which can contract, drawing bone ends together and causing pain. Femur fractures can also cause extensive internal bleeding. The recommended treatment for a femur fracture is a traction splint, which requires training to construct. In the absence of this training, you can hold manual traction on a femur fracture by grabbing the patient's foot and pulling hard in line with the long bones. The critical thing is that once traction is applied, you do not want to stop; but holding a femur in line is exhausting. You can tie something around your patient's ankle and foot and secure it to a tree to hold traction until help arrives. Treat all femur fracture patients for shock.

You can provide traction for a femur fracture by tying the patient's injured leg to a tree. DAVE ANDERSON

Sprains

Sprains involve injuries to your connective tissues: your tendons and ligaments. Severe sprains are impossible to distinguish from fractures without an X-ray, so if you can't tell in the field, immobilize the area.

Sprains are graded according to severity and range from minor ligament stretches to complete tears. A severe sprain can take months to heal, but an area with a minor sprain may be usable after RICE.

Assessing a Sprain

In the wilderness the most common sprains you can expect to encounter will be ankle sprains. Again, your first clue will be the mechanism of injury. Did the person roll her ankle on the trail? Did she hear a popping sound and feel a flash of pain? Those signs pretty clearly indicate a sprain, or possibly a fracture, while pain that comes on slowly is likely to be caused by overuse (see the section on tendonitis).

Sprains are also associated with discoloration, swelling, and pain. Deformity and point tenderness, on the other hand, point to a fracture. If you suspect a sprain, ask your patient to move the joint; point and flex her toes and rotate her foot in a circle in both directions. You may find that she has lost some range of motion and that certain movements cause pain while others do not. If the person can bear weight and endure a certain amount of use, you may be able to treat the injury in the field.

Treatment

Begin RICE (rest, ice, compression, and elevation) immediately. Apply ice or snow wrapped in a towel or T-shirt to the injury for 20 to 40 minutes

If you don't have snow or ice to use for RICEing your injury, stick the affected area into a cold stream for the same effect.
DAVE ANDERSON

every 2 to 4 hours for the first day or two to help reduce swelling. You can also stick the injured limb in a cold mountain stream to achieve the same result. Your goal is to constrict blood flow and numb nerve pain to help minimize inflammation.

- Wrap the limb in an elastic bandage to apply compression. Make sure the bandage does not cut off blood flow to the limb.
- Elevate the affected area above the heart to reduce blood flow and help lessen swelling.
- Administer an over-the-counter analgesic such as ibuprofen or acetaminophen to help control pain, and have the patient move the joint (circles, flexing, pointing) gently every few hours. Avoid movements that cause excessive pain.

TAPING ANKLES

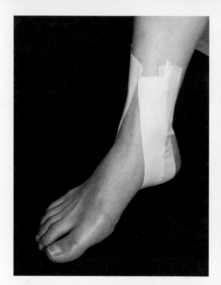

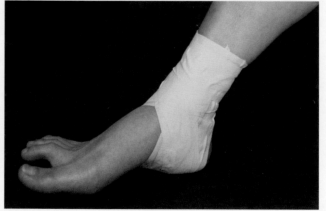

For minor to moderate ankle sprains, you can use tape to stabilize and support the joint enough to allow your patient to continue hiking if he or she desires.

Most ankle sprains occur when you roll your ankle to the outside. You can support this injury by taping the ankle. Start by creating stirrups that begin on the inside of your ankle, pass under your heel, and come up on the out—or injured—side.
DAVE ANDERSON

To provide further support, create two or three "figure eights" over the stirrups using a strip of tape. Start at the back of the ankle, cross over the top of the foot, pass under the arch, and back over the top of the foot, ending in the back of the ankle where you started.
DAVE ANDERSON

Tendonitis

Tendonitis, or the inflammation of a tendon, is relatively common on extended hiking or kayaking trips because of the repetitive nature of the activity. Tendonitis is usually—though not always—an overuse injury and in walkers is experienced in the knees and Achilles tendons. Boaters commonly get tendonitis in their wrists.

Signs and Symptoms

Tendonitis may cause some swelling, but often the main signs will be tenderness, pain with movement, and, in a few cases, a kind of crackly or grinding feeling in the area. Typically, tendonitis comes on slowly.

Treatment

Start with RICE and analgesics to control pain. You can also experiment with different techniques to limit motion in the joint or remove pressure on the tendon. Heel lifts can help with Achilles tendonitis, as can changing your shoes to remove any pressure on the tendon. Taping wrists for forearm tendonitis can help reduce the movement that causes pain for boaters. You may be forced to abstain from the activity that causes the pain until the inflammation goes down.

It's worth noting that tendonitis is often associated with technique. You may be someone who rocks back and forth on your feet when you walk, causing a lot of motion in your ankle joint, or you may flex your wrists too much when boating, putting undue pressure on the tendons in your forearm. Try walking flat-footed or switching to a non-feathered paddle to help avoid the motion that is causing pain.

A Few Final Thoughts on Athletic Injuries

Athletic injuries happen more commonly when people are cold, tired, dehydrated, and out of shape. You can help avoid this situation by warming up for activities, maintaining adequate hydration, resting, and making sure you are prepared.

WOUND MANAGEMENT

Cuts, scrapes, and blisters are common in the outdoors and usually don't cause problems if they are cared for properly. But failure to keep these wounds clean can result in infection, and suddenly an insignificant bug

Small cuts and scrapes—common in the outdoors—can become dangerous if not treated with care to avoid infection.
DAVE ANDERSON

bite turns into a medical emergency, so it's important to treat every opening in your skin seriously.

Bleeding

As mentioned earlier, most bleeding can be controlled by:

- Direct pressure
- Elevation
- Pressure points

Remember to wear gloves or place your hand in a plastic bag when you are around someone else's blood. You may need to apply direct pressure for a long time before the bleeding stops. Check the wound after a minimum of 5 minutes to see if clotting has occurred; if not, hold the dressing in place for another 10 or 15 minutes and then check again. Back up your direct pressure with elevation and pressure points: Together, you should be able to control most bleeding.

There are situations—usually tears of major arteries—where bleeding cannot be controlled by these techniques. In such extreme situations, you are advised to use a tourniquet. Tourniquets cut off all blood to the limb, so you risk permanent damage if they remain in place for extended periods of time.

PRESSURE POINTS

Pressure points are areas where major arteries run close to bones, such as in the upper arm or in the groin area. You can reduce blood flow to the limb below the point by pushing the artery up against the bone, thereby restricting the amount of blood moving through. Once the wound has stopped bleeding, gradually reduce the pressure on the artery, allowing blood flow to return to normal slowly. If bleeding resumes, start the process over again.

For major wounds, it can take anywhere from 5 to 20 minutes to stop the blood flow, so be patient.

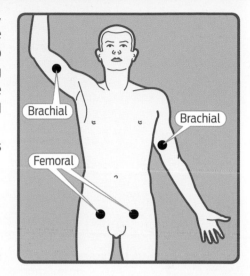

Pressure points of the body

Tourniquets should be placed 2 inches above the wound. Wrap a wide band around the limb, tie an overhand knot, place a stick on the knot, and tie it in place with another overhand knot. Twist the stick until bleeding stops and secure. Write "TK" on your patient's forehead so that treating physicians know immediately to look for the tourniquet. Seek immediate evacuation.

For serious wounds, leave the injury alone after you have controlled the bleeding and seek medical attention as quickly as possible. Trying to clean these injuries will just restart the bleeding. For less-serious wounds, or wounds where bleeding is minor, your next step is to clean the area.

If you are forced to use a tourniquet to control bleeding, write the time and "TK" on your patient's forehead so that the attending physician will immediately know to look for the tourniquet.
DAVE ANDERSON

Cleaning Wounds

Infection is a serious problem in the wilderness, so it's imperative that you keep all wounds clean. For most wounds, the best cleaning technique is to flush the area with water that is safe to drink. It's a good idea to carry a syringe in your first-aid kit to irrigate wounds with sufficient pressure, but if you don't have one, a clean plastic bag with a tiny hole in one corner will suffice. Hold the edges of the wound apart, and tilt the limb slightly so water can flow out. Flush the wound with a continuous high-pressure flow. Use about 0.5 liter of water and then stop and examine the injury. Pick out any bits of dirt, gravel, or sticks with sterilized tweezers. Flush the area again with another 0.5 liter.

You usually don't have to use any kind of disinfectant or soap if you use an adequate amount of water. Many disinfectants, such as povidone-iodine, are actually fairly caustic, even when diluted. If you have a particularly dirty wound or are worried about germs, say from an animal bite, you may want to clean with disinfectant. Just make sure to flush out the wound thoroughly with clean water afterward to remove all trace of the disinfectant.

Some wounds, such as abrasions, need scrubbing to get really clean. You can use a soap-impregnated sponge, available from first-aid suppliers, or a sterile gauze pad and soap for scrubbing. It may help to give your

The best way to clean a wound is to flush it with copious amounts of clean water. A needle-nosed syringe is the most effective tool, but if you don't have one handy, a plastic bag with a small hole in one corner will serve. DAVE ANDERSON

patient some mild analgesic 20 minutes or so before the cleaning to help dull the pain. It may also help to have him do the scrubbing himself if he's up for it. Pick out large foreign objects with tweezers first, scrub, and then irrigate thoroughly.

Once the wound is clean, let it air-dry. If you have a gaping injury and are carrying Steri-Strips in your first-aid kit, use the strips to pull the wound together, or improvise with strips of athletic tape. Start in the middle and work out toward the ends, interlacing strips from one side of the wound to the other like a zipper to help pull it together evenly.

Well-stocked first-aid kits often include occlusive dressings such as Tegaderm that help keep the wound moist, promoting healing. If you don't have such dressings, apply antibacterial cream to a sterile pad and place it over the cut. Use athletic tape to hold the dressing in place.

Check the fingers or toes on the affected limb to make sure you have not cut off circulation. If bleeding resumes, do not remove the dressing, as you'll destroy any clotting. Add more dressing material to soak up further blood.

An occlusive dressing keeps your wound clean and dry and allows you to monitor the area for infection.
DAVE ANDERSON

If you use an occlusive dressing on the wound, you can leave it in place for several days. Many of these dressings are see-through, allowing you to monitor for infection without disrupting healing. They are also waterproof, helping to maintain an ideal healing environment. In the absence of an occlusive dressing, try to keep the bandage and dressing dry. Change the bandage every day or so to help prevent infection. If the dressing is stuck to the wound, soak the area until you can remove it without ripping off scabs.

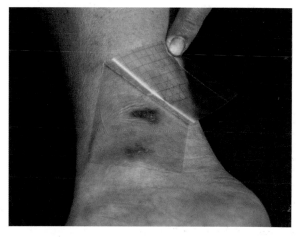

Infection

Signs of infection include increased redness, heat, swelling, and pain. As the infection becomes more serious, you may see red streaking leading away from the wound toward the heart; lymph nodes swell, and your patient may develop a fever. Ideally you won't get that far, however. Most localized infections can be treated easily if caught early.

Your first step for treating an infection is to re-clean the wound. You'll need to open it up or remove scabs to clean effectively. Soak the wound in warm water or antiseptic solution for 20 to 30 minutes several times during the day. Rinse with water that is safe to drink after each soak. Air-dry and re-dress.

Watch for signs of the infection worsening. Some people carry antibiotics specifically for skin infections, particularly when they travel overseas or expect to be far from medical care for an extended period of time. If you are carrying antibiotics for this purpose, administer them if you begin to see signs of deepening infection. Fever, red streaks, and swollen lymph nodes are all reasons to get your patient to a doctor as soon as possible. Infections on the face are particularly risky and merit rapid medical attention if they do not improve with cleaning.

BURNS AND BLISTERS

Burns

Burns are problematic in the field for a number of reasons: They are prone to infection, they can be extremely painful, and they can cause swelling, which may threaten airways if in the throat area.

Treating Burns

The first step in treating all burns is to remove the source. If your patient is on fire, have him stop, drop, and roll. Burns from wet caustic chemicals should be flushed with water for 20 minutes; dry chemicals should be brushed off the skin.

Once the source of the heat is removed, cool the burned area by pouring water over the burn. You can also use a cool, damp cloth for this purpose. Cool the area for several minutes.

Next, assess the injury. Burns are graded according to their depth and extent, with superficial burns involving only the outer skin layers being the least serious. Superficial burns do not involve blistering, but they are painful, as anyone who's had a good sunburn will know. Partial-thickness burns are more serious and cause blistering. These burns appear wet and mottled and are very painful. Full-thickness burns go all the way through your skin layers into the subcutaneous. Full-thickness burns appear gray and charred. They may be less painful than other burns because the nerves have been destroyed, but often your patient will have partial-thickness burns as well, so don't expect him to be pain free.

Superficial burns can be treated in the field, as can small, localized partial-thickness burns. Burns to the hands, feet, face, or genital area and burns that go all the way around a limb, as well as burns covering a large area, are more serious and should be attended to by a doctor. Cover the burned area with a moist dressing (2nd Skin works well for this), treat for shock, and seek help.

Blisters

Blisters are friction burns and are common injuries for hikers wearing new boots or covering long miles. Unfortunately they can put a serious glitch in your travel plans. Big blisters make walking uncomfortable or even impossible. Your best bet is to nip any blister in the bud. You'll know when something's going on: Most blisters start with a "hot spot" where the rubbing occurs. Stop and fix the problem right away.

Often blisters can be avoided by wearing comfortable, well-broken-in footwear and clean socks. But some people's feet are softer and more prone to blisters, and all shoes and boots are new at some point, so blisters happen. If you catch the injury at the hot spot stage, you're lucky. Today you can buy gel blister pads that pad the area and remove the friction, preventing the actual blister from forming. If you know you are prone to blisters, say on your heel, you may want to put one of these blister gel pads on the sensitive spot prophylactically. They aren't cheap, but they work.

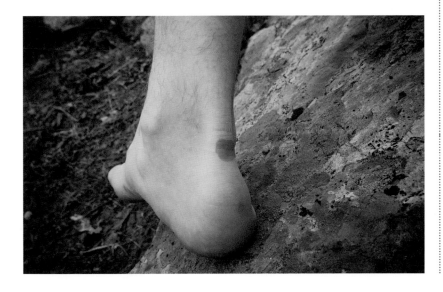

Stop if you feel heat from rubbing on your feet while hiking. A hot spot is easier to treat than an actual blister. DAVE ANDERSON

You can also use gel pads to cover small liquid-filled blisters, but if the blister is large, you may need to drain the area before you cover it up. The blister will pop once you start walking anyway, so draining it with a sterilized needle is a bit more controlled. After the blister is drained, clean the wound, bandage it, and watch for infection. If you have some kind of foam padding (mole foam or an Ensolite pad will work), you can make a doughnut to surround the affected area, remove the friction, and help alleviate pain.

A doughnut made from mole foam also can be used to stop the rubbing that caused your blister.

HYPOTHERMIA AND HEATSTROKE

Hypothermia

Hypothermia is one of the leading causes of problems, even death, in outdoor survival situations, so having a basic understanding of the illness is critical. You must know the environmental conditions that lead to hypothermia and recognize its signs and symptoms so you can respond should the situation arise.

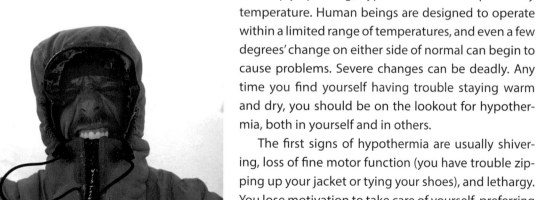

Your head represents approximately 10 percent of your body's surface area, which is a lot of area to lose heat from. Cover up when the temperature starts dropping. DAVE ANDERSON

Simply speaking, hypothermia is a drop in body temperature. Human beings are designed to operate within a limited range of temperatures, and even a few degrees' change on either side of normal can begin to cause problems. Severe changes can be deadly. Any time you find yourself having trouble staying warm and dry, you should be on the lookout for hypothermia, both in yourself and in others.

The first signs of hypothermia are usually shivering, loss of fine motor function (you have trouble zipping up your jacket or tying your shoes), and lethargy. You lose motivation to take care of yourself, preferring to sit around and shiver. As your body cools, these signs become exacerbated, and others join in: changes in personality or levels of consciousness, loss of gross motor functions (inability to walk), irritability, disorientation, strange behavior. At its worst, you lose consciousness. Victims of severe hypothermia are very sick; you can cause heart arrhythmia by moving them too quickly. These people need immediate hospitalization and still may not survive.

Preventing Hypothermia: How Do We Lose Heat?

1. **Radiation:** Our bodies radiate or give off heat as a by-product of metabolism and exercise—basic living—all the time.
2. **Conduction:** Temperatures want to be equal; that is, if you place your warm bottom on a cold rock, the rock will conduct or pull heat away from you until the two bodies reach equilibrium or the same temperature. Obviously, you cannot generate enough heat to bring a slab of granite to 98.6°F, so you'll be losing a lot of heat to the rock through conduction.
3. **Convection:** Moving air or water displaces the heat you are radiating from your body and replaces it with cooler air or water.
4. **Evaporation:** When sweat or moisture evaporates off our skin, it cools us down. This is a critical part of our body's temperature regulation capacities, but when in the outdoors, too much sweating can cause excessive heat loss.

How Do You Minimize Heat Loss?

1. **Clothing:** Since humans don't have much hair or any feathers, we rely on our clothing to protect ourselves from the elements. The best technique is to dress in layers that can be added and subtracted easily as temperatures change, because change they will. In the Rocky Mountains it is common for temperatures to fall well below freezing at night and rise to 70°F or higher during the day. These extremes can be even more dramatic in the desert, so you need to be prepared for just about anything.

   Think about the ways you lose heat when choosing your clothing. Insulating layers—down or synthetic parkas—help trap your radiant heat loss, as does a hat. Wind layers reduce the effect of convection, and wearing clothing that wicks moisture away from your skin or dries quickly—wool or some kind of synthetic fabric— helps reduce the negative effects of evaporative cooling. (In the desert, where you want to be cool, however, cotton is best, as it holds moisture and dries slowly.)

2. **Insulation from cold surfaces:** To reduce the effects of conduction on your body, you need to place a barrier between your body and the cold body that wants to steal all your heat. A foam sleeping pad makes a good butt pad, or you can sit on your backpack. In winter it is helpful to stand on a pad of some kind while you are in

camp to keep your feet warmer. If you don't have gear, improvise. Branches, dry grass, pine boughs, extra clothing, anything that will keep you away from the ground will help.

3. **Protection from moving air and water:** Your best bet to reduce your exposure to convection is to remove yourself from the offending environment. Get out of the water as quickly as you can; find a place where you are protected from the wind. Improvise a shelter of some sort, dig a trench in the snow, climb into a tree well, find an overhang, get behind a rock—anything that protects you from the wind will help.

    In hot climates the wind can be cooling, but it can also accelerate water loss. Use your judgment. Many backpackers prefer to seek shelter from the wind and the sun in the desert. They don't think the cooling properties of moving hot air outweigh the discomfort of its drying effect.

4. **Avoiding excessive sweating:** If you are more concerned with cold than heat, you want to try to minimize your sweating. Once you drench your clothes with sweat, you have to dry them again somehow. Usually that will be your body's job, and it takes a lot of energy (read "heat") to dry a soaking-wet T-shirt. In cold temperatures try to moderate your exercise so you don't overheat. Make sure you are wearing the minimum amount of clothing necessary to stay comfortable without sweating too much.

5. **Building a fire for warmth:** If you've been trained to be a low-impact camper, you've been told to minimize the use of fires, keep them small, and only use wood that is on the ground. In an emergency these rules go out the window. But don't abuse the privilege. If you are not really in danger, there is no need to build a bonfire.

    Nonetheless, if you are freezing and don't have any shelter or extra clothing, by all means, build a big fire. It can serve as both a signal for searchers and a way to help you stay comfortable if temperatures drop below freezing. Just take care not to start a wildfire.

Build a fire to stay somewhat comfortable if temps drop below freezing.
DAVE ANDERSON

FROSTBITE

Frostbite, or frozen fingers and toes, is another environmental injury frequently suffered by survivors of outdoor emergencies. Most common on your extremities, frostbite occurs when the liquids in your body freeze. Frostbite can cause serious tissue damage and may lead to amputation in extreme situations.

The first step in preventing frostbite is limiting exposure. Frostbite occurs in temperatures below freezing. Areas with obstructed blood flow—feet confined to tight boots or hands clinging to an ice ax—are particularly susceptible, as are places exposed to the cold, such as your cheeks and nose.

Like a burn, frostbite comes in different depths, affecting various skin layers. Superficial frostbite, or frost nip, is the classic white spot on your cheek on a cold ski day. Usually, all you need to do for frost nip is cover your face with your hands and blow. The warm air from your breath is enough to get the blood flow back to the tissue. The worst effect of frost nip is normally red and painful skin, similar to that of a sunburn.

As the freezing goes deeper, your signs will worsen. Your extremities may appear wooden, hard, and gray or waxy looking and feel numb. Frozen tissue is painless, so if you can still feel your toes, that's a good sign. It means you don't have frostbite—yet. You need to take care of cold toes before they freeze to minimize the damage. Take your boots off, change your socks, put your cold feet on someone's warm belly—get those toes warm rather than ignore the signs.

If you do get frostbite, you have a decision to make. The treatment is to rewarm the area rapidly in warm water (not so hot that it burns). But if you are in the wilderness and cannot keep your feet warm after they have been thawed, you may be better off keeping the tissue frozen. You may also find that once you rewarm a frozen part, you lose all function because of the pain.

Frostbite leaves the affected area white, hard, and painless until thawed. DAVE ANDERSON

If you have to walk out to get to help, you may choose not to rewarm a frozen toe or finger. Once frostbite is thawed, the injury is very painful and susceptible to refreezing. DAVE ANDERSON

Treatment

In the initial phases of hypothermia, the best thing to do is get your muscles moving to generate heat. Do fifty jumping jacks, run up a hill, dance around, get your heart rate up, and you'll warm up. If your clothes are wet, change into something dry or at least wring out the excess water if you have no spares, and put on a hat and dry socks. Start up the stove and have a warm drink. Eat a sugary snack. If you catch your chill quickly enough, these measures usually will be enough to take care of the problem.

If you begin to see more severe symptoms of hypothermia in your patient or yourself, you need to take dramatic action. The old treatment was to put the hypothermic person in a sleeping bag naked with another naked person. The idea was that the hot person would warm the cold one, which is true, but this technique can cause the warm individual to get chilled. Besides, most people probably wouldn't be comfortable getting naked with most of their camping mates. These days people advocate using warm-water bottles against the skin of the hypothermic patient. Place the patient in a sleeping bag with warm-water bottles under his armpits, in his groin area, against the palms of his hands. Make sure the bottles are not so hot that they could cause a burn.

You may want to wrap the sleeping bag in a tarp or tent fly—some kind of waterproof, windproof layer that will trap heat—and make a kind of cocoon around your patient. Cover everything but the individual's face.

If you are successful in warming your patient, remember that he will be exhausted from the experience and may need a few days' rest to get back to normal. If your patient is catatonic and unresponsive because of hypothermia, do not attempt to rewarm him in the field. He needs to be in a hospital. Wrap him in a sleeping bag, blanket, or something else that will prevent further heat loss, and seek immediate help.

Heat Exhaustion and Heatstroke

Heat injuries are common when temperatures rise and you are exercising in the sun. The most common scenarios include people passing out during marathons or while cutting their grass on a hot August afternoon. Heat exhaustion is usually relatively benign, but heatstroke, which can either follow untreated heat exhaustion or come on suddenly with no warning, is very serious and causes lasting problems or death.

The best treatment for heat injuries is to avoid them. If you know the temperatures are going to be high, alter your schedule to avoid extreme exertion during the heat of the day. Go on a night schedule: Sleep during the day and move at night, or at least take a siesta when temperatures are highest. Make sure that you stay hydrated and that you maintain your electrolyte balance by eating regularly throughout the day. Water without food can lead to a condition called hyponatremia, which is caused by too much water and too few electrolytes. Hyponatremia can be deadly, so be sure that when you drink you also eat. Diluted energy drinks are also helpful in maintaining your electrolyte balance on hot days when you are working hard.

Signs, Symptoms, Treatment

Hot, flushed skin; profuse sweating; and extreme fatigue usually indicate heat exhaustion. Heatstroke victims may be pale and no longer sweating, but not always. The most critical sign of heatstroke is a change in your patient's level of consciousness. She may be irritable, irrational, or confused. She may also pass out.

Heat exhaustion is treated by removing your patient from the offending environment. Get the affected party into the shade and cool her down by placing a wet, cold bandanna on her forehead. Have her drink. Usually your patient will begin to recover quickly, but it may take a day or two before she feels restored. Heatstroke victims need immediate attention from a doctor. You need to arrange for a helicopter evacuation for these individuals as quickly as possible. In the meantime, get the patient into the shade and begin cooling her with a damp cloth.

ILLNESS AND ALTITUDE SICKNESS

Illnesses

Illness in the field can be uncomfortable and scary. Most of us aren't doctors and can't tell the difference between a little bit of gas pain and a serious abdominal problem. Nonspecific gastrointestinal distress—or a bellyache—is relatively common on camping trips, often as a result of poor hygiene. You can feel pretty lousy as a result of this, but it's not going to kill you. Appendicitis, on the other hand, might. Upper respiratory illnesses can be equally mysterious: Do you have a common cold or pneumonia? How can you tell when someone is seriously ill or simply uncomfortable?

Here are a few guidelines to help you determine whether your patient needs to see a doctor. Try to make your patient comfortable and monitor him for 24 hours. If in doubt, get the person out. No one is going to criticize you for making a conservative call.

A moderate fever lasting more than 48 hours can be indicative of serious illness.
DAVE ANDERSON

Guidelines for Assessing Illnesses

These guidelines will help you assess a person's illness:

Fever: Any illness associated with a fever for more than 48 hours should be considered serious. High fevers are temperatures above 104°F and are often accompanied by delirium and convulsions, so you'll know it's bad. Moderate fevers between 102°F and 103°F for more than 48 hours are bad enough to consider evacuating your patient.

Breathing: For upper respiratory illnesses, any difficulty breathing that worsens over 24 hours may be a sign of more serious problems. Wheezing, shortness of breath, and anxiety are all signs of potential problems that demand medical attention. Monitor your patient and look for deterioration over time to help make your call.

Headache: Severe headaches that don't respond to pain medication, or persist over time and are accompanied by a stiff neck, are potentially dangerous symptoms that should be evaluated by a medical professional.

Abdominal pain: Pain that worsens over 12 to 24 hours and/or is accompanied by a spiking fever, tensed muscles, tenderness or hardness in the belly on exam, and vomiting or diarrhea are signs that your patient may be suffering something more serious than simple gastrointestinal distress.

Vomiting/diarrhea: Inability to tolerate fluids or food for more than 48 hours.

If your patient exhibits one or more of these symptoms, seek medical help. If you are unsure, seek medical help.

Altitude Illness

As we all know, there's less oxygen at high elevations, so our bodies have to work harder to supply ourselves with enough air. We begin to feel the effects of elevation at around 8,000 feet, although real altitude illness is more common above 10,000 feet. Altitude illness baffles scientists. They know what happens, but they don't really know why some people suffer more than others. There's no real rhyme or reason: Young, strong athletes can get sick as easily as older, out-of-shape couch potatoes; and some people who have traveled to altitude in the past without problems fall ill on their next visit.

Your best bet for minimizing your risk is to ascend slowly and give your body time to adjust, or acclimate. Physicians recommend ascending at a rate of no more than 2,000 feet per day, with 1,500 feet being a more conservative measure.

Altitude illness is categorized as acute mountain sickness (AMS), high altitude cerebral edema (HACE), or high altitude pulmonary edema (HAPE). HACE and HAPE can be deadly. Often, but not always, your body will be showing some signs of AMS before you come down with HACE or HAPE, so it's important to recognize all the symptoms to protect yourself and your team from the problem.

AMS

Many people assume headaches are normal at altitude; they are not. A headache is one of the first and most classic signs that your body is feeling the effects of altitude and is having trouble adjusting. Other signs of AMS include nausea, lightheadedness, disturbed sleep, lethargy, and loss of coordination.

If you exhibit these signs, the best treatment is to stop ascending and give your body time to adapt to the elevation. Keep hydrated, try to eat, and do some light exercise. Once your body adjusts and your symptoms dissipate, you can continue to ascend.

HACE

HACE is swelling of the brain and can kill you quickly if not treated. Signs of HACE are changes in levels of consciousness, headache, nausea, vomiting, loss of muscle coordination, seizures, hallucinations, and vision disturbances.

Treatment is immediate descent. Symptoms will begin to abate as you lose elevation, but expect to go down 2,000 feet or more—until all signs are gone—to ensure your patient is safe.

HAPE

HAPE manifests itself in the lungs and is associated with shortness of breath even at rest; fatigue; dry cough progressing to a wet, productive cough; rattling breath sounds; and loss of muscle coordination.

As with HACE, the treatment for HAPE is to descend immediately and as quickly as possible. Again, symptoms will lessen as you go down.

With both HAPE and HACE, you can attempt to reascend once your patient is free of all symptoms of altitude illness. But go slowly and watch for signs of a reoccurrence. It's not worth risking your life for one more summit.

Drugs

There are medications available that help our bodies acclimate or alleviate symptoms of altitude illness, although most doctors recommend that you allow your body to adjust naturally. If, however, you are planning a trip to high elevations, you may want to consult a physician about the wisdom of carrying these drugs just in case you or someone in your group falls ill.

YOUR FIRST-AID KIT

Everyone has an opinion on what needs to be in a first-aid kit. The truth is, you never know. Your best bet is to think about items that are hard to duplicate: gel pads, athletic tape, medications. Leave behind things that can be improvised: Cravats can be made from bandannas or T-shirts, bandages from gauze pads and tape.

Factors that affect the size and extent of your kit include remoteness, length of stay, number of people, type of activity, and the presence of children. Try to keep things to a minimum. Big, bulky first-aid kits tend to be left in camp, where they do you absolutely no good. (For information on how to prevent and treat bug bites, stings, and snakebites, see chapter 8 on outdoor hazards.)

On longer trips, a well-stocked first-aid kit allows you to deal with all sorts of illnesses and injuries.
DAVE ANDERSON

Some useful items include the following:

- Sterile gauze pads (assorted sizes)
- Ace bandage
- Occlusive dressing (e.g., Tegaderm)
- Gel blister pads (assorted sizes)
- Steri-Strips
- 35cc needle-nose syringe
- 1.5-inch roll of athletic tape
- Moleskin (one 4 × 7 sheet)
- 2nd Skin
- Trauma shears
- Povidone-iodine
- Topical antibiotic cream
- Nonprescription pain medication (e.g., ibuprofen, acetaminophen)
- Nonprescription antihistamine (Benadryl)
- Gloves
- Microshield or pocket mask
- Notepad, pencil, emergency contact information

Optional items:

- Gauze roll
- Cortisone cream
- Cravat or triangle bandage
- Thermometer
- Tweezers
- Adhesive bandages
- Soap-impregnated sponges
- Epinephrine*
- Antibiotics*
- Diarrhea medication*

*Consult with a doctor before using these medications.

Kid Care

When traveling with your kids, it's always best just to assume someone will come down with something—because if you don't pack kid-friendly meds, they surely will get sick. Bone up on their current dosages (based on weight), and stash a good supply of chewable children's ibuprofen and acetaminophen in your kit, along with children's Benadryl, anti-itch cream, and a soothing bug-bite balm, like AfterBite.

Be responsible for your fellow backpackers.
THINKSTOCK.COM

Crater Lake, Oregon.
THINKSTOCK.COM

Blackrock Summit, Shenandoah National
Park, Virginia. THINKSTOCK.COM

CHAPTER 10

OUTDOOR SURVIVAL

Wilderness or outdoor survival conjures up images of building fires using bow drills and shelters from pine boughs, collecting water drop by drop in a solar still, and gathering food by harvesting wild edible plants or killing small rodents in deadfall traps. These skills— also called primitive-living skills—are interesting to know and challenging to perfect but have little real relevance for most backcountry travelers, even those facing a so-called survival situation.

According to the dictionary, *survival* simply means "to live through something." The word *something* is vague, but when associated with survival, it usually means an ordeal that tests one's fortitude and knowledge. You survive trials and tribulations, emergencies, tragedies, scary situations. So outdoor survival means living through some difficult challenge in the wilderness, where you cannot call 911 for help and you may be forced to fend for yourself for hours, even days.

Most modern outdoor survival situations result from human errors: You get lost, injured, or in over your head. The focus of this chapter is on understanding how to minimize the negative effects when avoidance

Planning ahead is one way to avoid survival situations.
DAVE ANDERSON

Sometimes all your preparation comes to naught. Dense forest, off-trail travel, overcast skies can all cause you to become disoriented or lost.
DAVE ANDERSON

fails. Using a bow drill to light a fire is a cool trick, but when you are stuck out overnight, you are really better off having a lighter safely bagged in plastic and stored in your pocket to get a blaze going quickly. Likewise, knowing that you can eat cattails can be fun and may add some variety and flavor to your backcountry meals, but when you are tired, hungry, and lost in the wilderness, your tummy rumblings will be satiated more readily by pulling an energy bar or chunk of cheese out of your pack rather than trying to locate a wild plant to eat.

The best possible way to survive an outdoor emergency is to avoid one, and you can avoid many by being prepared and knowledgeable. Before you leave home, you begin the process by packing the appropriate gear, writing a travel plan, anticipating potential hazards or obstacles, making sure you are properly trained, and devising contingency plans. Once you are on your trip, you are constantly on the alert for hazards and take care to make sure your entire team is rested and well cared for to prevent making errors in judgment due to fatigue or injury.

That said, no one is perfect, and it is likely that you may run into trouble at some point if you spend a lot of time in the wilderness. Accidents happen, you get lost or separated from your party, someone falls ill, or you misjudge a hazard and end up in trouble far from help. The time has come when you need to breathe deeply and come up with a plan to get yourself out of trouble. For those times it helps to be ready both mentally and physically.

In chapter 3 we outlined the planning and conditioning steps you should take before you go on your trip so you are prepared; in chapter 5, we covered navigation techniques to help you stay found; and in chapter 8, we discussed outdoor hazards and identified ways you can avoid preventable mistakes. In this chapter we cover the survival knowledge you may need when things *do* go awry and you find yourself in a life-threatening situation. The techniques presented here will help you stay comfortable, calm, and healthy until help arrives or you can rescue yourself and get out of the wilderness.

YOU'RE LOST. NOW WHAT?

One of the leading reasons local search-and-rescue teams are called into action is to find lost hikers. It happens every summer all over the country: Hikers fail to show up at a designated meeting place on time; someone wanders off to relieve him- or herself, gets disoriented, and doesn't return to camp; or people don't know how to read their map or GPS and end up miles from where they planned. Getting turned around in the wilderness is actually pretty easy to do; the trickier skill is knowing where you are at all times.

Take advantage of high points and open terrain to get oriented to the surrounding landscape and familiar with obvious landmarks. DAVE ANDERSON

Ways to Stay Found

1. **Pay attention.** As you walk, take time to look around and make note of the landmarks you pass. Orient yourself to the landscape. Do the mountains trend north–south? Are there any major topographical features that can keep you clued in to the cardinal directions? For example, say you are hiking in view of Mount Rainier. Are you to the east, west, north, or south of the mountain? It's unlikely that orientation will change unless you are hiking very

long distances, so you can always look at the peak to get an overall sense of which way is which. Of course this technique is not very helpful when clouds obscure your landmarks, but on clear days it's a great way for you to place yourself in the landscape.

The sun can also help you get a sense of the cardinal directions. Make note of where it rises, watch how it tracks its way across the sky, and notice where it sets. If you check your watch at the same time, you'll be able to get a sense of time and direction by the sun.

Notice how things look as you move along. Verbalize the shape of the surrounding hills, identify places on your map, and look over your shoulder to get a view from another perspective. Don't keep moving forward if the landscape you see around you is not matching what you expected from reading your map. Your map will tell you if you will be traveling upstream or downstream; gaining or losing elevation; or moving above tree line, in a canyon, or out on a flat plain. If things aren't matching up, you need to figure out why.

2. **Pick out handrails and landings.** Handrails serve as guides, helping you follow a path. In the outdoors, handrails are natural features such as a long ridge or river that acts as a barrier, keeping you on the correct line of travel. For example, your handrail may be a river that you will be following for several miles along its northern bank. That means that if you are traveling west the river should always be on your left side. If suddenly the river disappears or you find it has magically switched to your right side, you should be clued in to the fact that something has gone wrong.

Natural features such as these valley walls act as handrails confining you to a specific path, helping you to "stay found."
DAVE ANDERSON

Landings are places where things change—as landings on a staircase are places to pause and change direction. In the backcountry a landing may be a trail junction, a river crossing, or perhaps a mountain pass. Once you encounter that landing, your handrails will change. A river may switch sides, or you may leave it altogether. You may find yourself traveling downhill after climbing for hours to reach a pass.

Pick out your handrails and landings in the morning before you start hiking. Make note of when you expect to reach specific points along your route. If you thought you'd cross a river at noon and 2 hours later you're still walking with no sign of water, you probably need to stop and look at your map.

3. **Look at the landscape *before* consulting your map.** If you have been hiking for several hours and your feet and back are getting sore, it can be very easy to look at your map and decide you are

It can be easy to lose track of where you are when pounding down a trail. Make sure to continue to pay attention to your surroundings to avoid missing key landmarks or trail junctions.
DAVE ANDERSON

someplace close to your destination. You can usually convince yourself that you've hiked farther than you have; and while you thought a mountain landmark was going to be bigger, with a little imagination you can usually make yourself believe it is that rounded knob in front of you, especially if that means you are less than a mile from camp. The phenomenon of making the map fit the land is not purely a habit of beginners. Most of us start to smell the barn when our legs are tired.

To avoid falling into this trap, your best bet is to pinpoint a few key points in the landscape around you before opening your map. These points need to be obvious features that you'll be able to identify on the map, such as the inlet or outlet of a lake, a large meadow with a river meandering through it, a low pass between distant peaks, or a prominent mountain. Usually it's best to choose a couple of different landmarks to help narrow down your options. Once you've looked around, pull out the map and locate your landmarks. Only after you've found those points is it worth trying to home in on your specific location.

4. **Keep track of time.** Make note of when you leave camp and what time you pass obvious terrain features. This will give you a sense of how fast you are moving and when you should expect to arrive at your destination or a specific spot. Most of us travel at about 3 miles per hour on relatively level trails carrying a light load. Add some elevation gain in, and you can expect to slow down. If you add an extra mile per 1,000 feet gained, you'll get a good approximation of your speed. Off-trail travel is usually slower. Regardless, every party moves at its own pace, so you'll want to pay attention at the start of your trip to get a better sense of what formula works for you.

Travel speed is useful primarily because it can serve as a gauge. If you calculated that you should reach your camp by 3 p.m. and you find yourself still hiking at 5 p.m. with no end in sight, you may have gone astray. If you are way overdue and there's no logical explanation for your tardiness (such as a 3-hour nap at lunch), stop and reevaluate. You may have made a wrong turn hours ago.

5. **Stay together while hiking.** You don't have to be right next to your teammates at all times, but you do want to be sure you have a system for communicating should the need arise. You may decide

that means you always have a designated leader out front and someone else bringing up the rear; you may have a rule that no one gets out of view; or you may decide that you will rendezvous at any decision point you encounter, such as a trail junction or river crossing. The key is to make sure that you do not become separated if something happens: A member of your party is injured, someone is uncomfortable crossing a stream, or part of the group feels too tired to make your destination. In and of themselves, none of these scenarios is particularly dangerous, but if half your group blithely journeys forward, oblivious to the difficulties faced by the others, you may end up miles apart before you know it.

6. **Know your campsite.** Take a few moments while you are setting up camp to familiarize yourself with your surroundings, especially if your camp is hidden in the trees and hard to see from a distance. Locate some landmarks that will help you home in on the site so that if you wander away to get water, go to the bathroom, or take a hike, you will have some markers to guide you back home. These markers may be a specific boulder, a unique tree, a trail junction, or a waterway—anything you can recognize from all directions.

Also follow these guidelines if you set your pack down and leave it for a few minutes while hiking. It can be surprisingly hard to find a backpack lying in the woods, so take a moment to look around before you leave. That helps ensure you know where to look when you finish your business.

7. **Know how to use your navigational tools.** You can carry a state-of-the-art GPS receiver and know exactly what your coordinates are at all times, but unless you can translate that information to a map, you can still be lost. Modern tools make staying found easier, but only if you know how to use them. Practice reading your map and using a compass or GPS at home. Seek instruction or assistance from someone who knows more than you if you find yourself confused.

Lost and Confused

In spite of everything, most people who spend a lot of time in the wilderness have been disoriented or flat-out lost at some point in their career. The land of 39-foot hills where the map's contour intervals are 40 feet, dense forests where you can see no farther than the next tree, and wide-open terrain without any distinguishing features—all are notoriously difficult to navigate through and, therefore, easy to become lost in.

So what do you do? First and foremost, don't panic. Stop, breathe, and evaluate your situation. Take off your backpack; sit down. As legendary mountaineer and founder of the National Outdoor Leadership School, Paul Petzoldt, used to say, "Stop and smoke a cigarette." The point is, slow down for a minute. All too often the first thing people do when they realize they are lost is to start moving rapidly back in the direction they think they came from; before you know it, they have wandered even farther astray. Nothing is going to happen to you in the next few moments, so settle down and come up with a plan.

1. **Retrace your steps in your mind.** Can you backtrack? Do you know where you came from? If it's just a matter of heading back down the trail, by all means, retrace your steps until you are back at a place you recognize, and then start over.

2. **Find a high point from which to observe your location.** Is there a nearby hill or open area where you can get a view of your surroundings? Look for major rivers, signs of humans, or recognizable landforms.

3. **Scout the area to look for recognizable features.** If you can't get to a viewpoint, consider scouting around to see if you can find something that will help you get oriented. The trick to scouting is

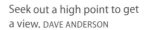
Seek out a high point to get a view. DAVE ANDERSON

not to get separated from your group or gear in the process. Scout in pairs, limit the duration of your exploration, and make sure you can retrace your steps and find your group and gear.

So You Are Lost: Do You Stay or Do You Go?

You've probably heard the old adage: Don't move when you get lost. In fact, if you are a parent, it is likely you've given your child this ultimatum. And often staying put is the best advice, but not always. To decide if you are better off sitting tight or moving, ask yourself:

- How long will it be before people notice your absence and come looking for you?
- Can you safely stay out overnight or longer waiting for help?
- Do you have shelter? Clothing? Water, food, and a source of heat?
- What is the weather doing?
- Is there a logical path to help?

You should attempt to walk out if one or more of these variables is true:

- The area you are in is unsafe.
- Bad weather is approaching, and you have no shelter.
- Nobody knows you are missing and won't notice for days, so a search is unlikely to be launched anytime soon.

If you decide to stay put, make yourself comfortable. It may be a while before help arrives. DAVE ANDERSON

- You have no way to communicate, and you are someplace where a signal—such as a smoky fire or flashing mirror—is unlikely to be noticed.

If you know that people are going to miss you and come looking soon, your best bet is to find an obvious place and stay put until you are found. This strategy is especially true if you get separated from your group. Make noise, build a fire, try to be obvious, but don't start moving until one of the factors previously listed begins to come into play.

Guidelines for Walking Out

If you determine no one is going to come looking for you and your best bet is to attempt to walk to safety, it helps to follow some basic rules of thumb to maximize your chances of being found:

1. **Attempt to hike to a road.** Roads lead to towns, farms, houses, and people, so if you can get yourself on a road, eventually you should be able to track down someone who can help you out. In the mountains all streams flow out to the flats, and unless you are near the ocean, sooner or later these streams will be crossed by a road. So start by following rivers downstream—stick to the bigger drainages and keep heading down; eventually you will come to some man-made feature. Trails will likewise take you to roads or towns at some point, so pick the direction that seems to be heading away from the mountains and start walking. In due course you will come to some help, at least in the continental United States. It may take you a while, but in today's world you will find people.

2. **Leave notes in obvious places.** Let searchers know of your intentions by leaving notes—or in the absence of paper and writing utensils, some kind of sign—at trail junctions, on the edge of meadows, or by other noticeable landmarks. Use a bright bandanna or something that will catch people's eyes to identify the mark.

Guidelines for Staying Put

Whether you are moving or staying put, your first goal is to make yourself noticeable. So when you stop moving for the day, and whenever you decide to remain in one location and wait for rescue, take time to make some kind of signal to help searchers see you. It can be surprisingly difficult to see a tent or hiker from the air, so use mirrors, smoke, patterns, and sound to make yourself as obvious as possible.

If you have no way to write a message, leave obvious signs that indicate which way you are traveling. DAVE ANDERSON

Finally, make yourself comfortable. If you are really, truly lost, it may take hours, even days before you are located, so take time to make a comfortable camp where you will be protected from the elements. Improvise a shelter, build a fire, and stay hydrated.

EFFECTIVE SIGNALING TECHNIQUES

Mirrors or shiny objects. Aircraft can often see the flash of a mirror easier than other signaling techniques.
DAVE ANDERSON

Geometric patterns, bright objects. Regular geometric shapes like squares are not found in nature, so they stand out. Use brightly colored clothing or other materials to create large shapes in open spaces to attract the attention of aircraft. DAVE ANDERSON

Smoky fires during the day, blazing ones at night. In daytime use green, wet wood to make a smoky fire most easily seen by searching aircraft. At night use dry wood to create a bright blaze, again most easily seen by searching aircraft. DAVE ANDERSON

Noise: yelling, whistle, banging pots. Make noise to attract the attention of searchers. The sound of banging pots or a whistle carries farther than your voice.
DAVE ANDERSON

HOW TO LOOK FOR A LOST PERSON

You may not be the one lost; it may be another member of your party who goes out fishing and fails to return. Before you run for the trailhead to call out the local search-and-rescue squad, it's worth conducting a search on your own, especially if you are traveling with a large group. The key is to be systematic in your searching.

Come Up with a Plan

Gather information first:

- Identify the missing person's last known location and time.
- Discuss the missing person's personality traits. Is he or she likely to panic and move, or will this person stay put? How reliable is this person?
- Brainstorm what gear the missing person may have with him or her.

Once you realize someone in your party is missing, it is imperative that you search in an organized, methodical way to avoid having someone else get separated. DAVE ANDERSON

Once you've decided on a plan of action, follow these steps:

1. **Organize search teams.**
   - Make sure no one is searching alone.
   - Each team should have marked maps and a clear sense of their location and the area they should search.
   - Set return times.

2. **Do an initial "hasty" search.**
   - Send searchers to obvious places: water, trails, and so forth.
   - Focus initial searches downhill of the last known point; people tend to trend downhill when traveling.
   - Leave notes in obvious places instructing the lost person to sit tight. Recheck these spots regularly.

3. **Do a "fine" search.**
   - When it becomes clear that you are not going to find the missing person easily, you need to shift your efforts into a more detailed "fine" search. At this point you will probably need to bring in outside help, as fine searches require lots of people power. If you have a phone, call 911 or send runners to the trailhead to seek assistance. Once help arrives, you will probably be required to turn over leadership of the search.

     While you wait for assistance to arrive, you can continue searching. Use the following guidelines to help improve your effectiveness and ensure your team is well cared for.
   - Organize your group into search parties of three or more with a designated leader. Give each team a specific area to examine, and designate a length of time to search. Your time frame will be determined by terrain, number of searchers, resources, and distances, so it may vary anywhere from 2 hours to 6 or even 8. Beware of fatigue. Make sure you do not overtax your volunteers and end up with more problems than you began with.
   - Individual search teams should spread out in a line, close enough together so they can see and talk to each other as they walk forward. Call the name of the missing person, and listen for responses. Mark the edges of the places you have searched. Note and flag any clues you may have found, but leave them in place. Repeat this process until the entire search area can be cleared (meaning no sign of the person has been located).

Lower Twin Lakes at Mammoth Lakes, California.
THINKSTOCK.COM

- Maintain one leader back in camp to serve as the Incident Commander. This person will keep track of search teams, determine search areas, and devise action plans, as well as make sure everyone is adequately fed and rested.

WATER

You can survive for weeks without food, but you won't make it long without water. Dehydration can kill in just a few days (or shorter in hot weather). In a survival situation, you'll want to prioritize finding water right after shelter and warmth.

Making Do: Finding Water

Streams, rivers, lakes, ponds, and puddles are obvious. But sometimes water is scarce, so you have to know where to look for it.

- Look in valleys or low areas where water will naturally drain.
- Locate lush, green foliage; water is generally nearby.
- Check rock crevices and caves where rainwater may have collected.
- Keep your eyes peeled for muddy, damp ground (then follow the "Make Water from a Sock" tip).
- Watch for animal tracks, especially where they converge. Animals always know the local watering holes.
- Look for swarming insects, which usually indicate a nearby water source.
- Watch the skies. Birds often circle above water.

Make Water from a Sock

Bear Grylls taught us this one (seriously!). If you find yourself in a mucky situation—surrounded by lots of wet clay, dirt, or mud but no water holes—fill your sock with wet glop, then squeeze until water makes its way through the fibers, either directly into your mouth or a vessel. Gross? You bet. But it's better than dying of dehydration.

Make a Transpiration Solar Still

If you have access to any sort of green vegetation, a plastic bag, and a tiny bit of cordage, you can create water. This method is simpler and more foolproof than a ground-based solar still. Just place the bag over live vegetation in a sunny spot, put a pebble in the bag to create a low spot in

Emergency Water Collection

When rain rolls in, gather water in any and all vessels you have: extra tarp material, rain jackets and pants, plastic baggies, stuff sacks, etc. Anything that holds water should be repurposed as a rain-catcher. Place bottles and pots near the low corners of an erected tarp to siphon off drippage.

Transpiration still tip: Place a small (clean) pebble in one corner of the bag. It will weight it, creating a low point where water will collect. KRISTIN HOSTETTER

which water can settle, tie it off at the top, and wait. The sun heats the bag and draws moisture from the vegetation, which collects at the lowest point of the bag. Depending on the sun and the temperature, you can collect up to several cups per day.

Tip: Use the largest clear (not black) bags you can find, and encase as much vegetation as you can in the bag. Pick a spot that will get full sun all day. If you have multiple bags, make multiple stills.

EMERGENCY FIRES

Jack London's short story "To Build a Fire" is one of the most gripping outdoor adventure tales of all time. Anybody who's read it can still remember the tension building as the man gathers his wood and prepares to light his one match—his only hope for survival—only to have the feeble flame doused by snow falling from the tree above. Fires can be tricky to build in the outdoors: Wet wood, rain, wind, snow, lack of flame—all can make your efforts frustrating, even futile.

Flame

The need for a reliable source of flame is one reason that many people advocate carrying a lighter in a plastic bag in their pocket at all times. If you keep your lighter dry and it has an adequate supply of fluid inside, you don't have to worry about whether you can start a fire in a driving rainstorm with a single match. If you are more of a purist and prefer matches, make sure you carry them in a waterproof container; again, it's always a good idea to keep them on your body somewhere in case you get separated from your backpack. (For additional fire-starting options beyond lighters and matches, see the section on campfires in chapter 6.)

Tinder

If you have some kind of flame starter, the key to your success is ensuring that you have sufficient tinder to sustain a flame until bigger sticks have time to catch fire. When it's wet and cold outside, gathering wood can become more difficult. Usually you just look for dead sticks on the ground, but if it has been raining for a week, that stuff is going to be soggy and slow to light. To find dry wood in these conditions, you need to be a bit more creative. Look around the base of coniferous trees. Often there

If you have a knife, you can make your own dry tinder.
DAVE ANDERSON

will be dead branches still attached to the trunk that stay dry in most rainstorms and work well as tinder. Or look under bushes and shrubs; you may find deadwood that is relatively dry here as well.

If you have a knife, you can make your own dry tinder. I've tried a couple of different techniques. One is to take a large dead branch and just whittle away at the sides until you begin to create dry shavings from the protected core inside. You'll need at least 3 or 4 cups of shavings—maybe more if the wood is really wet—to get a fire going, so don't stop too soon.

You can also make a kind of "broom twig," where you peel back shavings from a branch with your knife but leave one end attached so you end up with a lot of dry flakes of wood attached to the central stem. These broom twigs make great fire starters.

Wood

In addition to your pile of dry tinder, you'll need an assortment of sticks of varying sizes. Start small—pinky size—and move up to larger pieces. Make sure you have plenty of little stuff, though. If you get impatient and drop a large log on your flickering flame, you will undoubtedly douse it before you've begun. Again, focus your wood gathering under trees, rocks, and shrubs if it is wet out. If the wood has had some kind of protection, it may not be too saturated.

Building Your Fire

Backpackers who were in the Girl Scouts or Boy Scouts remember being taught how to make a central tepee from tiny twigs and surround it with a log cabin (kind of a Lincoln Log–type structure) made from larger sticks. That basic pattern still works today. The advantage is that it allows adequate airflow and gives some structure to your fire that ensures the wood is touched by flame. Start your tepee with a branched twig stuck into the ground surrounded by a mound of shavings. Lean your twigs against this central pole until you have a cone-shaped structure. Build your log cabin on the outside, and light the shavings. Once your tepee is burning, lay sticks across the top from side to side of the log cabin, increasing the size of the sticks as your fire gets established. Within a few minutes you should have a cheerful blaze to warm your hands and your spirit.

Once your tepee is burning, lay sticks across the top from side to side of the log cabin, increasing the size of the sticks as your fire gets established.

Technology

If you are lost with your backpack, by all means ignore the previous advice and douse your wood with a little white gas to get it going. This technique may not be the purest, but it is very effective. You can also place your twigs on a lit stove to get them burning. Be careful; playing with fire is dangerous, and white gas is particularly hazardous. Many people will fling burning bottles of fuel in a panic, lighting duff and grass in an instant, if not their partner too. To prevent such accidents, pour some gas on the wood, recap your fuel bottle, and place it well away from the fire site before you strike a match.

Remember, white gas will not explode. If your fuel bottle does happen to catch fire, place it on the ground and smother the flames with a metal cook pot.

Ethics

In an emergency situation, your safety preempts environmental concerns. Build a fire if you need to, and don't worry about scorched rocks or fire scars. You should not abuse this privilege by building a raging bonfire anytime your socks get wet, but in a life-threatening scenario, a fire is justified. Ease your conscience next time you go camping by cleaning up dirty campsites and trashed fire rings.

EMERGENCY SHELTERS

Getting out of the elements is often critical to survival in the wilderness. In some parts of the world—say, the Colorado Plateau in southeastern Utah—cliffs often form alcoves or overhangs where you can seek shelter and protection from rain, wind, and snow. Other parts of the world are less conducive to an easy hideout, and you may need to improvise a bit to come up with a protected shelter.

Survival Shelters

Even on day hikes, it's wise to pack some sort of "survival shelter." They typically weigh only a few ounces and pack down to the size of a sandwich, and if the stuff hits the fan and you find yourself stuck out there, they're lifesavers. There's no shortage of products out there marketed as "survival shelters." Be sure to get one with a silvery coating on at least one side so that you have the option of using it as a heat reflector. And remember: No matter what the packaging says, you will not be warm and cozy in or under these things. The reality is that you'll have an utterly miserable night, but you will make it through till morning.

If you have a poncho or a ground cloth, as well as some string, you may be able to rig up a tarp to keep the rain off. Grab a pebble, and place it in the corner of your tarp. Wrap the pebble up like a present and tie your string around it. Do this in each corner to make guylines for your shelter. Then attach the lines to trees or rocks to set up a wind block of sorts. Your best bet is to rig it at a steep angle on the windward side so that the tarp serves more like a sloping wall than a flat roof.

Here's a rundown of the most common types of commercially available products:

Space blanket. These thin Mylar sheets are cheap, ultralight, and ultra-packable, but they're fragile, generally small, very loud and crinkly, and often only good for one use. Example: Coghlan's Emergency Blanket.

These survival shelters can be rigged in numerous ways to help stave off hypothermia. Clockwise from left: Adventure Medical Kits Sport Utility Blanket, Heatsheets Emergency Bivvy, Coghlan's Emergency Blanket. KRISTIN HOSTETTER

If time is short and you need shelter fast, rig a lean-to using tarp material. If it has a reflective side, like this one, make sure it's facing down toward you so that it can reflect your own body heat back at you, as well as any heat created by a fire built in front of it.
JOE FLOWERS

If you need more incentive to carry some sort of shelter material, here you go. Any of the emergency shelters listed above can be used in myriad ways to help a survivor. Think outside the box!

- Collect or hold water.
- Place silvery side face up to attract rescue.
- Reflect heat from a fire.
- Use as a ground cloth.
- Use as a waterproof gear cover.
- Carry firewood.
- Augment/fortify a natural-materials shelter (see pages 329–33).

Emergency bivvy. Thin, stretchy polyethylene body sacks have taped seams and a heat-reflective inner coating. They are generally more protective (for one person), more durable, reusable, and can boost the warmth of a sleeping bag by up to 15°F. But they're slightly heavier and bulkier, more expensive, and less versatile for augmenting built shelters. Example: Adventure Medical Kits Heatsheets Emergency Bivvy.

Multipurpose emergency blanket. These often look like Mylar blankets but are much thicker and more durable, made of a woven, ripstop material. Although heavier and bulkier than the above options, they'll last way longer and often include corner grommets to help with rigging. Example: Adventure Medical Kits Sport Utility Blanket

Plastic sheeting. Clear plastic fabric found at any home improvement store can be cut to any size. It's rugged, cheap, and can help fortify any self-built shelter from rain and wind.

Natural Shelters

Overhangs, boulders, and caves can all serve as shelters from the elements, but there are other natural shelters that can fill that function as well. Dense stands of trees with low-hanging limbs often keep much of the rain or snow away. You can also crawl into thick bushes to get some protection. Remember, however, that you are invisible once you burrow

You can seek
natural shelter in a
hollowed out area
under a tree root.
DAVE ANDERSON

down in the trees, so take care to leave some sign of your presence nearby in case searchers visit the area while you are resting.

Tree-Branch Lean-To

In forested areas you can create a lean-to from dead limbs to serve as a shelter. Gather a bunch of large dead branches—about the size of your arm in diameter and 4 feet long or more. Find a boulder or downed tree, and lean the branches up to create a small cavelike space beneath. Try to overlap the branches, or place grass or leaves in between to fill in the spaces.

Debris Huts

Debris huts work best in cold situations when sustaining a fire all night long isn't an option. It can take more than several hours to build a good one, but once finished, the thick walls of leafy insulation can keep you warm in well below freezing temperatures. The basic idea

is to build an A-frame structure with a long ridgepole that you situate about crotch high at the head end, tapering down to foot height. Place ribs (sticks) all along the ridgepole, and then pile it high with dry debris such as leaves and pine boughs. Walls should be at least 2 feet thick. Drag more dry debris inside the shelter to provide bottom insulation and to fill any empty space inside the cavity.

Snow Shelters

Snow is a good insulator and can be carved and sculpted into elaborate shelters that are great for keeping the elements at bay. If you are out in the winter or up high enough in the mountains to encounter year-round snow, a shovel is an integral piece of backpacking equipment. With it you can build a snow cave or other form of shelter that protects you from the wind and cold. Temperatures in a snow cave usually hover right around freezing, which will feel balmy if it's below zero outside.

You can still take advantage of snow's insulating properties without a shovel. Your shelter won't be as comfortable, but it will help. Hollow out a shallow trough in the snow with your hands, line the bottom with a sleeping pad, backpack, spare clothes, or pine boughs—anything to keep you off the snow—then climb in and cover yourself with something. Again, you'll need to improvise. Anything can work—a tarp, tree limbs, blocks of snow, even your backpack will help keep you warm.

You can also use tree wells—the moat-like structures that form around the base of trees in the snow—to provide you with some protection from wind and snow. You'll also need something to keep you off the ground and to cover you up.

BUILDING A SNOW SHELTER

The fastest, easiest type of snow shelter is a quinzhee. Basically, you make a huge pile of snow and then methodically hollow it out from the inside. It's fun to practice in the yard with your kids after a big storm. Some key points:

- Take it slow so that you don't work up a sweat. In frigid temps, hypothermia can be right on the heels of sweat.
- Let your snow pile set for 20 to 60 minutes before digging into it.
- Keep the walls at least 5 or 6 inches thick to avoid collapse.
- Poke an air vent through the top to prevent carbon monoxide buildup.
- Pile excavated snow into walls on either side of the door to block wind.
- Use your emergency blanket as a ground cloth.

Six Rivers National Forest, Bigfoot Scenic Byway, California THINKSTOCK.COM

INDEX

survival situations, 309–33
   avoiding, 309–16
   fires in, 320, 324–27
   shelters in, 327–33
   water collection in, 323–24
   See also lost hikers
sweating, 225–26, 229, 296
sweep position, 57
symbols, map, 87

talus, 253–55
tarps, as shelters, 4, 327
temperature, air
   and elevation, 228
   in weather, 232
   See also cold conditions; hot
      conditions
tendonitis, 287
tent(s), 1–5
   alternatives to, 4–5
   bear encounters in, 79
   cooking inside, 111
   placement in backpack, 53
   vs. snow shelters, 218
   what to keep inside, 128
   in windy conditions, 2, 222
tent poles, 9, 53
tent sites. *See* campsites
ticks, 23–24, 59, 263
tidal areas, 251
tinder, for emergency fires, 325
toilet paper, 119–22
tornadoes, 220, 223
tourniquets, 200–09
trail running, 69–70
travel time, 45, 46, 314
tree line, food storage above, 131–32
trees
   climbing, in bear encounters,
      76–79, 124

food storage in, 124, 125–26,
   127–28
   hazardous, 110, 267–68
   as natural shelters, 329–32
trekking poles, 18–19
   in rain, 58
   in snow, 61
   in steep terrain, 214, 255
   in stream crossings, 59, 249
   as tent supports, 3, 4
triangulation, 96–97
trip planning, 35–53
   contingencies in, 48–50
   equipment in, 40–43
   experience level in, 39
   lack of, as hazard, 208–10
   meals in, 50–52, 137–38
   packing backpack in, 52–53
   physical fitness in, 38–39,
      212–14
   research in, 35–36, 49
   route planning in, 44–48
   self-assessment in, 37–38
   team composition in, 39
tsunamis, 251

umbrellas, 19
United States Geological Survey (USGS)
   maps, 84, 88, 100–101
Universal Transverse Mercator (UTM),
   98–101

vehicle campgrounds, 122
vestibules, tent, 2

walking out, after getting lost, 317–18
wasps, 264–65
wastewater disposal, 111, 131,
   140–42
water consumption. *See* hydration

water crossings. *See* stream crossings
water sources
   campsites near, 109, 139
   finding, 323–24
   treatment of, 13–15, 111–14,
      323–24
waypoints, 102–3
weather, 216–47
   hazards of, 216–30
   ingredients of, 232–33
   See also specific conditions
weather forecasting, 230–47
   by clouds, 233–41
   by dew, 245
   by fog, 247
   fronts in, 242–44
   by frost, 246
   in trip planning, 36, 50
weight
   food, 51
   pack, 1, 8–10
   sleeping bag, 5–6
   tent, 3
widow makers, 110, 267–68
windy conditions
   in bear country, 66–67
   cooking gear for, 12
   hazards of, 220–23
   mechanics of, 230–31
   tents in, 2, 222
   tips for dealing with, 221–23
   and weather forecasting, 233
wolves, 260
wool, 25, 28, 157
wounds, 274–75, 287–92

zero-impact camping, 129, 130
zip-lock bags, 9, 51, 112, 127, 130, 131